Christmas '93

Karl,

Hope you enjoy this book

with lots of love,
Karen, Andrew,
James + Thomas

JOHN WILSON'S

GO FISHING TECHNIQUES

ANGLIA
Television Limited

B■XTREE

A CHANNEL
FOUR BOOK

First published in Great Britain in 1993 by Boxtree Limited

1 3 5 7 9 10 8 6 4 2

Edited by Helen Douglas-Cooper
Designed by Penny Mills
Colour Origination by Rainbow Graphics, Hong Kong
Printed and bound in England by Butler & Tanner Ltd,
Frome and London for

Boxtree Limited
Broadwall House
21 Broadwall
London SE1 9PL

A CIP catalogue entry for this book is available
from the British Library.

ISBN 1 85283 436 6

CONTENTS

FOREWORD

In this, my third *Go Fishing* book, the format is as different as the first was from the second. Apart from a short resumé of the history of *Go Fishing* to bring everyone up to date and a recollection of those magic moments that have occurred during eight consecutive years of researching and making fishing programmes for television both abroad and within the British Isles, this book is all about techniques.

Some have appeared previously in my books, others have not. Some are suitable for the beginner, while others require a certain amount of practice to perfect. However, the beauty and richness of our sport lies in the diversity it offers and it is this that sees most of us through a lifetime of weathering whatever Mother Nature throws at us.

Good Fishing.

John Wilson
Great Witchingham
1993

DEDICATION

This book is for the marshmen of Norfolk
whose efforts keep our Broadland heritage alive
for the enjoyment of all; and for friends such as Richard Starling,
Francis Russell and Eric Edwards,
without whose help my programmes
could not happen

CHAPTER ONE

THE HISTORY OF *GO FISHING*

It is an irrefutable fact, as many of my friends and well-wishers take great delight in pointing out, that when I first became involved in making fishing programmes, and *Go Fishing* with Anglia Television was born the best part of a decade ago, my hair was an even dark brown in colour. Who knows, perhaps it would have gone prematurely grey anyway. What I do know, however, is that rearranging and gearing one's life around your chosen subject brings great rewards, and I am very fortunate in being able to earn a living from doing what I like most. Not, I might add, that making a fishing programme necessarily means I get to enjoy an inordinate amount of actual fishing.

During the course of a five-day shoot, for instance (the budgeted time span we need to put together half an hour of fishing for TV) I am lucky, taking everything into consideration, even getting a fair crack of weather, if I fish for two full days on camera. Generally I have to make do with less than one full day's fishing (in terms of hours) over the duration of the shoot, with an hour here, three there, and so on – often between showers.

Take our series back in the Anglian region shown nationally in 1993, for instance, but made during 1992. We are, of course, always having to work a year up front. The laborious, yet most pleasant job of editing and post-production work, etc. make it that way, of course. Anyway, take the Broadland Pike programme we made on the River Thurne system of interconnecting Broads and tidal channels during that last week of September. What an unbelievably horrible week's weather. Most dedicated fisherman would, of course, welcome the rain because the aquifers all over the country had been greatly depleted during these past few consecutive drought years to a dangerously low level. So who am I to moan about a much needed deluge. But I wear two caps, and to someone presenting and co-producing fishing programmes, however, the last week in September, 1992 was an absolute nightmare. So allow me to provide a running outline of that particular five day shoot.

Day ONE, for instance, as usual, found the crew full of optimism, gathering at the Kingfisher Hotel in Stalham at midday. We

Filming a Go Fishing *introduction invariably takes longer than the fishing itself, as John and the crew experienced outside the Gateway of India in Bombay, prior to their mahseer adventure.*

secured a conference room in which both to store our equipment and to use as a TV room during the evenings for watching the day's rushes. So in what remained of suitable afternoon light, we decided to grab a few general views around Broadland – windmills, boats, wildlife, etc.

On Day TWO the shoot started in earnest with five miserable faces at breakfast watching the rain fall incessantly. Boy, was I popular for arranging a 5.30 am alarm call four mornings running. After lunch, the rain miraculously cleared up for me to provide, on wobbled smelt deadbaits, some wonderful pike action and a tackle introduction for the two cameramen, Ron

Tufnell and Paul Bennett, with fish of 19lb and 27½ lb (my fourth largest pike ever from the Broads) plus a lost smaller fish – all coming in the space of just two hours. Yes, the wine certainly flowed that evening.

On Day THREE rain again stopped play for the entire morning, but we did manage some afternoon footage shot in fine drizzle (unless really heavy, rain never seems to show up on video) of my arrival scene, towing the boat and the rowing sequence leading up to anchoring on the Broad. As you have gathered by now, rarely are our programmes actually filmed in the same sequence that they appear on television. That is sorted out in the editing.

No wonder Wilson and his guide, Stu McKay of Lockport Bridge Dam, are smiling. Canada's Red River in Winnipeg is full of 20–30 lb channel catfish like this whopper, which duly obliged for the Go Fishing *cameras.*

On Day FOUR any chance of our being able to film some pretty sunrise or dawn sequences was once again thwarted by continual rain, which cleared for just three hours around midday, enabling me to hook, but unfortunately lose close to the boat a long, lean fish of around 18 lb, plus hook into and jump a few jacks. We then just had enough time left to film a short nature trail introduction and a piece about the Norfolk Naturalists Trust Centre at Hickling Broad, before the rain came down yet again at around 4pm, forcing us to head back to base. I am often asked why it is we choose not to continue filming in heavy rain, because it is obviously still possible to catch fish. And the answer is sim-

ple. During heavy or persistent rain, especially when accompanied by even gentle winds, everything looks flat and uninteresting on film due to the low light values – not to mention the rain spots continually running down the lens. In colour photography, a reasonable level of light is, of course, imperative. It is what makes colours come alive and sparkle, and I doubt very much whether viewers, even fanatical fisherman, would still be watching after half an hour of doom and gloom, even with the occasional fish.

Day FIVE and our final chance of a few pretties was our worst, and almost a total write off, once again due to persistent rain which never stopped from the 5.30 am alarm call for breakfast. People ask me why is it we need five days to make a programme (hinting, of course, that it takes me that long to catch the fish). If only they knew!

In these closing stages, fortunately with the meat of the programme (those lovely big pike) well and truly in the can, as they say, our only option was to record some voice-over tracks with Francis Russell, the warden of Hickling Broad in the reed shed at Whiteslea, plus knock off a few general views, despite the poor light. And that was it. Sopping wet, we made our way back to the hotel to sort through the damp equipment and label up the used tapes before wrapping. Statistically, I had (in terms of hours) experienced rather less than a full day's pike fishing on camera. However, as always, with an experienced crew at the ready, we were able to assemble useable footage for yet another *Go Fishing* programme despite the rain. There was more than just a little help from Francis Russell, Richard Starling and Richard Hobbs of the Norfolk Naturalist Trust, too.

As I mentioned in my first *Go Fishing* book written in 1988, the series initially got under way through my good friend, James Forte, now living in Ontario, Canada. He introduced me to Peter Akehurst, who directed the first four series. The first two of these were produced in-house with Anglia TV crews, and the second two independently for Anglia by Wizard Productions.

Apart from a few episodes in Sweden and Southern Ireland, all were British based, and consisted of six programmes per series. Then came series five, a 12-episode international extravaganza produced for Anglia by Pretty Clever Pictures and directed by Paul Martingell, who later became my partner and co-producer of Kazan River Productions, through which *Go Fishing* is now made. We named the company after one of the mighty lake trout rivers in the North-West Territories of Canada, where every member of the six-man (one lady) crew, including Martin Founds of Anglers World Holidays, who arranged the locations, all caught massive great lake trout in excess of 20lb and masses of specimen grayling. What a place. Melissa Robertson, our production assistant for that series, actually boated a 30-pounder. Talk about beginner's luck. And if I sound like an insanely jealous television presenter, you're right.

On a more serious note, I was only kidding, it seems to be an unsavoury British trait that once someone has finally, after much hard work, reached the summit of their profession, they become fair game to all and sundry, not unlike a coconut shy. Naturally, it was lovely receiving so many accolades during our numerous *Go Fishing* programmes on the way up. However, since the programmes have become well established, the inevitable British 'knocking' disease has come along – based I am sad to say, on a mixture of jealousy and self-defeatism. I have exceedingly broad shoulders as far as nit-picking criticism is concerned, but at times I really do wonder what makes other fishermen tick. For instance, in the letters page of *Trout and Salmon* during 1992 a few fellow fishermen were accusing me of not being able to cast with any sort of 'form' to quote one idiot, of laughing too much, and, believe it or not, of actually daring to enjoy the fight of a fish.

It all makes you wonder, doesn't it? Out there are guys who, it would seem, never see the humour in anything, cast with competition perfection – dare I say, sterility – regardless of how knackered they are, and when they hook into a fish, apparently cannot enjoy the ensuing fight until the poor creature has been despatched.

Well, let me say for the record, right here and now, I certainly never set out to give the impression on screen that I am any more than an average fly fisherman, and because I seldom have the chance of using certain techniques, spey casting for instance, I am rather less than average. I can even recall actually saying as much on television. Nevertheless, through stealth, observation and watercraft, which are the important values in fishing, wherever you practise it, I manage to catch most of the species I am after, whatever the location. So keep sending those letters in to the media folks, good and bad, positive or negative, on the assumption that the old adage of 'any publicity is good publicity' just could be right.

And talking of letters, I guess I have now answered thousands of letters from viewers; not always straight away, but eventually I endeavour to send everyone a reply on such varied topics from the sex problems of a certain female (honest) to mums and dads wanting me to take little Jimmy out fishing on his birthday. And how I wish I could please each and every one. But as there are only so many free hours in a seven-day week, I hope viewers understand when I respectfully decline, due to being

too busy making, editing or researching more *Go Fishing* programmes. Because it is perfectly true.

The statistics for *Go Fishing* are that it regularly attracts an audience of between 2 and 3 million when screened nationally on Channel Four. Many of these are, of course, non-anglers, as the viewership breakdown carried out by commercial television proves. It is, indeed, extremely satisfying to know that our purposefully edited balance, comprising fish-catching action and wildlife, together with the natural beauty of the countryside, is so well received by such a large cross-section of television viewers. At times the fisherman wants to see more fish-catching, and I can honestly relate to his wishes, but the programmes are just 24 minutes long, and it is impossible to please everyone. I also want others to understand our sport and the reasons why we sit there in the damp and the cold for so long: for the raw beauty of our flora and fauna, and the ever-changing elements. And it is my belief that angling as a whole will suffer far less criticism with the media if *Go Fishing* can continue along these lines with something for everyone. Who knows, if our running time were, say, 45 minutes, then perhaps we could please a larger percentage. Perhaps not! Either way, *Go Fishing* has survived a seven-year run from 1987 to 1993 as angling's only regular UK television programme, with no less than 48 episodes, 36 of which are available on video cassettes. It has been shown abroad in 10 countries from Japan to Turkey and I sincerely hope that health and television programme commissioners will allow me to bring you more.

11

Everyone lends a hand to help cameraman, Ron Tufnell, assemble the underwater unit used for capturing the antics of dolphins beside the boat in the blue seas off Madeira.

John and director, Paul Martingell, discuss a point with on-line editor Ralph Forsdick (centre) at Anglia Televison studios in Norwich.

We have spotlighted some truly fabulous fishing in no less than 12 different countries, and actually caught on camera over 70 different species of fish, from dace to mahseer. If you include those caught during my research trips to exotic locations yet to be filmed, but there for the making, this figure jumps to more than 100 separate species. It has, of course, been a most illuminating part of my life, stretching over almost a decade – if an 18 month waiting period is included, from the time the first pilots of *Go Fishing* were put together to when the first six part series was made and screened, first on Anglia Television, and subsequently on Channel Four. For those interested in exactly what we have caught during 48 programmes, the list of the largest fish of each species and the location in which they were caught should prove interesting.

I have tried my very best to provide a balance of coarse, sea and game species in the hope of pleasing everyone. I have to admit, however, that until the twelve part international series which contained a wealth of exotic sea fish from barracuda to sailfish, British sea fishermen were not particularly well catered for. The reasons for this boil down to the fact that most of my local Norfolk beaches are flat and have correspondingly low horizons offering only minimal location excitement and a limited variation of camera angles. I didn't fancy risking an entire 30 minute programme on what, at best, would be codling up to 10 lb – perhaps very much less. If you add typical British weather, you have all the ingredients for a potential turn off. I hope to turn people on – both anglers and non-anglers. (OK, so I chickened out!)

FACT FILE

A list of the largest fish of each species actually caught by John on camera in 48 *Go Fishing* programmes

FRESHWATER

Barbel	9lb 12oz	River Wensum, Norfolk
Bream	7lb 2oz	River Shannon, Ireland
Brown trout	6lb 9oz	Norfolk gravel pit
Bullhead catfish	3lb 1oz	Red River, Canada
Carp	25lb 12oz	Austrian lake
Channel catfish	32lb 8oz	Red River, Canada
Chub	4lb 10oz	River Wensum, Norfolk
Crucian carp	3lb 14oz	Swedish lake
Dace	1lb 1oz	River Kennet, Berkshire
Grayling	3lb 3oz	Kazan River, Canada
Grey mullet	3lb 1oz	River Ebro, Spain
Ide	4lb 7oz	Klaralven River, Sweden
Lake trout	26lb 9oz	Kazan River, Canada
Mahseer	65lb	River, Southern India
Manyame salmon	5lb 1oz	Zambezi River, Zimbabwe
Nile perch	53lb	Lake Victoria, Kenya
Perch	2lb 7oz	Suffolk lake
Pike	27lb 8oz	Norfolk Broads
Rainbow trout	5lb 2oz	Norfolk gravel pit
Red-bellied bream	2lb	Zambezi River, Zimbabwe
Roach	2lb 10oz	River Wensum, Norfolk
Roach/bream hybrid	3lb 2oz	River Bann, N. Ireland
Robustus bream	4lb 3oz	Zambezi River, Zimbabwe
Rudd	2lb 2oz	River Shannon, Ireland
Sea trout	9lb 4oz	Mörrum River, Sweden
Salmon	10lb 6oz	River Bann, N. Ireland
Sik	3lb 2oz	Klaralven River, Sweden
Steelhead trout	14lb 11oz	Copper River, Canada
Tench	6lb	Norfolk lake
Tiger fish	14lb 2oz	Zambezi River, Zimbabwe
Vundu catfish	60lb	Lake Kariba, Zimbabwe
Wels catfish	4lb	Norfolk lake
Yellow catfish	3lb 12oz	River, southern India

SEAFISH

Barracuda	21lb	8oz	Gambia River
Bass	4lb		Essex coast
Big-eyed tuna	80lb		Madeira
Bullhead catfish	3lb	2oz	Gambian river
Cod	22lb	7oz	Alderney, Channel Islands
Dogfish	2lb	8oz	Essex coast
Eel	2lb	14oz	Essex coast
Garfish	1lb	3oz	Alderney, Channel Islands
Kujeli	6lb		Gambian river
Lemon shark	300lb		Gambian river
Ling	21lb		Alderney, Channel Islands
Pollack	18lb	8oz	Alderney, Channel Islands
Tope	39lb		Lough Swilly, Ireland
Thornback ray	10lb	6oz	Essex coast
Sailfish	76lb		Malindi, Kenya
Yellowfin tuna	15lb		Malindi, Kenya

(Tiny species not included)

BIGGEST FISH LOST ON CAMERA

FRESHWATER

Mahseer   80–100 lb estimated   River, southern India

SEA

Suspected Black Marlin

400–500 lb estimated   Malindi, Kenya.

Lost after two hour battle.

I am often asked which locations I personally consider to have been the most exciting of those featured in *Go Fishing*, and I have to admit that this is a difficult one. For starters, I have a permanent love affair with India, and the mighty mahseer is, I believe, the most exciting and awesome of all the fish I have caught. By the same token, the mind-blowing sunsets of Africa – Zimbabwe and Lake Kariba in particular – make a person want to return time and time again. Owing to the fact that they actually tail-walk following a lengthy, deep-down battle, I was totally surprised by the power and sheer endurance of the Nile perch in Kenya's fabulous Lake Victoria, the second largest sheet of freshwater on the planet. And I suppose for

sheer 'gut-busting' stamina, the big-eyed tuna makes a cissy out of the strongest man. Certainly those averaging just 50 to 80lb in Madeira's water fought like fish twice their size. It is, in fact, quite humiliating to put on all the strain a 12-stone man can muster for 20 minutes against an unseen force, only to find, when it finally surfaces, that it weighs no more – and is indeed smaller – than your dog. But so it goes.

I guess what I am trying to say is that I drink it all in greedily, although if I were limited to just the one choice, with its perfumes, its poor, proud, wonderful people, I would choose to spend time with guides Suban and Bola and, of course, the mighty mahseer, in Southern India.

CHAPTER TWO

GO FISHING
TECHNIQUES

A regular, but in my opinion, rather negative comment from a minority of our viewers is that they cannot enjoy our *International Go Fishing* programmes nearly as much as those based in the UK because they will never get to visit the same locations, which is a great shame. But then I think the organization of British travel agents would give them an argument, seeing that more and more people are now travelling abroad for their holidays. I would even take some to task by suggesting that it all depends on how you proportion out your income. My current car, for instance, is an elderly A reg. Saab that has over 130,000 miles on the clock and is worth little more than the yearly fee Norwich Union charge me to insure it. Personally, I have never much worried about 'looking good' or whether I have the latest registration letter on my number plate. Yet I have friends who change their Granadas or Escort GTXs or GTIs every two or three years, drink like fish, smoke 40 cigarettes a day and spend a fortnight in Benidorm each year, who then take

When enjoying the art of long trotting, John loves nothing better than to search for big grayling in the crystal-clear water of Hampshire's River Dever.

great delight in telling me if only they were lucky and could afford to fish where I do, they would enjoy similar results. And of course, the irony is that in many cases, they would.

I do accept, however, the fact that you cannot please everyone, but I feel it is rather strange that some fishermen are even reticent about learning new techniques. Some of those featured in *International Go Fishing* programmes, for instance, adapted correctly, could considerably improve sport even on their own local, difficult fisheries. It works in reverse, I can tell you. On location far away from home, when I haven't a clue which species a particular water holds and how to catch them, those very same tried and tested British techniques have scored time and time again.

Methods perfected to solve the problems encountered while fishing in other parts of the world really do open up a whole new exciting area of diversity, whether your adversary lives in salt or in tropical freshwater. Items such as baitcasting outfits, downriggers, echo-sounding fish-finders, certain clothing products, carbon poles, weedless popping lures and spinner baits (the list is endless) are all imported innovations, comparatively new to the British angler, yet few would now wish to be without them.

So please use this technique chapter with a completely open mind. Accept that while downrigger trolling may look complicated, it could easily be adapted for British pike inhabiting those really deep loughs and reservoirs, which rarely see a baited hook. And what about baiting the hook of a small spinner with a bunch of red worms? My sport with perch and chub has improved no end since first learning of this ruse while fishing for the predatory bream and tiger fish in Africa's Zambezi River. I could go on – and do, of course, throughout this chapter, outlining a galaxy of techniques that I enjoy using, most of which have, at some time or another, been featured in my television programmes, and including a few which have not.

COARSE FISHING TECHNIQUES

FLOAT FISHING IN STILLWATER

To enjoy modest-size species like perch, roach, rudd and bream, where possible I would always choose to present the bait beneath a float rather than by ledgering, due to the fact that the tiniest bites can be struck and the bait can be offered in a most natural manner anywhere between the surface and the bottom of the water being fished. To catch fish from small stillwaters, or when the shoal is fairly close into the margins of large lakes and pits, there is nothing to beat the joy of light float fishing using a 13 ft waggler-style rod and a 2 lb reel line.

LIGHT MULTI-PURPOSE ANTENNA RIG

I suggest a simple multi-purpose rig as shown in fig.1A, incorporating a fine-tip antenna (such as a stillwater or blue) holding two No. 1 for calm water or taking up to 3AA for windy conditions. The stability provided by the body allows you to shot the sensitive tip down to the merest 'dot' so that the tiniest bite registers.

Plumb the swim carefully so the bait just comes to rest on the bottom once the two shots have settled. A bite can be determined at any time throughout the bait's descent (fig. 1B), or once it comes to rest on the bottom. The majority of bites happen 'on the drop' because the shoal (most typical of summer rudd) is situated in the upper water layers. Then move the float down and try these higher levels. In really deep water, say 10–12 ft or deeper, the 'layer' at which the shoal holds may change at any time, so when bites slow up try different levels until you relocate the main shoal. Remember to cast well beyond the area being loose fed and dip the rod tip beneath the surface while cranking the reel handle a few turns in order to sink the line. This is a most important procedure for all stillwater float fishing, otherwise any slight draw or chop on the surface will drag the rig and thus the bait along unnaturally.

If the bait is not taken on the drop, but lies untouched on the bottom for several minutes, one ruse that sometimes prompts an immediate response from lethargic bream in particular, is to wind the float quickly towards you, 1–2 ft at a time. This momentarily whisks the bait attractively upwards, allowing it to freefall again.

Light baits, such as a single caster on a size 20 hook, fall much more slowly and thus more naturally on a finer hook length. Even roach to 2 lb and bream up to 3 lb can be comfortably handled on a 1 lb bottom, so experiment whenever bites are not occurring but you are certain fish are in the swim.

When bream are packed tightly together, feeding in earnest from carpet of groundbait or loose feed on the bottom, lack of space may prevent them from moving off with the bait and providing you with a sailaway bite on the float-tip.

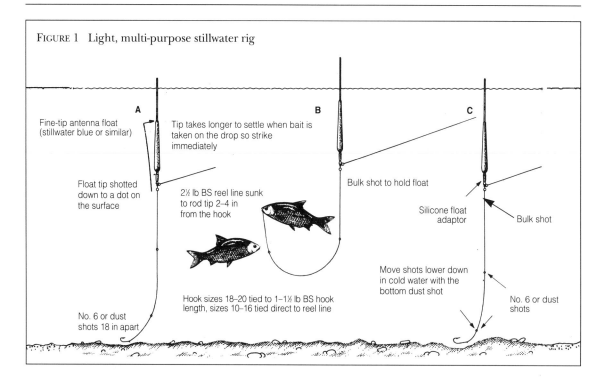

FIGURE 1 Light, multi-purpose stillwater rig

A

Fine-tip antenna float
(stillwater blue or similar)

Tip takes longer to settle when bait is
taken on the drop so strike
immediately

Float tip shotted
down to a dot on
the surface

2½ lb BS reel line sunk
to rod tip 2–4 in
from the hook

B

Bulk shot to hold float

C

Silicone float
adaptor

Bulk shot

Move shots lower down
in cold water with the
bottom dust shot

Hook sizes 18–20 tied to 1–1½ lb BS hook
length, sizes 10–16 tied direct to reel line

No. 6 or dust
shots

No. 6 or dust
shots 18 in apart

Instead, with their bodies angled downwards and their protrusible mouths fully extended, they hoover up food and right themselves to chew on the spot.

By far the best shotting pattern to indicate this kind of bite is to slide both shots down to within 4–6 in from the hook. The bait is now anchored and presented lift-style – so that when a big roach, hybrid or bream sucks it up and rights itself, thus dislodging the shots, the float-tip rises in a glorious lift. To encourage more deliberate float-tip indications, do not be afraid to juggle about with that all-important distance between hook and bottom shots to see what works best.

In really cold water conditions move both dust shots lower down, with the bottom (tell-tale shot) one just 2–4 in from the hook, and strike at the very slightest indication no matter how insignificant (fig. 1C).

LOADED DART 'ON THE DROP'

When deliberately presenting the bait 'on the drop' to rudd or roach working the upper water layers during the summer months, especially shoals patrolling tight up against marginal reeds, along the opposite bank of a canal, or a reed promontary reaching out into the lake, use a small loaded float like a zoomer or a 'dart', which sails through the air ahead of the bait as in fig. 2.

The secret when fishing on the drop is to catapult the loose feed out and cast over it immediately, so that both bait and feed sink simultaneously.

With heavy baits use no shot on the

20

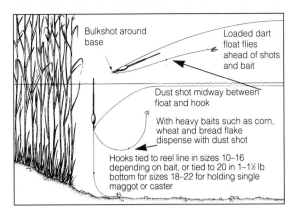

FIGURE 2 Dart rig for fishing on the drop

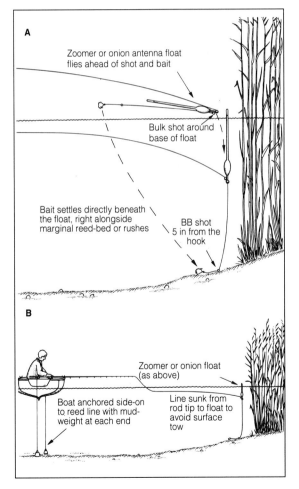

FIGURE 3 Zoomer rig

line, but a single caster or maggot may need the addition of a dust shot midway between float and hook. The bait is quite liable to be sucked in any second from the moment it hits the surface. So be ready.

Tie hooks in sizes 10–16 direct to a 2 lb reel line for baits such as bread flake and sweetcorn. To achieve the slowest possible descent with small baits like casters or punched bread use a 1–1½ lb test, 20 in hook length and fine-wire hooks in sizes 18–22.

THE ZOOMER RIG

This is a deadly float rig with species such as tench, big bream and even wild carp for placing the bait close up to reed-lines or against lily-beds in clear water conditions, where bites materialize only if the bait is presented in their habitat (fig. 3A). Simply rig up an onion or zoomer with the bulk shot at the base of the float. After plummeting the depth accurately, pinch on a BB shot around 5 in from the hook, so it comes to rest just on the bottom. Then, because the float precedes the hook and shot, you can allow it almost to bump against the reed-line before stopping the cast, knowing the bait will angle back down through the water to settle mere inches away from the leading reeds, in full view of patrolling fish.

This method also pays dividends on even-depth, clear-watered lakes and meres where dinghies or punts are used (fig. 3B). If beds of marginal reeds, rushes or sedges are the only cover, that is where the fish will be. Row up quietly to within practical casting distance and position the boat side-on to the reed-line.

As the float cannot be wound back with the rod tip held beneath the surface to sink the line (which would only bring the bait away from the reeds), take along a small (medicine) bottle of neat washing-up liquid and dab a finger-full over the spool every so often. The line will then sink willingly and instantly, after which you can very gently tighten up without pulling the float away from the reeds. Hold the rod whenever bites are expected.

Keep catapulting fragments of loose feed like sweetcorn, maggots, casters or worms along the reed-line for a distance of several yards either side of the float, and you might be able to encourage fish to work the area all day long.

As a last resort when bites appear to have finally dried up once the sun rises high in the sky, try this favourite old all-or-nothing ruse. Row over to reeds and with an oar spend 15 minutes clouding up the bottom silt. Then return to your anchorage and commence fishing. It is particularly effective with the ever-inquisitive tench.

Though the float may be light, this is certainly not a light-tackle method. You will need all of a 6 lb test line to subdue even modest-sized fish of 2–3 lb.

'TIPPED' PEACOCK WAGGLER RIGS

For presenting the bait to species like perch, roach, rudd, bream and tench in stillwaters where casting distance or choppy conditions immediately rule out the light rigs already mentioned, the float to use is the tipped waggler. It can be shotted to offer the bait on the drop or at any depth from a few feet beneath the surface to hard on the bottom.

A good general rig is shown in fig. 4A, with the bulk shot required to reach the swim grouped around the float so that it casts like an arrow, leaving two small shots down the line near the hook. If you plumb the swim carefully so the bait just touches bottom at the end of its fall, bites on the drop will register by the float tip failing to settle in its final position, and at any time afterwards when the bait touches bottom.

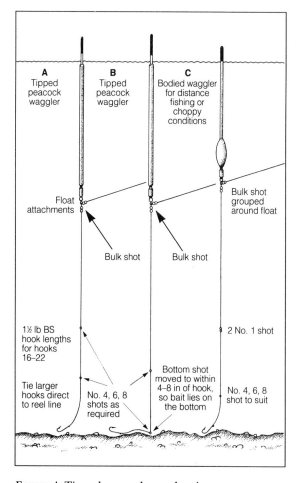

FIGURE 4 Tipped peacock waggler rig

When fish occupy the lower water layers, the bait might need to be nailed to the lake-bed to indicate a bite. If so, then fish slightly over depth and juggle about with the lower shots, ensur-ing the bottom one is somewhere between 4 and 8 in from the hook (fig. 4B). This is an excellent general shotting pattern for bottom-feeders like tench and bream.

At all times remember to overcast and wind the float back over the shoal with the rod tip below the surface to ensure that the line is sunk.

For the often long and continual casting involved in waggler fishing in stillwater, I increase the reel-line strength to 2½ lb test and use a 14 ft rod for long-distance work. Otherwise a 13 ft suffices. To facilitate a quick change, the swivel, push-in float attachment allows you to change from a tipped to a straight waggler (to improve visibility at distance), and for rough conditions select a bodied waggler for greater stability (fig. 4C).

When offering large baits like a bunch of maggots, sweetcorn, stewed wheat or breadflake, tie hooks direct to the reel line. For a more delicate approach, especially in clear water, use a 1½ lb hook length and hooks in sizes 16 and smaller for maggots and casters.

Unless shoals are truly enormous (it is easy to overfeed rudd and roach) keep loose feed to hook-bait fragments only, regularly introduced by catapult, as opposed to heavy helpings of cereal feed. A few small balls to get them interested is fine but thereafter loose-fed casters or maggots on the little-and-often principle will do fine.

The only exception to this is when the swim is full of bream, when you may need to keep cereal feed going in to hold them.

Incidentally, one of the problems encountered while after the better-quality bream in a swim full of mixed sizes, where small bream plus roach or rudd occupy the upper water layers, stems from an over-sensitive shotting pattern, which allows smaller fish to intercept the bait on the way down.

To remedy this, rearrange the shotting load to take the bait straight down to the bottom on to the noses of the larger bream. Simply move half the bulk shots from around the float and group them with the lower shots just 10 in from the hook.

LOADED PEACOCK WAGGLER/SLIDER RIG

To reach distant deep water the peacock loaded waggler, owing to its built-in weight at the base (the equivalent of 2 to 4 swan shot wagglers are available according to distances required), will get your bait there and, because so little shot is required, will allow the bait to be presented delicately.

As can be seen in fig. 5A and B, it is shotted in exactly the same way as the tipped waggler to register bites both on the drop and on the bottom. In really deep swims during the summer months when roach and rudd especially occupy the upper water layers, start with the float set to just 3 ft deep and deepen off 1 ft or so every cast until bites come. The 'loaded waggler' is a great float to use 'slider fashion' for bream where depths in excess of 10–12 ft present problems with

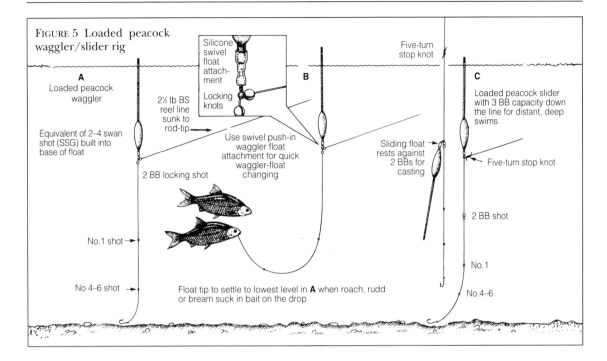

FIGURE 5 Loaded peacock waggler/slider rig

A
Loaded peacock waggler

2½ lb BS reel line sunk to rod-tip

Equivalent of 2–4 swan shot (SSG) built into base of float

2 BB locking shot

No.1 shot

No 4–6 shot

Silicone swivel float attachment

Locking knots

Use swivel push-in waggler float attachment for quick waggler-float changing

B

Five-turn stop knot

Sliding float rests against 2 BBs for casting

Float tip to settle to lowest level in **A** when roach, rudd or bream suck in bait on the drop

C
Loaded peacock slider with 3 BB capacity down the line for distant, deep swims

Five-turn stop knot

2 BB shot

No. 1

No.4–6

the fixed float. For a loaded slider that accepts an additional shotting of 3BB down the line, for instance (as in fig. 5C), split this up into three groups 18 in apart above the hook so the float rests against the 2BB for casting.

Remember not to close the bale arm immediately after casting in order to let line peel off as the lower shots take the bait down through the bottom of the float. Remember also that once the slider knot hits against the bottom of the float, bites on the drop will be indicated if the

tip fails to settle at its lowest position on time. It will in fact settle in three increments. When the 2BBs hang, when the no. 1 shot hangs, and finally when the no. 4 or 6 shot hangs. So learn to count each down accordingly, striking instantly at anything out of the ordinary.

BODIED WAGGLER OR 'DRIFTBEATER' RIG

If you want to float-fish for species like tench that are actively feeding considerably further than, say, a couple of rod lengths out, particularly in windy weather, the line must be sunk or the float will drag under. This means you cannot strike upwards, and immediately rules out the simple 'lift rig' using a length of plain peacock quill.

To reach greater distances, you require a float taking a fair shotting capacity –

Top left When presenting casters or maggots on light float tackle, Dave Thomas always shots the tip right down to indicate the slightest bite.

Left Nothing beats the loaded peacock slider rig for presenting the bait far out into large stillwaters, demonstrated here by Terry Smith with a fine bream from Ireland's Garadice Lake.

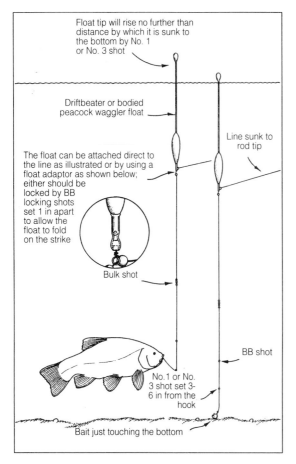

Float tip will rise no further than distance by which it is sunk to the bottom by No. 1 or No. 3 shot

Driftbeater or bodied peacock waggler float

Line sunk to rod tip

The float can be attached direct to the line as illustrated or by using a float adaptor as shown below; either should be locked by BB locking shots set 1 in apart to allow the float to fold on the strike

Bulk shot

BB shot

No.1 or No. 3 shot set 3-6 in from the hook

Bait just touching the bottom

FIGURE 6   Bodied waggler or driftbeater rig

anywhere from 3AA to 2½ swan shot – and this means using a bodied waggler or a driftbeater. The float is locked by a BB on both sides, with the bulk shot set at mid depth, leaving a small shot (no. 1 or no. 3) to go near the hook, and a BB between it and the bulk shot (fig. 6).

To facilitate a quick change of float as surface conditions alter, use a swivel float attachment into which the float can instantly be pushed or removed. Lift bites on this rig are obviously not going to make the float come flying out of the water. However, with the bottom shot

close to the hook, if the float is 'lifted' the float top will rise the same distance as it is sunk by that shot. So, after casting and winding the rig back over the swim with the rod tip beneath the surface to sink the line, memorize the level of the float in the water when the tip eventually settles once the BB shot is 'hanging', and by how much more it sinks when the bottom shot hangs the bait just on the bottom.

In all probability most bites on this float rig will consist of a slow disappearance of the tip; you reply with a strong scything, sideways strike, keeping the rod tip low to the water to pick up maximum line and put the hook home. Gentle lift bites will occur, so watch for the tip rising.

FLOAT FISHING FROM A BOAT

The enjoyment to be had from going afloat to catch species like roach, rudd, tench and bream in both still and running water is enormous. It is often the only way to tackle bream shoals inhabiting areas that are completely unapproachable from the bank. Such is the situation on my local Norfolk Broads, for instance, most of which are surrounded by peaty, swampy margins with thick beds of tall reeds. Being largely underfished, these areas contain shoals that rarely see a baited hook and provide consistently good sport.

Boat-fishing also permits tempting, overgrown backwaters and other inaccessible parts of river systems well away from all the popular areas to be reached. So if you own a suitable car-top dinghy, or dinghy plus

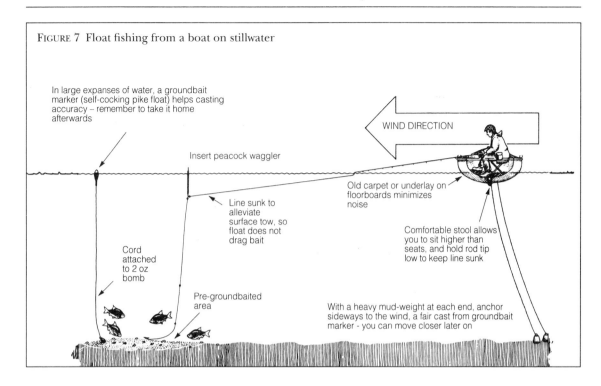

FIGURE 7 Float fishing from a boat on stillwater

In large expanses of water, a groundbait marker (self-cocking pike float) helps casting accuracy – remember to take it home afterwards

Insert peacock waggler

WIND DIRECTION

Old carpet or underlay on floorboards minimizes noise

Line sunk to alleviate surface tow, so float does not drag bait

Comfortable stool allows you to sit higher than seats, and hold rod tip low to keep line sunk

Cord attached to 2 oz bomb

Pre-groundbaited area

With a heavy mud-weight at each end, anchor sideways to the wind, a fair cast from groundbait marker - you can move closer later on

trailer, or can arrange to hire one, give boat-fishing a try.

You need to be very well organized in a boat (fig. 7), and the first consideration should be a pair of heavy mud-weights on adequate-length ropes for keeping the boat anchored in windy conditions. There is nothing more irritating than suddenly to drift away from a feeding shoal because the mud-weights are too light.

Sound carries very easily on water, and one slight klunk on the gunnel or seat can be heard by fish hundreds of yards away, so be especially quiet when rowing up to a potential swim prior to lowering the mudweights. Be very deliberate and slow in all your movements from stowing the oars to preparing nets and bait buckets. Take time to make the rods up and arrange all the large items neatly in the boat either before you set off, or long before you reach the swim. Take along an old piece of carpet or carpet underlay to cover the floorboards, as this will minimize noise. Several hours spent in a boat encourages fidgeting, which in turn creates still more vibrations, so take along a comfortable folding-chair if there is enough room in the boat. If not, use a pad of thick foam on the seats, which in most boats tend to be rather on the low side.

If you are sitting high above the surface, you will be able to control the float more comfortably and effectively, as you can dip the rod tip and sink the line to counteract surface drift. Exact float control is imperative when out in a boat, facing the elements. Remember that if you keep too tight a line between float and boat, whenever the boat moves back and forwards on the anchor ropes, the bait will be pulled unnaturally along the bottom. For this reason, and assuming the surface will be broken (flat calms for most of the day are quite rare), by far the best rig is the tipped peacock waggler set-up in fig. 4. The lift method in fig. 4C can usually only be used effectively in really calm conditions, and even then you need to hold the rod to counteract the pull of the boat.

To ensure good sport from an early-morning start if your quarry is bream or tench, try rowing out to pre-bait the swim the night before, not forgetting to mark the swim in some way. It is sur-prising just how far out you can be when you make a calculated guess as to the exact position of the swim when you return to a large expanse of water, even when you go to the bother of lining up one feature with another on shore. You can construct a marker from a length of cord, with a 2 oz bomb tied to one end and a loaded (self-cocking) pike float on the other end. Drop the marker over the side of the boat once you have scattered the groundbait about. In the morning, as you approach the spot, use binoculars to look for signs of fish movement, or their bubbles, over the groundbait. Be sure to position the boat sideways-on to the wind (with a mud-weight at each end) at a reasonable cast length away from the marker so as not to spook the fish. If during the session the bream are feeding so confidently you feel the boat could be repositioned a little closer, simply lift the mudweights at each end and use the wind to drift silently forwards.

It is always better to fish from further away to start with, because you then have the option of moving closer later, rather than anchoring too close and scaring the fish initially. Don't forget to take the marker home at the end of the session.

When anchoring in rivers, you should anchor bows-on to the current. To do this, put down the bow mud-weight first (if alone in the boat, this is the easier way round), and let out at least several feet more rope than the depth requires. Once the boat comes round to settle steadily, lower the stern weight on a fairly tight rope. When the flow is too strong for you to use standard waggler techniques, use the stret-pegging rig shown in fig. 25, or simply swap over to a quivertip set-up (see 'Quivertipping', p. 67).

THE FLAT FLOAT (LAYING ON) RIG

When tackling dense reed-lines along your own bank, either from wooden staging or from marshy ground, it is a waste of time to cast out over the reeds and expect species like tench and carp to feed in open water, unless the water is well coloured. They are much more likely to be mere feet away, working through the reeds or rushes.

Such swims demand a stealthy approach, sitting or kneeling a few feet back from the waterline with a bait hanging right beneath the rod tip just 2 to 3 yd out, where fish will be feeding between the stems. Ledgering is an option, but invariably spooks large, deep-bodied, patrolling species such as bream, tench and carp. Even if the sound waves of a heavy lead going in doesn't scare them, the line stretched 'hauser' fashion

Provided you are well concealed, you can take even big carp like this 20-pounder from the margins, mere feet away on float tackle.

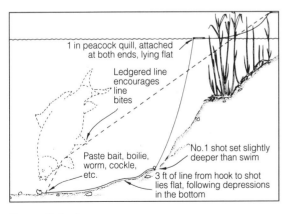

FIGURE 8 Laying on

from bait to rod tip most certainly will. They simply fade away when they sense the line or accidentally bump into it, and promptly vacate the area in blind panic.

Neither occurrence is likely to produce a specimen in the bottom of the net, but the problem is easily solved by the flat float rig shown in fig. 8. The float is not cocked because if it was, water displacement caused, for example, by a carp's tail, could move the line and dip the float momentarily (the float sometimes twitches when fish are in the swim, enticing you into striking when there is not a bite). When a fish does move off with the bait, however, the float sinks from view as the line from bait to rod tip straightens.

The rig is simplicity itself to construct. Attach 1 in of peacock quill (a tiny waggler will do nicely) to the line with a silicone rubber band at each end. After tying on the hook, set the float well over depth so that at least 3 ft of line lies along the bottom. Then fix on a small shot (a No. 1) below the float, slightly deeper than the swim. The rod can then be placed in two rests. Alternatively, it can be held.

Fishing right in among marginal stems means that prebaiting is not really necessary because the fish are already there. However, you will need to creep about in order to catch them at such close quarters. Just scatter a handful of bait fragments among the stems every so often (worms, cockles, bread flake, boilies etc.) to keep fish moving through the swim. Although the float may be light, this is certainly not a light tackle method. You need to relate line strengths to the species expected. For tench, bream and modest-sized carp, 6 lb test should suffice. For carp into double figures and larger, opt for a 10–12 lb reel line coupled to hooks of suitable size and strength.

FLOAT FISHING FOR CRUCIAN CARP

To catch crucians regularly, a very carefully shotted light float rig is imperative, the best floats being a fine-tipped antenna or a short, narrow-diameter length of peacock quill fished in 'mini-lift' style. The object is to see those tiny bites for which crucians are renowned and which often barely register on the float tip (fig. 9B).

For this reason the single shot (a No. 1, BB or AA depending on float size) should be not more than 2 in from the hook. Try moving it even closer, to 1 in away, because sometimes this alone can make all the difference between seeing bites or not. The secret, after casting in and tightening up so the float cocks, is to wind down even further so the tip is just the merest 'blimp' on the surface. Strike the slightest movement.

When crucians are really feeding confidently, denoted by clusters of small bubbles regularly rising to the surface, the float might even lift completely out of the water and lie flat, as the carp tilts its head up after sucking up the bait and dislodges the shot. Or the tip will sink positively as the crucian characteristically runs along the bottom. Many more bites will barely register on the float, so you need to hold the rod throughout and be eagle-eyed.

To stand a better chance of hitting bites from crafty crucians that just lie on the bottom blowing the bait in and out, rig up a light antenna float with a dust shot 2–3 in from the hook, with the bulk

shot set at mid depth (fig. 9A). After carefully plumbing the swim, adjust the float so the bait is literally a fraction above the bottom. As with the lift rig, strike at the slightest movement on the float tip. Remember to keep loose feed or small balls of groundbait going in on the little-and-often principle, and they might be encouraged to feed all day. A ruse always worth trying when they are particularly dour is to gently wind the float in 6 in at a time, which makes the bait lift upwards enticingly and fall gently down to the bottom again. Baits which are inherently buoyant like bread flake or

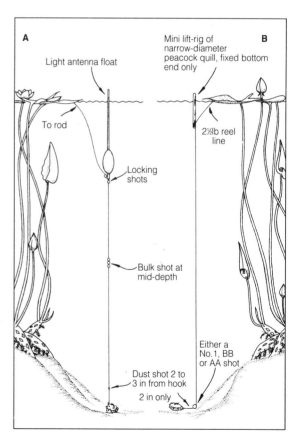

FIGURE 9 Float fishing (left) and mini-lift rig (right) for crucians

casters, or which are expected to move, such as worms, work best when 'twitching' in this way to encourage bites.

Incidentally, both these rigs work effectively for tench that are biting particularly shyly.

THE 'LIFT' METHOD

No other float-fishing technique has been so exhaustively described as the famous lift method. Yet even now, almost 40 years after the Taylor brothers first popularized the method back in the 1950s with their huge catches of tench from the lakes at Wooton Underwood, the vast majority of anglers still get it wrong because they fail to grasp the basic principle of the lift. Once and for all, let me explain how this great technique actually works.

The lift is particularly successful with, and suited to, the tench as a species because of the way in which they stand on their heads to suck in bottom-fished baits. They then return to an even keel while chewing the food and spit out the hook because it is indigestible. This is why an angler whose lift rig is incorrectly shotted (the shot being too far away from the hook) will reel in time and time again with empty maggot skins on the hook, without seeing the slightest indication of a bite.

The essence of fishing the lift is to set the float (a length of peacock quill or commercial waggler) a little overdepth, attached bottom end only with a piece of silicone tubing and *not* locking shots. I'll say that again: *not* locking shots. You do not want any shots anywhere near the float. All the shot loading, a BB, an AA, or

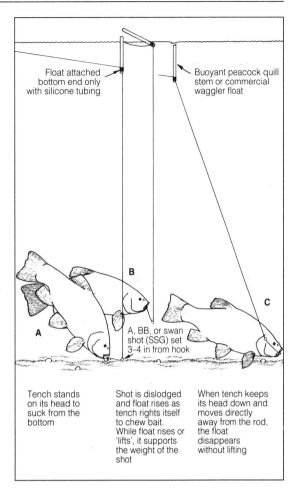

FIGURE 10 The mechanics of the lift method

a single swan shot (depending on casting requirements) must be fixed just 3–4 in from the hook (fig. 10A). When the tench sucks up the bait and rights itself, thus dislodging the shot, the float starts to 'lift' (hence the method's name) and may even fall flat. But more importantly: while it is 'lifting' it is helping to support the weight of the shot. Of course, once the float lies completely flat (fig. 10B) the tench is fully supporting the weight of that shot and could eject the bait. This is why you should always strike as the float lifts.

31

Using the famous lift method, John's partner, Paul Martingell, takes time off during a Go Fishing *shoot on a beautiful Austrian lake to prove he can catch carp in addition to directing the cameras.*

Some anglers suffer a mental block at this stage; because the float is still visible they do not consider the bite worth striking. You cannot risk waiting for such a positive indication because the tench will probably drop the bait in the meantime.

If, however, from the moment it sucks up the bait the tench keeps its head down and carries on going directly away from the rod, the float without any pre- warning whatsoever (occasionally it might 'bob' first) will simply disappear (fig. 10C). And this is the beauty behind the lift method – it allows you to interpret exactly what is happening down below.

When you expect bites at regular inter- vals, you will convert considerably more (even the tiniest lifts and dips) into tench in the net if you hold the rod throughout. It may only take a split second to reach down and grab a rod that is set in rests, but the tench can blow the bait out even quicker. Besides, an immediate strike allows you to bend the rod into a full curve and apply sufficient pressure against a tench hooked beside potential snags and to get it well under control before it can retaliate.

There is another advantage in holding the rod when fishing the lift. By gently moving the bait along the bottom you can encourage difficult tench to make a quick decision and grab the bait. This works especially well when the bait is presented over a clean bottom – either silt, mud or gravel – because as you slowly give the reel handle half a turn (providing the line is tight from float to rod tip) the inherent buoyancy of peacock quill will help the shot move along the bottom. Initially it will go under as you start to wind but will pop up again a second or two later. In the meantime, a tench may be aroused by the bait's sudden audacity in moving away, and make a sudden grab for it, resulting in a very quick 'lift' or 'dip'. If you are holding the rod you can strike these bites instantly, producing tench that would otherwise not be caught.

Tench can invariably be induced into feeding by bait movement, especially with baits that move anyway like maggots and worms. And there is no better way of moving the bait while remaining ready to deal with an instant bite than presenting the 'lift' rig.

For 'twitching' the bait over an uneven bottom, use a longer (and thus more buoyant) peacock quill than the shot requires. For example, if it is set shallower than the swim depth, the float should cock but with a good 2 in above the surface. Then reset it so that it is slightly over-depth and cast out, gently tightening up until only 1 in of the tip is visible (fig. 11A). You will know the set-up is correct when you wind down too much and the float lifts the shot along the bottom and keels over. Just tighten up again, as this is exactly what it is supposed to do (fig. 11B).

The lift can be used effectively with most baits (except really large mouthfuls), and sometimes it pays to juggle

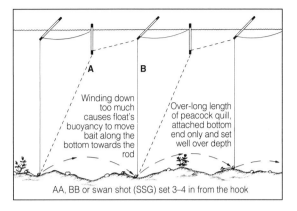

FIGURE 11 Using the lift rig to twitch the bait along an uneven bottom

about with the shot, moving it a little closer to the hook or a little further away than the recommended 3–4 in. When tench are especially shy in clear water conditions, I use a single BB (it is almost impossible to fish the lift effectively with a smaller shot) pinched on just 2 in from the hook, and select a short, super-slim length of quill.

This super-sensitive rig is great for provoking the 'bubblers', tench that are rooting just beyond the marginal lilies quite close in, where the bubbles of individual fish can be identified. Make a calculated guess as to which direction the tench is heading in and cast a little to the right or left of where bubbles last erupted. Keep casting to rising bubbles until an instant bite occurs.

When bites are not forthcoming, but fish are obviously in the swim attracted by the loose feed, you can make the hook bait more appealing and easier to suck up without the tench feeling the initial weight and presence of the hook by threading the bait on to a 'hair' (fig. 12).

Because an upward strike is imperative

with the lift method to pick up the slack created by the tench lifting the bait and shot, it can only be used as a close-range technique. If you want to float-fish for tench that are actively feeding considerably further than, say, a couple of rod lengths out, particularly in windy weather, the line must be sunk or the float will drag under. This means you cannot strike upwards, or continue to use quite the same rig, nor can you use just a single shot.

Carp and bream also stand on their head to take a bait from the bottom, as indeed do large rudd. The lift method is therefore successful with all these species. Particle baits rigged on a hair, fished in conjunction with the lift method, is a deadly way of getting wily old carp, for instance, to bite.

Lift-float fishing at night

Tench and carp that inhabit very clear waters, or lakes and pits where marginal cover is sparse, are more inclined to feed close into the bank under the cloak of darkness. They then become nicely catchable with the lift method. Use a peacock quill fitted with a luminous element so that you can see the float easily.

For fishing close in just beyond the rod tip, and regular sessions at night, it pays to invest in a 500/600 microlambert (the most powerful) betalight luminous element, which is easily glued and whipped into the top of a peacock stem (fig. 13A).

For the occasional night trip, and for fishing out well beyond the rod tip, use a luminous 'starlite' chemical element, which is very bright. It is easily slipped on to the tip of the peacock quill with a short length of clear tubing that comes supplied with the element (fig. 13B).

These wonderful inventions come in a choice of three sizes. They consist of a clear plastic tube containing two chemicals which, once you bend the tube and

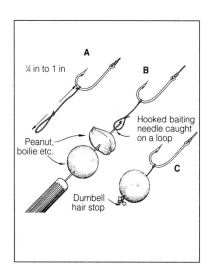

FIGURE 12 Adding a hair to a hook on a lift rig

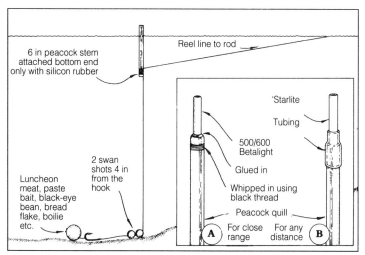

FIGURE 13 Lift-float fishing at night

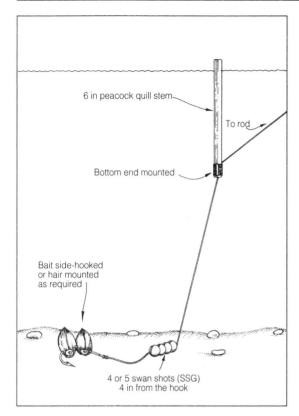

6 in peacock quill stem

To rod

Bottom end mounted

Bait side-hooked
or hair mounted
as required

4 or 5 swan shots (SSG)
4 in from the hook

FIGURE 14   Converting the lift into a bolt/shock rig

shake, mix together and become luminous for about eight hours.

As bites at night tend to be far more positive than those experienced in the daytime, resist the temptation to wind the float tip down so only the merest tip is visible, or you will be forever striking at ghosts. By all means hold the rod to capitalize on bites when they are occurring frequently, but when times are slow, try to relax by positioning the rod close to hand, supported horizontally on two rests.

Wherever there is a slight draw on the surface, the float might be slowly dragged under. Simply push the back rod rest down a little to angle the tip of the rod upwards, thus lifting sufficient line off the surface for the float tip to reappear. You will gradually learn these little tricks. You will also quickly discover to switch on a torch *only* when it is absolutely necessary (such as when the line is tangled), because night vision is instantly ruined by torchlight.

The lift/bolt rig

To adapt the basic lift method into a 'shock' or 'bolt rig', with or without the bait presented on a hair for carp, simply pinch on 4 or 5 swan shot instead of the usual two (fig. 14). This invariably stops nuisance fish like bream and tench from pushing the bait about and giving false bites. Be prepared to hold the rod all the time because it is rather tricky fishing, especially when the bait is close to lilies or beside jungle swims. When a carp grabs the bait and instantly panics off, it feels the extra shots as the hook pricks home and it moves at incredible speed.

FLOAT LEDGER RIG

When contemplating float-fishing for roach, perch, rudd, bream or tench at distances beyond the casting potential of the previously mentioned lift, bodied waggler or driftbeater rigs, it makes sense to take all the shots off the line and put them on a mini ledger link stopped 10 in from the hook (fig. 15). With this float ledger rig, extremely long distances can be covered and the bait can be presented into areas where the ledgered bait is not practical, such as swims 40 yd out where a ledgered line cannot be sunk because of a large patch of lilies between the swim and the bank. The float ledger is also the best

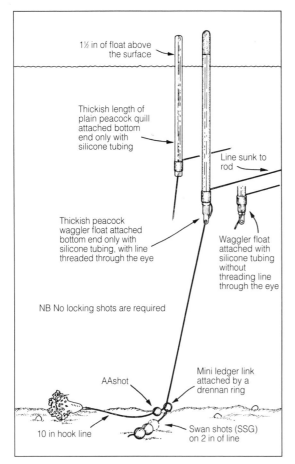

1½ in of float above the surface

Thickish length of plain peacock quill attached bottom end only with silicone tubing

Line sunk to rod

Thickish peacock waggler float attached bottom end only with silicone tubing, with line threaded through the eye

Waggler float attached with silicone tubing without threading line through the eye

NB No locking shots are required

Mini ledger link attached by a drennan ring

AAshot

10 in hook line

Swan shots (SSG) on 2 in of line

FIGURE 15 Float ledger rig

Opposite Ex-world champion, Ian Heaps, squeezes a small ball of cereal feed to keep the rudd and bream feeding while he uses the long pole-short line method.

can see this easily at distance – about 1½ in should do.

POLE FLOAT RIGS

Because the line can be held immediately upwind of the float without its being dragged under or off course and thus affecting bait presentation at distances of up to 30–40 feet out, the degree of sensitivity gained from pole fishing has no equal. Only in extremely gusty conditions or when you fancy a change is it pertinent to sink the line and change to waggler fishing or ledgering.

The renowned 'short line-long pole' method where only 5–6 ft of line exists between float and pole tip is arguably the most deadly of all match fishing techniques. Tackle rigs are not really so different from running line set ups except that shots are not used close to the float.

To offer a small bait such as caster or maggot on the drop to summer rudd, which love the warmer upper water layers, or to super-wary roach or dace in a clear water canal, the set up in fig. 16A is perfect. If a bite does not happen on the drop or when the bait has been touching bottom for a while, it is easy with the pole to move the float (and thus the bait) several inches either to the right or left, or to whisk it up off the bottom a couple of feet and let it fall again, or to lift the rig completely out, flipping it straight back in again to encourage bites on the drop. Plummeting of the swim is critical

rig for presenting a static bait in extremely windy conditions, when either surface pull or underwater tow continually belly the line and submerge the tip of a delicately shotted float rig.

Strangely, in rough weather bites are invariably quite bold, and I can recall several outings when even using three or four swan shots on the mini ledger, large fish such as bream and tench have moved them and actually given a lift bite. Most registrations, however, will consist of a positive sinking of the float tip, so ensure that enough of the tip is visible so that you

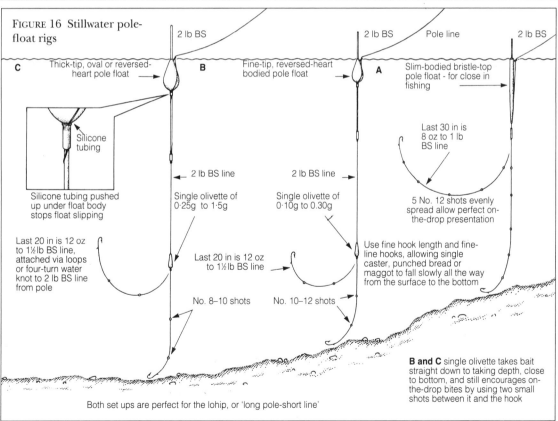

FIGURE 16 Stillwater pole-float rigs

C

Thick-tip, oval or reversed-heart pole float →

Silicone tubing

Silicone tubing pushed up under float body stops float slipping

Last 20 in is 12 oz to 1½ lb BS line, attached via loops or four-turn water knot to 2 lb BS line from pole

B

2 lb BS

Fine-tip, reversed-heart bodied pole float →

2 lb BS line →

Single olivette of 0·25g to 1·5g

Last 20 in is 12 oz to 1½ lb BS line →

No. 8–10 shots

A

2 lb BS   Pole line   2 lb BS

Slim-bodied bristle-top pole float - for close in fishing →

Last 30 in is 8 oz to 1 lb BS line

5 No. 12 shots evenly spread allow perfect on-the-drop presentation

2 lb BS line

Single olivette of 0·10g to 0.30g

Use fine hook length and fine-line hooks, allowing single caster, punched bread or maggot to fall slowly all the way from the surface to the bottom

No. 10–12 shots

B and C single olivette takes bait straight down to taking depth, close to bottom, and still encourages on-the-drop bites by using two small shots between it and the hook

Both set ups are perfect for the lohip, or 'long pole-short line'

37

during the winter months when the fish's metabolism has slowed down and bites are gentle dips of the fine tip. Most will come in that narrow band of water immediately above the bottom and so that is exactly where your bait needs to be all the time. The rig in fig. 16B is ideal because the single olivette takes the bait straight down and the two tiny shots between it and hook will still register any 'on the drop' bites. When fish are situated a fair way out into very deep water two things are important: a float tip thick enough to see easily; and a heavy enough olivette to take the bait straight down to the feeding zone (fig. 16C). Again by using two tiny shots between the olivette and hook, 'on the drop' bites will register by the tip not settling properly so watch it like a hawk. If the occasional specimen

roach or rudd is on the cards and super-light tackle is imperative to initiate bites then use the elasticated tip set up.

Hit-and-hold tactics

Certain types of summer venues on still-waters dictate that if you want quality fish you must present the bait in among or alongside thick beds of tough lilies. For those inevitable hit-and-hold tussles that will follow, a 5–6 m telescopic glass or glass/carbon-mix pole can be wound up nicely into a cushioning bend, dispensing altogether with the need for shock absorbing elastic. Such a tool may be held single-handed and supported along the forearm like a rod, and its soft action is your buffer and insurance against breakages. An unpainted quill is fished with the simple lift method.

FLOAT FISHING IN RUNNING WATER

WAGGLER FISHING

Wagglers have neat bottom eyes permitting a speedy change from one float to another with the help of a silicon float adapter, which is sleeved on to the line. In addition, by grouping the bulk shot either side of the waggler, locking it in the desired position (remember to leave a gap between the shots), not only is casting more accurate, like an arrow, but the float easily 'folds' flat to the line on the strike and so does not impair hook penetration.

A 2 or 2½ lb reel line is perfect for most waggler fishing used in conjunction with a 13 ft waggler rod and a simple shotting pattern for slow currents.

The waggler/lift rigs (slow currents)

Use of the waggler in running water provides a choice between anchoring the bait to the bottom or presenting it trundling slowly over the river-bed at current pace. And for both methods the straight peacock waggler is best, because unlike the insert waggler, whose tip is drawn under too easily, its inherent buoyancy allows small baits to be trundled smoothly over an uneven bottom without the tip dragging under and registering false bites.

For dragging small baits like casters or maggots along the bottom in very slow currents in search of dace, roach, chub and bream, group most of the bulk shot around the float, which should be set at least 1 ft over-depth. Then dot several small shots at equal distances (say, every 18–20 in) down the line, finishing with a dust shot (fig. 17A) For the best presentation in windy weather, sink the line as though fishing in stillwater and strike sideways. In calm conditions ensure that the line floats, allowing reasonable slack and a distinct bow from float to rod tip so

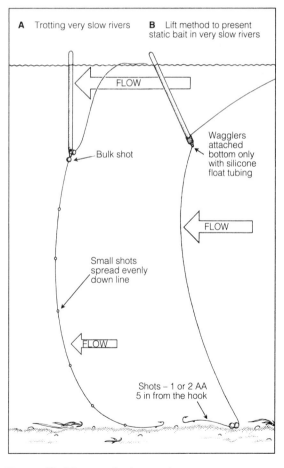

FIGURE 17 The waggler in running water

The roach of small, shallow rivers with a gentle flow respond best to waggler fishing. Safely in the net is a 2 lb plus specimen for John's tackle-shop manager, Andy Jubb of Norwich.

that the bait is not drawn inwards and away from the feed line.

For those occasions when species like bream refuse to accept a moving bait and show interest only in one lying static, put your faith in the lift method (fig. 17B). By adding a starlight luminous element to the tip of the waggler good catches of bream can be made at night by fishing 'lift style'.

I particularly enjoy using the waggler to present small baits like maggots and casters to chub in the smaller rivers during the winter, when the weeds have gone, provided that the flow is not too strong. In clear, low, cold water conditions when chub in shallow rivers tend to pack beneath definite habitat swims like over-hanging or sunken willows and are loathe to leave such protection, there are times when, unless the bait is teased into spots no ledger could ever reach directly under the edge of the branches, you won't catch any chub.

With the float set to present the bait just off the bottom it is cast a few feet upstream from the trees (fig. 18A) and allowed to be carried downstream unchecked alongside the branches. Any attempt to keep a tight line, as with the ledger (fig. 18B), will draw the bait away from the fish.

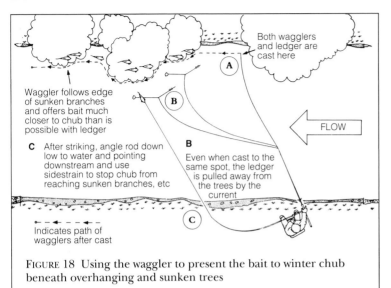

FIGURE 18 Using the waggler to present the bait to winter chub beneath overhanging and sunken trees

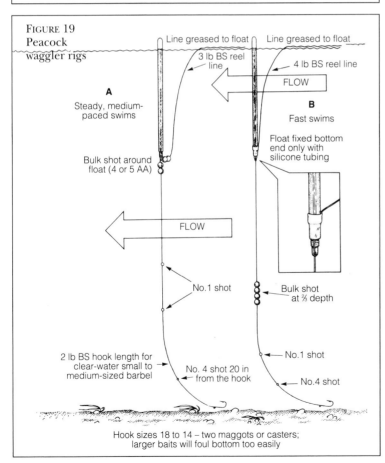

Loose feed should be kept to a minimum initially and should be catapulted well upstream to allow for current speed. If baiting with a single caster or maggot, stewed hempseed or tares are excellent loose-feed attractors, but feed sparingly in very cold conditions. Just half a dozen seeds every other trot down will suffice.

Waggler in steady, medium-paced to fast swims

To offer a moving bait in deep rivers of medium pace or deep eddies in weir-pools, choose a waggler carrying a fair shotting capacity when seeking big fish like chub and barbel.

For ease of casting, and to hit the same line consistently, do not be afraid to rig up a really big, thick peacock waggler that takes plenty of shot – between 5AA and 6AA. For long, medium-paced swims where there is time for the bait to find its level slowly, bulk most of the shot around the float, leaving room down below for a couple of No. 1s and a No. 4 20 in above the hook (fig. 19A). In order every so often to mend the bow that forms between rod tip and float as it is carried downstream unchecked, grease the line above the float with mucilin. The bow is impossible to mend if the line is sunk.

If the bottom is clean, smooth sand or gravel, the float tip may be shotted reasonably well down. Where the river bed is uneven, however, leave a good 1½ in of the tip above the surface, encouraging the buoyancy in the peacock waggler to drag the bait over the river-bed without the tip being submerged. When a barbel or chub grabs the bait, you will be in absolutely no doubt of a bite. In really clear water, the hook link can be reduced to make spooky fish bite, but no lighter than 2 lb test. Remember to keep feeding exactly the same line with the catapult on every cast to ensure that barbel move over the bait at some point along the swim. A loose feed mixture of hemp and casters works well in clear water with double caster, caster and maggot, or double maggot on the hook.

To waggler-fish fast swims, shallow or deep, I prefer to bulk most of the shots at around two-thirds depth, with a No. 1 and a No. 4 between them and the hook (fig. 19B). The float is not locked to the line in the normal way, but held tightly by silicone tubing. I also feel happier switching over from a 3 lb to a 4 lb reel line in stronger currents – and ensure the line for at least 5 or 6 yd above the float has a liberal coating of mucilin.

Laying on with the waggler

This technique is ideal for catching roach, bream and tench from deep, slow-moving water. It permits the bait to be presented 'layed on' over bottom weeds such as the subsurface cabbage of the yellow water-lily, instead of falling through them and

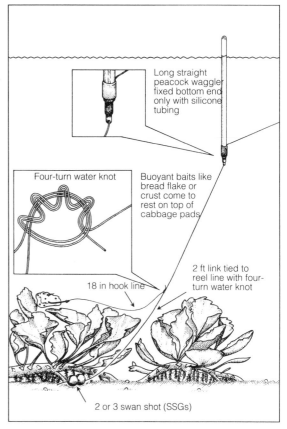

FIGURE 20 Laying on with the waggler in slow moving water

thus being hidden from feeding fish.

You need a very long waggler to fish this method effectively. The swan shots (fig. 20) are not responsible for cocking the float, so you can use as many as you like to aid casting and provide the weight necessary to carry them down through the cabbage leaves to the river-bed. Tighten up quickly after casting so that the waggler cocks with a good inch of the tip above the surface. This ensures that the very last thing to settle is the bait, which will rest in full view on top of the cabbages, where the fish can see it. A large piece of fresh, white bread flake, pinched tightly in just one small area along the hook shank, comes to rest extremely gently. Also effective is a balanced offering of crust on the shank and flake on the bend. Even better still is a ½ in cube of plain bread crust tipped with a single maggot to make it gyrate.

Fishing the stick float

The reason for fixing top and bottom is purely one of control. As the line is not actually threaded through any part of the float, changing from one to another is indeed accomplished in a matter of seconds. But overall it is the sensitivity in control of the stick float and subsequent finesse in presentation of small baits like casters, maggots, hempseed, elderberries and tares, which sets the technique apart. Fishing the stick float should be considered a technique that only really works effectively at short range – a length of one and a half rod lengths or a distance beyond which loose feed cannot accurately be thrown by hand.

As soon as you try to control a float cast any further, it will be pulled away from the line being fed and at which the shoal is lying as it is taken downstream by the current. So first and foremost think of presenting the stick to roach, dace and chub occupying marginal and close-range swims only. Beyond this – use the waggler.

Consider the basic shotting pattern of the wire-stemmed stick float for instance in fig. 2I. Sometimes bites happen when the

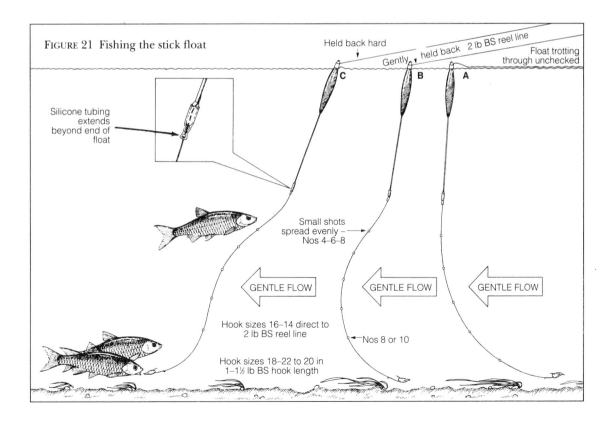

FIGURE 21 Fishing the stick float

Held back hard

Gently held back   2 lb BS reel line

Float trotting through unchecked

C   B   A

Silicone tubing extends beyond end of float

Small shots spread evenly – Nos 4–6–8

GENTLE FLOW   GENTLE FLOW   GENTLE FLOW

Hook sizes 16–14 direct to 2 lb BS reel line

Nos 8 or 10

Hook sizes 18–22 to 20 in 1–1½ lb BS hook length

Known for his prowess with all float-fishing techniques, Dave Thomas accounted for this lovely roach haul on the stick float from Ireland's River Inny.

the tip it keeps just above the surface to indicate instantly the very slightest and most hesitant of bites. A single buoyant caster presented slowly just above bottom in conjunction with hempseed fed very sparingly is a wonderful winter combination for chub, roach and dace. An elderberry or tare on the hook plus loose fed hemp is also a winner.

BIG STICK/BALSA TROTTER RIG

For presenting the bait to big roach, chub or barbel hugging the bottom of

float is trotted along, set overdepth and completely unchecked (fig. 2IA). More bites are usually instigated, however, by constant light-fingered control of the stick float. Bites also happen when gently holding back (fig. 21B), which momentarily speeds up the bait's forward movement. And by holding back hard for several seconds (fig. 2IC), the bait is whisked away from the bottom to flutter enticingly ahead of the float.

For a really slow search of the swim, particularly effective in cold water conditions when roach for instance are loathe to give chase, slightly overshot the float so that if left to trot through unchecked the tip would actually disappear. But of course by gently controlling and holding back on

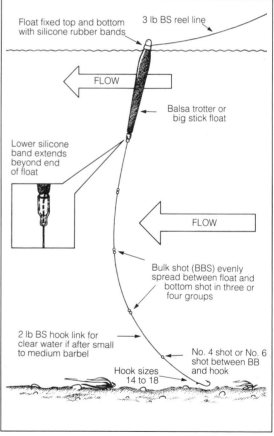

FIGURE 22 Big stick, balsa trotter rigs

deepish swims where the pace is steady, I like the sensitivity of big sticks and balsa trotters. I even step down to a 3 lb reel line if there are no snags or marginal rushes and reeds.

The shotting load can be spread evenly in three or four groups (depending on swim depth), with a small shot, a No. 4 or 6, between the lowest group and the hook (fig. 22). Try slightly overshotting the float so that you can ease back gently (as though stick-float fishing for roach) all the way down the swim with a fairly controlled line from rod to float tip. Do not be afraid to set the float well over-

John subdues a scrappy grayling using a centre-pin reel and a long-trotting float rig – the most effective set up for exploring narrow, overgrown rivers like this carrier of Berkshire's River Kennet.

This 2 lb roach was caught during a Go Fishing *programme from a deep, turbulent weir-pool using a four-swan-shot 'loafer' float to keep the bait down close to the bottom.*

depth so the bait literally bumps bottom all the way down the swim. Bites are invariably a bold sinking of the tip which looks exactly like the bottom.

If the water runs crystal clear and bites on a heavier set up do not happen, be prepared to step down to small hooks, sizes 16 and 18 on a 2 lb bottom. But you should only do this if you are sure you have room to play a barbel should you hook one without the problems caused by nearby snags. I am talking here about small to medium-sized barbel, up to 4–5 lb. If there is any chance whatsoever of a specimen barbel inhabiting the swim, my advice is to stick with heavier tackle capable of landing it.

LONG-TROTTING RIGS

When using a 2½–4 lb line and long trotting the smaller rivers for big roach, grayling and chub, I use the simple rig shown in fig. 23, which incorporates the stumpy chubber float.

Because it has such a wide tip and is easily seen even at distances of up to 30 yd, and because for its size it carries a good shotting load, this float is ideal. In fast water there is no point whatsoever in messing about with complicated shotting rigs, especially in water less than 4 ft deep. Simply put the entire shotting load within 1 ft of the hook, so the bait is presented right down there just above bottom (fig. 23A). In swims of considerable depth where the pace is moderate, bunch the bulk shot within 3 ft of the hook and pinch on a BB or an AA in between (fig. 23B).

I prefer to slightly overshot these chunky floats and keep a fairly tight line as they are taken downstream by the flow: alongside overhanging trees, around the back eddies in weir-pools, through deep centre channels, around acute bends overhung by willows and so on. It is very much a moving game whereby, carrying the minimum of tackle, I can offer the bait to fish inhabiting numerous interesting and demanding swims along the river's twisting course. If roach and chub are the quarry I avoid all areas of heavy turbulence and extreme shallows, preferring the long, easy-paced glides where experience suggests they are most likely to be shoaled up. With grayling in mind, however, no run, no matter how fast, turbulent or rocky, is passed without running the float through a couple of times. This is such a good probing, searching, exploring method, and it works best during mild winter weather when, with the weed growth gone, fish keep permanently on the look out for food items brought down to them by the current.

For attracting roach and chub there is nothing to beat mashed bread as loose feed in coloured water, with either flake or small cubes of crust on the hook. In clear water, on the other hand, particularly

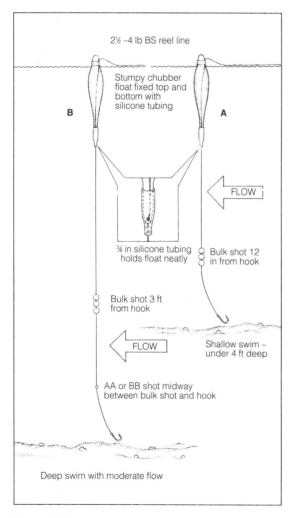

2½–4 lb BS reel line

Stumpy chubber float fixed top and bottom with silicone tubing

B

A

FLOW

⅜ in silicone tubing holds float neatly

Bulk shot 12 in from hook

Bulk shot 3 ft from hook

FLOW

Shallow swim – under 4 ft deep

AA or BB shot midway between bulk shot and hook

Deep swim with moderate flow

FIGURE 23 Long-trotting tactics

when you are after grayling, maggots or casters have the edge. Grayling, especially, love trotted brandlings.

In classic barbel rivers, which are quite shallow and thus easy to wade and where shoals hug the clean gravel and sandy runs between beds of long, flowing streamer weeds, it is an absolute joy to catch barbel and chub by long trotting. You get the best results by climbing quietly into the river in thigh boots or chest-waders (a sound investment), and wading slowly to an upstream position, from which the bait can be trotted almost directly downstream. This permits excellent presentation because the float is not dragged off course when it is controlled or held back. The bait can be trundled down in a natural way along the desired line by gently breaking the float's passage and occasionally swinging it upwards by holding the float back hard momentarily.

As the barbel feeds from the bottom and the layer of water immediately above the river-bed where food particles are washed along by the current, your bait needs to be presented either dragging bottom (only possible where the river-bed consists of clean sand or gravel) or within a few inches of the bottom. Any higher and it will ride above the barbel's head, out of its feeding zone. In the summer months when the water runs both warm and crystal clear, barbel will take, and can sometimes be observed, moving upwards and across the flow to intercept loose-fed casters and maggots as they fall and tumble downriver. Such occasions are responsible for those unmistakable bites that drag the float quickly beneath the surface within a second or so of your

holding it back to waver the bait upwards. Generally speaking, however, barbel want their dinner to move slowly along or just above the river-bed.

Ideal baits for trotting are the big four, maggots, casters, worms and bread, with sweetcorn bringing up the rear. As for ledgering, I rate hempseed highly for loose-feed attraction and often put a couple of handfuls into the top of each swim when long trotting, prior to follow-

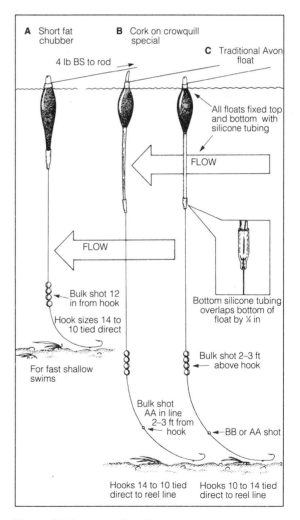

FIGURE 24 Long-trotting rigs

47

Anglers fishing this picturesque tidal pool on the Hampshire Avon at Christchurch use long-trotting tactics to catch sea trout, mullet and coarse species.

ing through with a bunch of maggots or casters, plus loose-feed helpings of the same every other cast. It's only fair to state that at no time when trotting for barbel should you expect to enjoy a bite every other trot down, as you might when roach fishing.

It goes without saying that when wading, an indispensable item of tackle is the bait pouch or apron, and so too is a tackle waistcoat. There is nothing more infuriating than having to make frequent trips back to the bank in order to change floats or hooks.

I generally opt for a trotting line of around 4 lb test. I use a centre-pin reel in

conjunction with a 13 ft, carbon waggler rod, but for tackling swims with particularly heavy weed, bullrushes or an extra strong flow, I increase the power to a 12 ft, 1¼lb test curve, carbon Avon, which harmonizes nicely with a 5 lb or 6 lb test line.

Really shallow, fast runs are most effectively fished with a short, fat float (long floats could easily spook the barbel) such as the chubber, with all the shot bulked 12 in above the hook (fig. 24A). Keep running the float through unchecked, inching it up the line on each cast until the bait is dragging bottom so hard that the float pulls under. Then pull it down a shade and commence fishing. This is a far easier method of finding the depth than plumbing the entire length of the swim.

In deep, steady runs where extra shots down the line are imperative for presenting the bait smoothly and trundling it along in a natural manner, I use cork on crowquill floats. These specials take up to 6AA and are best rigged with most of the bulk-shot loading set in a line 2–3 ft above the hook with a No. 1 or a No. 3 between the float and the hook (fig. 24B) – this rig is very simple but most effective.

When the water is deep and swirling, the float to use is the traditional Avon. Its bulbous, oval body and thick tip permit maximum shotting capacity for a stable trot through and ensure that the bait searches slowly, close to or actually along the river-bed (fig. 24C). To achieve the correct depth, follow the procedure for chubbers. In really long swims, however, of 20 or 30 yd, it is not uncommon to find a hump on the bottom that would present the bait too high throughout most of the trot if it is set to the shallowest depth. The remedy is to hold back hard on the float just before the hump or similar obstruction (such as a weed clump) to ease the end tackle over it and then continue the rest of the run through.

STRET PEGGING

One of the most effective and fascinating close-range float-fishing techniques to use in flowing water is the art of stret pegging. It is a combination of float ledgering and laying on that ensures the bait is always accurately placed and lies perfectly static on the bottom. So long as the intended species occupy a deepish run close into

the bank beside man-made pilings alongside marginal sedges or reeds, natural laybys and so on, then almost regardless of the flow, stret pegging is indeed the only way of watching a float with the bait layed hard on. It is a superb method both summer and winter, especially during exceptionally cold conditions when fish are loathe to chase a moving bait. As can be seen from fig. 25A, the float (a short length of unpainted peacock quill) needs to be fixed top and bottom and set considerably deeper than swim depth so the current forms a bow in the line between float and bottom shots. This to some extent relieves the pressure on the float, enabling it to lie flat and the bait to

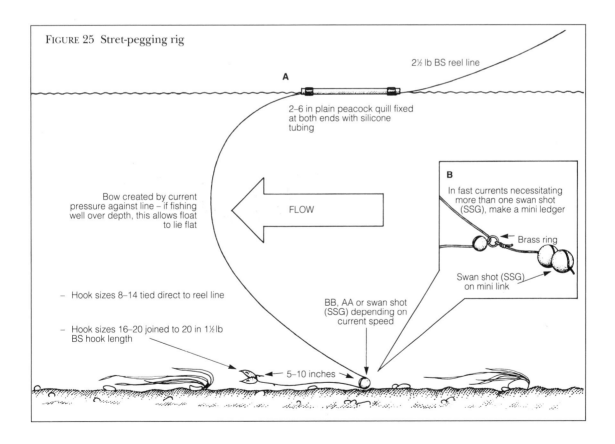

FIGURE 25 Stret-pegging rig

A

2½ lb BS reel line

2–6 in plain peacock quill fixed at both ends with silicone tubing

B

In fast currents necessitating more than one swan shot (SSG), make a mini ledger

Brass ring

Swan shot (SSG) on mini link

Bow created by current pressure against line – if fishing well over depth, this allows float to lie flat

FLOW

– Hook sizes 8–14 tied direct to reel line

– Hook sizes 16–20 joined to 20 in 1½ lb BS hook length

BB, AA or swan shot (SSG) depending on current speed

5–10 inches

remain static with just a single BB, AA or swan shot (depending on current force) pinched on the line 5–10 in from the hook.

When the flow is too fast for a single shot to hold bottom, construct a 'mini ledger' using a small ring plus 1 in or so of thick line, to which a swan shot or two are added, as in fig. 25B.

If seeking species like dace, perch, roach and bream, reel line is 2 ½ lb test (in conjunction with a 13 ft waggler rod) and when I use this technique for catching specimen roach or bream I tie hooks in sizes 8–14 direct for baits like bread flake and crust or stewed wheat etc. When you are after modest-sized fish and there is a need to step down much lighter, such as in clear, cold water conditions, add a 20 in length of 1½ lb test hook length enabling you to use hooks in sizes 16–20 holding smaller baits like maggots and casters.

Always sit looking down river and make the cast downstream and across so the rig swings inwards (fig. 26). Put the rod on two rests with the tip angled upwards so

no line actually lies on the surface or the float may be swept around. Most bites are positive with the float simply gliding under, sometimes preceded by a gentle twitching or shaking. When presenting bread flake, introduce a few balls of mashed bread well upstream allowing for current speed so it comes to rest close to the hook bait. With maggots and casters simply use a bait dropper to deposit them with accuracy in strong currents or deep water.

For larger species like chub and barbel, line strength is increased to 5–6 lb coupled to an 11–12 ft, 1¼ lb test curve, Avon-style rod. To combat stronger currents, larger, more buoyant floats are imperative, along with mini ledger rigs or a block-end feeder to anchor the bait static on the bottom (fig. 27).

Stret pegging is a great flood-water technique when rivers run tea coloured and lap the banks and most species seek out all the choice slacks or move into the mouths of sidestreams where they join the main river. To attract roach, dace, bream etc, put down a couple of bait droppers full of maggots or casters and follow in with your stret pegging rig. In mild weather you will not wait long for a bite. In cold weather if the maggots come back sucked to mere skins without any noticeable registration on the float, reduce the hook length to just 3 or 4 in.

Lobworms really sort out quality roach, chub and barbel when the river is in high spate. Loose feed by scattering a handful of broken worms into the swim several yards upstream of the point where you intend them to settle close to the hook bait. To fool easily spooked chub and

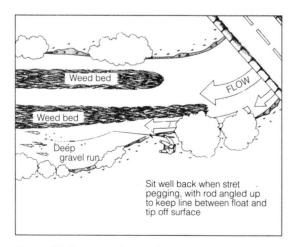

FIGURE 26 Stret pegging tactics

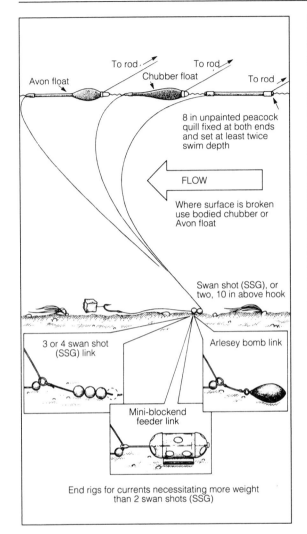

FIGURE 27 Heavy stret-pegging

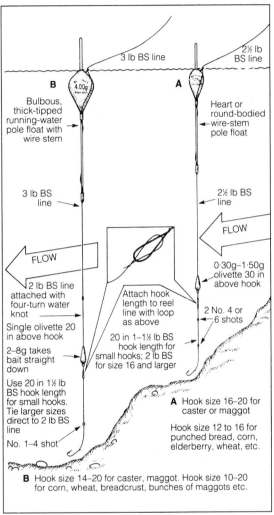

FIGURE 28 'Long pole–short line', or to-hand rigs

barbel, try presenting the bait (meat cubes, corn etc.) on a hair.

POLE FLOAT RIGS

To present the bait at reasonably close range or in gentle currents, the rig in fig. 28A, utilizing a heart or round-bodied wire-stem float carrying somewhere between 0·030 and 1·50 gm, will cover most situations. Presentation is of course far superior with the long pole–short line technique provided that species like roach or dace are situated no further out than, say, 11 m.

There will be numerous occasions – when trotting the float way beyond the pole tip alongside trailing branches on the opposite bank of a small river, for instance, or fishing along the centre bowl of a canal into water 12–4 ft deep – that demand a full pole length of line out, so that when you swing in a small fish or the hook for rebaiting it comes directly 'to hand' – hence the expression.

When fishing into really deep water, the 'to hand' method is extremely effective and much quicker than unshipping the pole after each cast to unhook or rebait, although with an excess of line between float and pole tip, the sensitivity of the presentation can be impaired in strong winds. When presentation to hand becomes totally impossible, think about swapping over to the waggler or a feeder outfit. Or try drawing the shoal closer in by feeding along a shorter line so the long pole–short line method can be employed.

The beauty of using the pole in running water is that you can hold back gently on the bulbous-bodied float to slow the rig down and trundle the bait naturally through the swim really close to the bottom, like the loose-feed fragments. Choose the size of float required to combat the current speed (always go heavier rather than lighter), and a simple bottom rig as shown in fig. 28B to deliver the bait straight down to the feeding zone, which, if after bream or roach, is that first foot of water immediately above the bottom. Fix the single olivette around 20 in above the hook, with a No. I to No. 4 shot midway between. If the shot is moved closer to the hook, this will sometimes improve bite registration, so do not be afraid to move it around.

If you find groundbaiting with accuracy rather difficult when fishing at 9–11 yd out, try touching the surface with the pole tip and use this as a marker when employing the 'long pole–short line' technique. Loose feed such as maggots, casters and hempseed are always best catapulted (leave the pole tip in the water, freeing both hands for catapulting). To ensure that it arrives around the hook-bait when trotting in really deep water, either lock the casters or maggots up in a small ball of firmly-squeezed breadcrumb groundbait that won't break up until it touches bottom, or use a small wire-mesh bait dropper. The latter are really effective for loose-feeding bait such as casters and maggots, except when you are using an elasticated tip.

When easing the bait slowly through the water, concentrate on holding the pole really steady so that the float is not lifted or jerked. This is best achieved by holding it either across your knee or with the butt end lodged between crotch and seat, your strongest hand supporting it in front at arm's reach. This sounds more painful than it is, and it adds a couple of valuable feet to the pole's maximum distance with the fixed line.

Deep, flowing water

Fig. 29 shows two simple but heavy rigs for catching species like bream and roach/bream hybrids living in deep, flowing water where the bait needs to be taken straight down to the feeding zone immediately above the bottom and offered very slowly or even static.

In order to combat deep water and these strong, steady currents, monstrous bulbous-bodied pole floats with wire stems and carrying anything upwards from 5 to 10 gm may seem over the top,

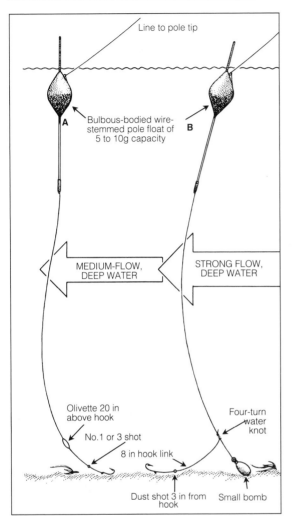

Line to pole tip

A

Bulbous-bodied wire-stemmed pole float of 5 to 10g capacity

B

MEDIUM-FLOW, DEEP WATER

STRONG FLOW, DEEP WATER

Olivette 20 in above hook

No.1 or 3 shot

8 in hook link

Four-turn water knot

Dust shot 3 in from hook

Small bomb

FIGURE 29 Pole fishing

but they are perfect for the job. Anything less would not allow the bait to be presented slow enough. The object is to get the bait straight down to the bottom, then ease back gently on the big float as the bait runs through. You will see from fig. 29A that all the weight is locked up in the single olivette, which is fixed just 20 in above the hook, with a no. 1 or 3 shot set halfway between.

When the flow is simply too strong or the bream only want a static bait (a complete lack of bites suggests this) dispense completely with weight on the line by adding a 6 in link of heavier line, as in fig. 29B.

For this method I prefer the flick tip and tie the rig directly to the small ring glued into the end. If big bream are expected then the rig should be made up on 6 lb test, with hooks from size 14 to 12 tied on a lighter 2 ft length of 3 lb test. Larger hooks, size 10 and 8, are better matched to 4 lb test when bream are being cautious.

PRESENTING FLOATING BAITS

FREELINING IN RIVERS FOR CHUB

Some would say the most exciting way of catching chub during the summer, when weed-beds furrow the surface and make other methods impractical, is with floating crust or wasp cake. For close-range swims a completely free line treated with mucilin so it floats easily and does not hinder the bait's passage downstream is all that is required. A fairly large hook is best for crust, and a size 6 or 4 (depending on bait size) is ideal. There is more than sufficient weight in a 10p-sized piece of crust for casting and if you think not, simply dunk it momentarily.

Floating crust

To entice chub up to the surface, away from the cover of weed-beds or overhung hideaways, and to persuade them to suck in crusts confidently, sit or crouch well upstream of the swim and introduce a batch of loose crusts into midstream every couple of minutes. Half a dozen at a time will do nicely. Don't worry if the first few batches are ignored (you need at least a couple of large tin-loaves for a morning's crusting), it is all part of the ritual or game anglers and chub play with each other. Sooner or later up will come a huge pair of lips, and in a huge oily swirl down will go one of the crusts, then another and so on. Float your crusts down until each crust disappears as soon as it reaches a certain spot. Then put your hook in the next crust. It is just like

floater fishing for carp, probably the most heart-stopping technique of all.

When the first swim dries up because too many chub have been removed or you botched the first strike and put them all down, wander downstream following your batches of previously uninspected crusts, some of which by now will have attracted chub in other spots.

Wasp cake

As an alternative and wonderful change bait to floating crust, try fishing in the same way with wasp cake.

It has a sweet, honey-like smell to which the chub quickly becomes addicted. Once aroused, chub will charge several feet through clear water to intercept a piece of floating cake ahead of other shoal members. It is therefore a most selective bait because as long as your cast puts a piece of cake alongside a noted specimen, unless you strike too early it is as good as in the net. As with bread crust, always wait for the fish's lips to close, for it to get its head down beneath the surface and the line to tighten before banging home the hook. A 5–6 lb line is mandatory.

THE FLOATING WORM

Carefully inject a little air from a hypodermic syringe into the head of a large lobworm to make it float tantalizingly on the surface (fig. 30) and you have a wonderful way of tempting at least three species. In stillwaters, among lily-pads and around the lapping branches of overhanging willows, both perch and carp will quickly gulp in a floating, gyrating lob, whether it is freelined using its own weight or transported to the swim with the aid of a small controller float such as the tenpin.

Chub love them too, and the floating worm is a great bait for tempting those educated, well-fished-for specimens, living in popular stretches of a river and which always seem to hole up in the snaggiest, most inaccessible spots. Drift the worm downriver, using the current to peel line from an open pool, taking it over weedbeds etc., into the shallowest runs beneath overhanging trees; and then give a gentle twitch when the chub have it in their vision. This technique produces the most fabulous, aggressive, visual takes from the surface. However, you need to be quick off the mark to extract a good chub from a tangle of branches, using a heavy-hand, hit-and-hold technique. A 6 lb test line is therefore imperative.

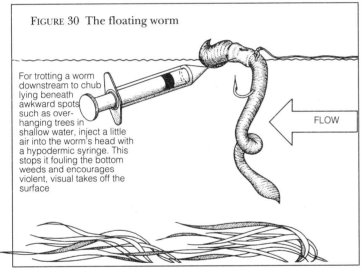

FIGURE 30 The floating worm

For trotting a worm downstream to chub lying beneath awkward spots such as overhanging trees in shallow water, inject a little air into the worm's head with a hypodermic syringe. This stops it fouling the bottom weeds and encourages violent, visual takes off the surface

FLOW

THE FLAT PEACOCK QUILL RIG

When roach and rudd especially, are working the upper water layers during the summer months and are more interested in sucking in food literally from the surface, make up a flat peacock quill rig (fig. 31) with the shots fixed at both ends of the float, and strike when it glides across the surface as opposed to going under. It is a rig that creates minimal resistance to surface takers and a fascinating way of catching both small and specimen-sized rudd.

At close quarters it is often possible to watch the bait being sucked in and forget the float altogether. Just remember not to allow too much of a bow to develop between rod tip and float, otherwise striking could be impaired. A good dubbing of mucilin on the line will

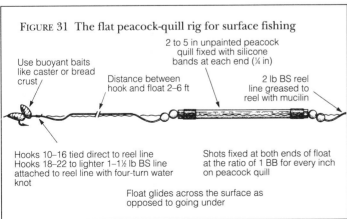

FIGURE 31 The flat peacock-quill rig for surface fishing

2 to 5 in unpainted peacock quill fixed with silicone bands at each end (¼ in)

Use buoyant baits like caster or bread crust

Distance between hook and float 2–6 ft

2 lb BS reel line greased to reel with mucilin

Hooks 10–16 tied direct to reel line
Hooks 18–22 to lighter 1–1½ lb BS line attached to reel line with four-turn water knot

Shots fixed at both ends of float at the ratio of 1 BB for every inch on peacock quill

Float glides across the surface as opposed to going under

ensure it floats well, allowing you to lift and mend the line every so often.

To loose feed, catapult fragments a little in front of the rig and slowly draw your hook bait among them. Casters are perfect bait for this technique but make sure you use all floaters or you might discourage the rudd from surface feeding. Loose feeding with scraps of breadcrust catapulted well upwind also attracts rudd and when they start splashing and nibbling at the bread use a small cube of breadcrust on the hook. This rig also works well in really shallow rivers for dace and chub, both of which are partial to floating casters.

CONTROLLER FISHING FOR CHUB

To drift floating crust into distant swims without the current bellying the free line into an unstrikable situation, the answer is to thread on a small loaded controller (like the ten-pin), which adds weight for casting (smaller baits such as casters can then also be used). More importantly, it allows the line to be mended occasionally while the bait floats downstream.

Stop the ten-pin 4 to 6 ft above the hook with a nylon stop knot and small bead (fig. 32). Stop the ten-pin 4 to 6 ft above the hook with a nylon stop knot and small bead.

Floater fishing in stillwaters

Except for small overgrown lakes and pits, in which freelined crusts can be placed or drifted alongside bushes or

This fisherman is well concealed, and needs to be in order to extract wily chub from such a shallow, clear-water stream.

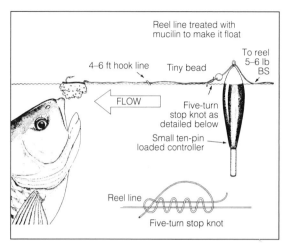

FIGURE 32 Floating controller fishing

sunken trees close to the chub's hideouts, the loaded controller offers the most effective way of getting the bait out to chub patrolling the surface. Loose attractor crusts should be catapulted well upwind around the float and the entire batch allowed to drift naturally with the wind or surface pull.

Keep paying out line as though trotting. Every now and then lift any bowing line off the surface with the rod held high, and lay or flick it upwind so that it is reasonably straight again. When fishing really large waters you have to decide on a point beyond which striking would be impaired because of the possibility of pricking and losing a chub. So strike the crust off and retrieve for a new cast.

Never wind the crust back across the surface. Only pike fall for such lack of thought, while the chub become craftier.

MARGIN FISHING FOR CARP

To catch carp slurping down floating baits like crusts or mixers which have either

Loop of line loosely held

Bale arm closed

Bait flows on the surface without any line lying on the water to scare the carp

Bait can be crust, mixer biscuit, etc.

FIGURE 33 Margin fishing (daytime)

Closed bale arm

Silver foil cylinder on line between butt ring and reel

Line is kept clear of water to prevent it scaring carp

FIGURE 34 Margin fishing (dusk onwards)

been scattered among the marginal growth or drifted there with the wind, there cannot be a more simple rig than using just the hook itself. If the fish are directly below the rod tip, lower the floater down so it rests on the surface without any slack line lying on the water. Hold the rod loosely yet expectantly with the reel's bale arm closed (the clutch properly set), and in the other hand hold a loop of line pulled from between butt ring and reel (fig. 33). This you let slip through your fingers when a carp closes its mouth over the bait and submerges with it, before whacking the rod back to set the hook.

Many carp anglers would rate this particular form of marginal floater fishing as the most exciting technique of all and I would certainly not give them an

argument. It is extremely satisfying, but demands tremendous stealth as you need to crawl into a position where a bait can be lowered among patrolling surface-feeding fish.

When surface activity is slow and the appearance of carp is not expected until the light starts to fade (either due to weather or clear water conditions) quietly set the rod on two rests, again with the bale arm closed, and instead of holding the loop of line between butt ring and reel, hang on a lightweight coil indicator. A cylinder of silver foil is perfect (fig. 34).

When fishing this method over marginal lilies, wind the bait in so it comes to rest alongside the pads and lay the line over them (fig. 35). Don't for a moment imagine the carp cannot see even small floaters presented in this way. They are looking up into bright light, and can even identify the form of a floater resting completely on top of a lily-pad. On numerous occasions I have witnessed carp knocking pads to dislodge a seemingly invisible (to them) unreachable floater. And they are not satisfied until such food is in their stomachs.

When using pieces of floating breadcrust over pads, or drifting them across the surface in open areas, if carp are

suspicious of the floating bread use a crust/flake cocktail.

Start by sliding a piece of crust up over the eye of the hook and then squeeze on a giant piece of flake. Slide the crust down again and gently squeeze a part of the flake on to the crust, thus 'locking' them together. Hopefully they will hold together until a carp investigates and 'knocks' them apart, whereupon the flake will slowly start to sink. At this point the carp can stand it no longer and promptly sucks in the flake.

Watch the line carefully and hit any positive movement instantly. One of the most suspicious and difficult of all carp to hook on floating crust is the grass carp. Rarely do they gulp the bait in and go charging off. More often than not, they simply hold the crust between pursed lips for several seconds before swallowing it and turning away. Be sure that the bait has completely disappeared before striking to this type of bait, or you risk pulling the hook away and missing the fish.

FIGURE 35 Fishing over lilies

CONTROLLER FISHING FOR CARP

When carp will only accept floaters presented further out because the water along the margins is either too clear, too shallow or both, making them feel vulnerable, casting weight is required in the form of a self-cocking controller like the 'ten-pin', which is available in four sizes. Rig up the ten-pin as shown in fig 36. Loose-fed floaters like small biscuits, boilies and so on can all be catapulted into any given area alongside features, and the hook bait deposited accurately among them. Or better still, cast out the

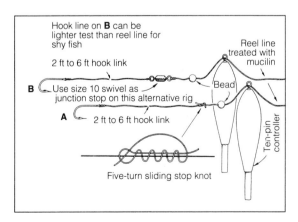

FIGURE 36 Floating controllers

Carp in small, densely stocked fisheries quickly become suspicious of floating baits presented directly on the hook. The answer is to use a hair-rigged bait.

With a grass carp and a mirror carp, these young anglers enjoy the rewards from presenting surface baits close in among the lilies.

controller and hook bait well up wind; then catapult the loose feed around it, allowing the floating food to drift down wind while playing out line from an open (well-filled) spool.

Carp are invariably more wary of accepting surface baits once they have associated them with danger than they are of bottom-fished baits. But by fishing as light as you dare, using much finer line than normal, for instance 6 lb test instead of 10 lb test if conditions permit, and by fishing in low light at dusk, dawn or even well on into darkness, most problems can be solved. Carp refuse the bait because they can see the line and hook, or because the bait behaves unlike all the free offerings around it due to the weight of the hook and drag from the line. Carp prove this time and time again by mopping up all the free floaters, but not the one on the hook. The problem is not so much getting them to accept floating food but to accept the hook bait. Even familiar unattached baits like pieces of bread crust are taken down, maybe not so quickly on waters regularly fished, but disappear they eventually will. Particle baits create far less suspicion, and sooner or later one will be sucked in, provided carp respond.

In contrast to bottom baits, at least it's possible to actually observe the reaction of carp and consequently do something about the way in which the bait is refused. Anything and everything is worth trying. Go for a much longer hook link to create less drag; or smaller hook; two floaters instead of one, which provides greater buoyancy; grease or even degrease the hook link, and so on.

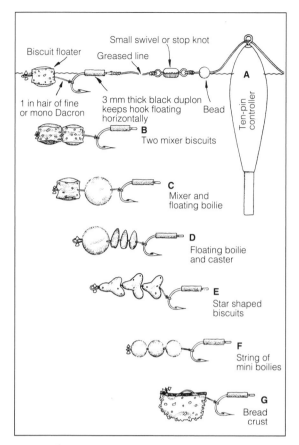

FIGURE 37 Hair-rig floaters

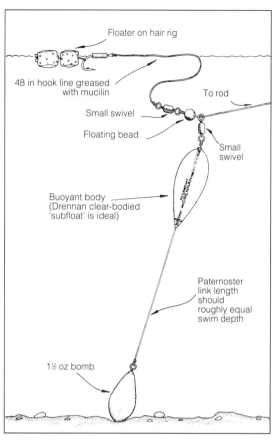

FIGURE 38 Anchored floater for distance fishing

If all else fails, put your faith in the hair rig (fig. 37) and offer the bait off the hook. There are all sorts of variations worth trying along these lines. Go down in hook size: try two or even three floaters on the hair instead of one; or a cocktail, one biscuit and one boilie together on the same hair, a boilie and casters, and so on.

Because the line actually passes through the top of the controller, when a carp moves away with the bait the line will visibly tighten and 'lift' across the surface. Hold the rod all the time with the bale arm closed ready for action. Straighten

any bow in the line formed by wind drift, leaving just a little slack so as not to scare interested fish through resistance. Keep your eyes fixed on the float's red top and identify your hook bait among the loose ones, striking on sight if you suddenly see it go without the line actually moving or whistling through the float.

THE ANCHORED FLOATER

The answer to distance problems is the anchored floater presented on a sliding, buoyant paternoster rig (fig. 38). When the rig lands and the bomb touches

61

bottom, the buoyant float body rises up to the swivel and supports the reel line just a couple of feet below the surface with the bait floating nicely above. Tighten up gently with the rod set horizontal in two rests, ensuring the line is sunk, and clip on an indicator, such as a bobbin or monkey climber. Keep the bale arm closed. When a carp sucks in the floater, the reel line runs freely down through the paternoster swivel, up goes the indicator and you are in business with a hefty strike to pick up any loose line. For this kind of long-range floater fishing, keep your eyes peeled on the area of the hook bait so that you can anticipate a probable run, and scatter loose floaters around the anchored hook bait.

LEDGERING IN STILLWATER

FREELINING

If you spend any time at all observing carp, for instance, and how they relate to a baited hook, you will soon understand why the simple method of freelining the bait without any foreign bits on the line (floats, shots, bombs, tubing, etc.), other than the hook, is the most sensitive method of all. Unless the carp picks up the line with its large pectoral or pelvic fins, or brushes up against it and does a runner, it will trundle off confidently with the bait.

Large baits heavy enough in themselves to disguise the hook and neutralize its weight, such as the insides of a whole swan mussel, a lump of trout pellet paste or a lobworm, are each also heavy enough to cast accurately from a well-filled spool without added weight. Freelining is therefore a method that can only be practised at close range where species like carp, catfish, eels and tench are attracted to natural habitats.

Anglers who have only ever float-fished for tench, using light float tackle in heavily fished waters and straining their eyes for those tiny dips or lifts of the float tip in order to strike, would not believe the way in which tench run off with a freelined bait. But then, with an unweighted bait the tench have no reason to be fussy. They

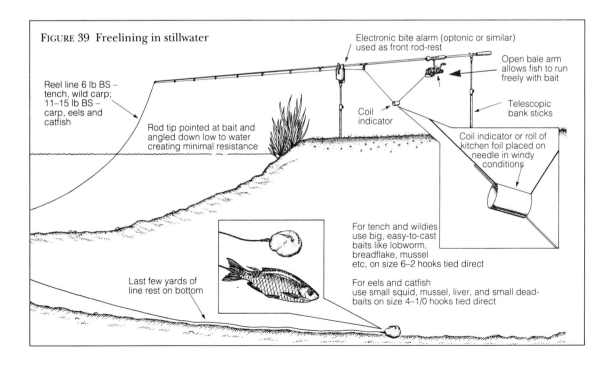

FIGURE 39 Freelining in stillwater

Electronic bite alarm (optonic or similar) used as front rod-rest

Open bale arm allows fish to run freely with bait

Reel line 6 lb BS – tench, wild carp; 11–15 lb BS – carp, eels and catfish

Rod tip pointed at bait and angled down low to water creating minimal resistance

Coil indicator

Telescopic bank sticks

Coil indicator or roll of kitchen foil placed on needle in windy conditions

Last few yards of line rest on bottom

For tench and wildies use big, easy-to-cast baits like lobworm, breadflake, mussel etc, on size 6–2 hooks tied direct

For eels and catfish use small squid, mussel, liver, and small dead-baits on size 4–1/0 hooks tied direct

simply suck it in and move off looking for the next meal, lifting the line in a glorious, unmissable, almost carp-like run.

If immediate bites are expected, do not bother with indicators. Hold the rod and keep your eyes glued to the bow in the line from rod tip to surface. If not, hang a lightweight foil indicator on a 2 ft drop between butt ring and reel, after positioning the rod on two rests with the tip pointing directly at the bait (fig. 39). Whack the hook home just before the indicator slams against the butt ring.

With minimal resistance on the line, the tench is just as likely to swim towards the rod and give a 'drop back', where-upon the indicator suddenly falls to the ground. This is a good reason for always keeping the bale arm closed when freelining, enabling you to go straight into a 'wind-cum-strike' routine in order to pick up the line and punch the hook home.

When freelining into darkness or when tench activity is on the slow side, rig up an electric alarm in conjunction with the foil indicator so you can relax. You can certainly afford to, because bites are nearly always positive.

When freelining for eels, carp and catfish at night, in addition to stepping up line strengths to 11–15 lb test, it is wise to leave the bale arm open. This allows the fish to make a positive run, peeling several feet of line from the open spool. You then close the bale arm and strike the hook home.

SWINGTIPPING

Conceived by Jack Clayton of Boston to identify the shy bites of Fenland bream,

the swingtip is, in theory, the most sensitive ledgering bite indicator ever invented and works with equal effect when ledgering for other species like roach, rudd and tench. Because the swingtip screws into the tip-ring and hangs down in front of the rod, resistance to a biting fish is minimal compared to quivertips, ledger bobbins or monkey climbers. And in certain circumstances, in shallow water in particular, bite amplification sometimes occurs; a long swingtip will move further than the distance a fish pulls the bait.

It is important to remember that swing-

When stillwater bream are biting shyly, the most sensitive indicator of all is the swingtip, used here to good effect on an Irish lake by Terry Smith.

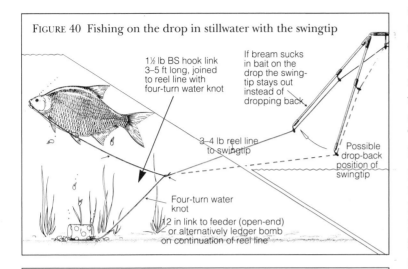

FIGURE 40 Fishing on the drop in stillwater with the swingtip

1½ lb BS hook link 3–5 ft long, joined to reel line with four-turn water knot

If bream sucks in bait on the drop the swing-tip stays out instead of dropping back

3–4 lb reel line to swingtip

Possible drop-back position of swingtip

Four-turn water knot

12 in link to feeder (open-end) or alternatively ledger bomb on continuation of reel line

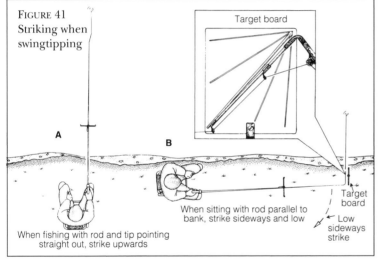

FIGURE 41 Striking when swingtipping

Target board

A

B

Target board

Low sideways strike

When sitting with rod parallel to bank, strike sideways and low

When fishing with rod and tip pointing straight out, strike upwards

occur on the drop within seconds of the ledger bomb or feeder hitting the bottom – a common occurrence during high summer, when bream tend to layer off bottom above the feed. The best rig (as it is for all bream ledgering) is the simple fixed paternoster. For this, join a 3–5 ft lighter hook link to the 3–4 lb reel line 2 ft above the bomb or feeder, which should be tied direct to the line using a four-turn water knot (fig. 40).

After casting, put the rod in the rests quickly and tighten up to the bomb, watching that tip like a hawk. It will slowly drop backwards after each turn of the reel handle until the line is reasonably tight from bomb to rod. A bite on the drop is easily registered by the tip failing to ease back when it should, because a bream (or another species) has sucked in the bait and stopped the process.

Buoyant baits such as casters, or a caster and maggot cocktail, are excellent for on-the-drop fishing. To engineer as slow a fall as possible, use a long, light hook length of about 1½ lb test – and a small, fine-wire hook. Because they are so very small and light, size 20 and 22 hooks holding a single maggot fall extremely slowly indeed.

tips are only effective in still and very slow-moving water. In fact to counteract even the slightest current, you need to use a loaded swingtip to which weight has been added. For most stillwater situations, except when strong winds rip down the lake or pit causing a heavy undertow, a standard, lightweight swingtip is ideal.

Swingtips are great indicators to use when bream fishing on hard-fished waters. They are also good for registering bites that

Once the bait has settled on the bottom and a fish moves directly away from the rod with it, the tip will respond in a positive upwards movement, often straightening out horizontal with the top joint. On other occasions, the tip will rise or suddenly fall no more than ¼ in; treat these as positive bite indications, as though float-fishing. After all, if the float-tip with just ¼ in showing above the surface suddenly disappeared, you would strike and expect to hit into a fish. Ledgering, like float fishing, is all about using the correct indicator for the occasion, and interpreting each movement accurately.

When bites are coming thick and fast, do not bother with rod-rests. Get used to holding the rod handle comfortably beneath your forearm with the tip pointing directly at the bait (fig. 41A). Bites become much easier to see if you allow the rod-tip to angle downwards so that the swingtip is just an inch or so above the surface. Then strike upwards in one smooth, sweeping action. Any abrupt movement could wrap the swingtip around the rod-tip if you miss the bite. When bites are not happening with regularity, or it is too cold to hold the rod and concentrate, or bites are barely discernible movements, set the rod on two rests at an angle parallel to the bank and use a target-board positioned immediately behind the tip. Bites, even tiny indications, show up surprisingly well, and to strike you simply ease the rod from the rests in one long, sweeping sideways pull all the way backwards, pulling the line through the water as you would a waggler on a sunk line. Do not lift it up against the surface tension, as this greatly reduces the effectiveness of the strike (see fig. 41B).

Consistent accuracy in casting is imperative when swingtipping, so on every cast concentrate on putting the bait into the feed area. The only exception to this is when the swim is so full of moving bream that line bites occur on almost every cast. Possessing such incredibly deep bodies and large fins, bream cannot help but pick up the line when they are tightly packed. The swingtip might suddenly flip up and drop back with equal speed – obvious line bites these – or it could straighten out, to all intents and purposes like a positive bite. Line bites from roach and rudd are very rarely experienced, but from bream they are a real problem.

Eventually you will learn to distinguish between liners and genuine bites, but whenever you strike and miss what looked to be a positive bite, don't waste time winding in to inspect the bait. Drop the rod-tip immediately after striking and allow the rig to settle again. Besides, now the rig will be closer to you, in a less populated part of the shoal where line bites should be minimal. In fact, casts made to where you consider the outer edge of the feeding shoal to be, as opposed to the centre, are a good plan of attack. You experience less bites, but they are invariably positive lifts resulting in hooked bream, instead of the constant irritation of liners. In addition, bream hooked on the perimeter of the shoal and bullied quickly away will never spook the others, whereas a big fish hooked from the most dense part of the shoal

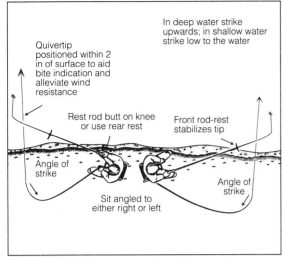

FIGURE 42 Quivertipping in stillwater

FIGURE 43 Stillwater quivertip or swing-tip ledger rig

and then played for several minutes through the others while they are trying to feed, might just unsettle them.

QUIVERTIPPING

Generally speaking, bites in static water are not going to register on the tip as boldly as those in running water, so opt for a finely tapered, super-sensitive tip. If using screw-in tips, one of 1½ oz test curve is suitable, although in extremely cold weather a step down to a 1 oz tip will improve bite registration.

To alleviate wind disturbance, position the rod on two rests (I use a front one only and rest the rod butt on my right knee for a quick strike) with the tip just a couple of inches above the surface – where, incidentally, bites show up better. Angle the rod to either left or right (whichever is more comfortable) and follow through along the same line on the strike. If the water is very deep, strike upwards; if it is shallow strike low to the water (fig. 42).

The end rig is the faithful fixed paternoster, with a bomb on the end if you wish to loose-feed by catapult or groundbait by hand only. Substitution of an open-end swimfeeder for the bomb, however, dramatically increases the chances of immediate bites because it deposits a pile of crumb and bait fragments right where it matters alongside the hook bait (fig. 43).

Note how the hook length is tied to the reel line and varies in test according to the hook size. This in turn is dictated by the bait and to some extent by the species and size of fish expected. When using maggots, for example, start with a 3 ft hook link, but if they return sucked to skins without a bite registering, start reducing the hook link until hittable movements are seen on the tip. Sometimes species like bream and tench will run along the bottom with the bait and

These Irish roach were caught on quivertipped maggot by Martin Founds of Anglers World Holidays, who not only advises customers about where to catch, but fishes himself.

pull the tip slowly all the way round. At other times they chew the bait on the spot, showing only the merest indication on the tip, as will immature rudd, bream and roach. When this happens, do not be afraid to reduce the hook length to somewhere between 6 and 10 in of 1½ lb, and hooks down to 18s and 20s.

You can often create a response by winding in gently a half or one full turn of the reel handle, should a fish think its food is getting away. And this ruse works especially well when baiting with worms. I am sure it is the gyrating movement of the worms, plus their internal juices, that really excite bream, rudd and tench. On

another day they might refuse worms, corn or maggots, and show interest only in fluffy, white bread flake. So always be prepared to experiment when bites are not forthcoming. Change baits, use cocktails and move the bait along every so often to goad them into grabbing hold of it.

Watch out for the tip slowly but decisively dropping back, a sure sign a fish has moved towards the rod and in so doing has dislodged the feeder. To encourage drop-back bites, use just enough lead on the feeder to enable you to tighten up after casting but not so much that the bait will be dropped. The only situations on stillwaters when I would use more lead than is necessary are either to aid casting, or to get the bait down quickly through deep water, past the attentions of nuisance shoal fish like roach and rudd to the bream feeding on the bottom.

Whenever you can, get used to holding the rod and support it on the front rest only; and make sure the line will lift off cleanly at whichever angle you strike. This way, you can make small movements of the bait, and reply to snatchy bites, much more easily. Dampen the breadcrumbs going into the feeder only very lightly so they explode as it touches bottom, sending a cascade of attractive feed all around the hook bait. If the breadcrumbs are too wet they could clog the feeder, and remain inside it until you pull in for a recast. Loose-fed hook fragments can be added to the crumb, or you can sandwich a quantity of hook baits like maggots, corn or casters, or even finely chopped worms, between a plug of breadcrumbs at each end of the feeder.

When specifically quivertipping for bream at the start of the session it is a good ploy to lob out a few balls of groundbait (stiffened well for throwing) by hand to get them feeding. Then keep them interested and moving around within the area through the feeder's regular arrival carrying extra food, whether bites are coming or not. And this is the secret of feeder-fishing: consistency in casting accuracy and consistently introducing those tiny piles of free nosh. Bream really respond well to these tactics, as do most other species.

DISTANCE LEDGERING

When you are expecting to hit into tench and bream at distances of 40 yd plus in lakes and gravel pits, a standard ledger rod is not up to the task. This is particularly true with specimen bream, which are always difficult to hook. At this distance I use an Avon-actioned, 11 or 12 ft carbon rod of 1¼ lb test curve for maximum line pick-up, and a 6 lb test line. I also change bite indicators, switching to the ledger bobbin.

This clips on to the line between buttring and reel, and falls harmlessly to the ground on a retaining cord, even when I make a hard, sweeping strike. For daytime ledgering I use the fluorescent-red ten-pin bobbin, and after dark the luminous glo-bobbin, which incorporates a betalight element. The glo-bobbin can of course be used around the clock.

Whenever long periods of inactivity are likely – for example on waters where there is a low density of bream (often the case with 'big-fish-only' lakes and pits), or

during the hours of darkness when long periods of inactivity are liable to occur – it is comforting to have an electric alarm incorporated into the set-up, and the Optonic indicator is ideal. An alarm, or 'buzzer' as they are called by carp anglers, allows you to appreciate fully the surrounding wildlife, and also to scan the surface away from the area being fished with binoculars for signs of bream activity.

Indeed, I wish I had a £5 note for every bonus fish that has graced the landingnet as a result of winding in and placing a bait on top of a bream (or tench) I had seen breaking the surface. Watching a pair of bobbins (two rods are an advantage when covering a large area) for hour upon hour is not just dull; you are missing out on much of the pleasure that ledgering has to offer.

This is a clear-cut case where electronic wizardry earns its keep. However, do not turn the volume up so loud that everyone on the next lake hears it. Apart from the irritation this causes to other anglers, you are also informing them of your success. Incidentally, to stop bobbins blowing about or steadily rising with the underwater tow and registering annoying false bites, pinch two or three swan shots on to the retaining cord immediately below the bobbin.

As for rigs, the faithful fixed paternoster ledger is still top of the list, but slightly changed. For distance ledgering, and for presenting baits over thick bottom-weed so they come to rest on top in full view, I use a bomb or feeder link of 4–5 ft and a hook link of around 10–20 in joined to the reel line with a four-turn water knot (fig. 44).

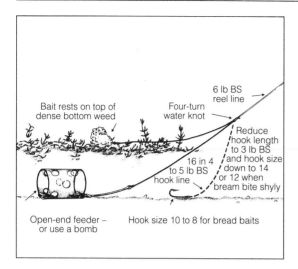

FIGURE 44 Distance ledgering on stillwater – fixed paternoster

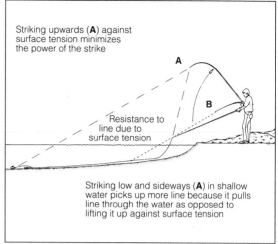

FIGURE 45A Striking when ledgering 1

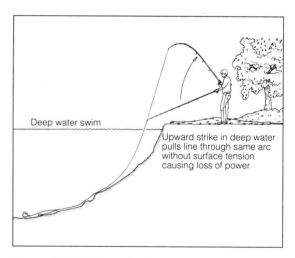

FIGURE 45B Striking when ledgering 2

Where only small numbers of large bream are present and regular helpings of groundbait not required, I usually put out a few balls by catapult and stick to a bomb ledger. On the other hand, where there are large shoals capable of continually mopping up loose feed and crumb groundbait, the open-ended swimfeeder is indispensable, especially when you are casting distances beyond accurate catapult range.

The further out you present the bait, the greater will be the problems of setting the hook, especially a large hook, so remember to follow through on the strike in a full, scything movement, keeping the angle at which the line is lying beneath the surface. Remember that in really shallow water a low, sideways strike will pick up more line because it pulls it through the water as opposed to lifting it upwards against the surface tension (fig. 45A). On the other hand, when presenting the bait into deep-water swims, an upwards strike is more advantageous (fig. 45B).

Try to tighten up gently after casting, to sink the line fully, so that it settles in a straight line between feeder or ledger and rod tip, not in a huge belly. Then clip on the indicator. A little washing-up liquid dabbed around the line on the spool will help it sink quickly, so keep a bottle handy. In strong winds, endeavour to fish directly into the wind. Otherwise, pinch a swan shot or two on to the bobbin line to stop any underwater tow bellying the line between feeder and rod tip, thus reducing the effectiveness of the strike. Remember that if the line is not reasonably tight from ledger to rod, the hook becomes more of a problem to set the further out you fish. This may occur when you are fishing over dense beds of soft weed if the rod is set too low to the surface. Bite indication will be hampered if the line actually rests on the weed, resulting in a much reduced movement of the bobbin. The remedy here is to set the rods as high as you can, keeping as much line as possible off the weed.

TWITCHER HITTING

During high summer when tench are at their most active but suddenly become preoccupied with loose feed deposited by the feeder, and as your casting becomes more accurate thereby concentrating good numbers of tench into a comparatively confined area, tiny twitch bites – 1 to 2 in lifts or drops of the bobbin – will become commonplace. This happens to a much lesser extent with bream.

Now is the time to reduce both the bobbin drop so that small movements are more noticeable, and the hook length to just 6 in enabling you to see bites much earlier, but retain the 10 in feeder link (fig. 46). Quite simply the tench are no longer moving away with the bait to another patch of food, they are consuming it on the spot. Bites which merely lift or drop back the

bobbin by ¼ in may seem to be the work of small fish instead of tench, but that is because they have become so preoccupied and so confident, with an excess of food spread around them, that they have little reason to move.

If on a standard hook tail (18–20 in long) you repeatedly reel in sucked maggots or sweetcorn skins, or your worms have had all the goodness crushed out of them, the bait must have been sucked back to the pharnygeal teeth, chewed for a while, and then spat out. It is wise to strike promptly at the slightest twitch or jiggle of the bobbin once the twitching cycle begins – once you have shortened the hook length.

On calm days you can forget the bobbin altogether after tightening up, and simply watch the line itself where it enters the water, hitting the slightest lift or drop back no matter how seemingly insignificant.

If bites prove conspicuous by their absence, and you believe tench are still in

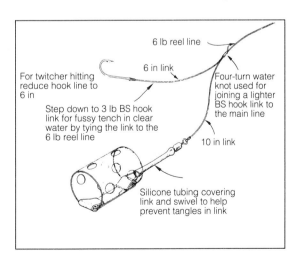

FIGURE 46 Twitcher hitting rig

Not only tench and bream give twitch bites on a ledgered bait. John took this fine perch by twitching a lobworm along the bottom until the predator could resist it no longer.

are not forthcoming, it is worth trying anything. However, don't be tempted to go down to a lighter hook length than the tench can be safely extracted with. Consider the weed growth, snags, and the general size of the fish expected and only step down accordingly.

I like to try to stimulate bites by constantly changing hook baits (regardless of what has been fed in), from maggots to corn, flake to worms and back again. Occasionally a buoyant bait presented on the drop will bring immediate action simply because it's different. Or try offerings like casters and crust cocktails, casters and corn, flake and maggots, and so on. Never be afraid to experiment. Try twitching the bait in, pausing for 30 seconds or so between each half or full slow crank of the handle. This of course is suicidal in thick weed, but where the bottom is reasonably clean it is a deadly technique that often leaves you next to no time between twitches to reset the bobbin before it is yanked upwards.

As you might with a float, try and relate movements of the bobbin to what is actually happening at the end of your feeder rig. For instance, wherever the bobbin jerks upwards a couple of inches and then suddenly falls completely slack in a glorious drop back, this is not the fish first moving away and then turning around and swimming back towards the rod, as you might be forgiven for thinking. It is the ledger rig tightening (as the bobbin

the swim – as may be the case in the middle of the day when parts of the terminal rig look far more obvious in very clear water – it is time to reduce the hook length from 6, 5 or 4 lb to just 3 lb, and to step down in hook size, presenting smaller baits. While a number 10 hook holding four grains of corn or five maggots may be the taking formula at 6 am, by 11.30 am, when the sun is high above the water, those same tench may not provide you with a hittable bite until you offer them a size 16 holding two casters. When bites

Opposite With rods set up high above the surface, enabling him to pick up maximum line on the strike, Charlie Clay is rewarded with a big gravel-pit bream hooked at 70 yd plus.

jerks up) immediately before the tension becomes too great and the feeder is pulled towards the rod, whereupon the bobbin suddenly drops. The tench has in fact been moving towards the rod from the moment it picked up the bait. These are always definite bites, because the tench is not going to let go, and a long sweeping strike to mend the loose line nearly always connects.

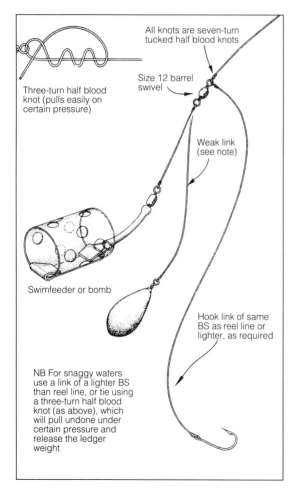

Three-turn half blood knot (pulls easily on certain pressure)

All knots are seven-turn tucked half blood knots

Size 12 barrel swivel

Weak link (see note)

Swimfeeder or bomb

Hook link of same BS as reel line or lighter, as required

NB For snaggy waters use a link of a lighter BS than reel line, or tie using a three-turn half blood knot (as above), which will pull undone under certain pressure and release the ledger weight

FIGURE 47 Constructing a fixed paternoster using a barrel swivel

SNAGGY SWIM RIG

In really overgrown waters where the ledger link may become snagged while I'm trying to extract a big tench or bream from snags or weed-beds, I use a weak link or tie just a three-turn half blood knot, which will pull free at a certain pressure (fig. 47). Thus, using a barrel swivel does have its advantages, including the option of being able to change the hook link from long to short or from lighter to heavier quickly without having to dismantle the entire end rig, using simple seven-turn 'tucked' half blood knots.

BOLT-RIG TENCHING

The shock, or bolt rig was first devised for carp fishing, but also works well for wary tench. It is especially useful when fishing for tench that share carp fisheries, and which have been weaned on to carp baits, namely boilies and hard particles such as peanuts and black-eyed beans.

As can be seen from fig. 48, a rotten bottom is used on the bomb link, tied on to the main line with a four-turn water knot. If it snags up in weed you can continue to play the tench, losing only a 1½ oz bomb. Reel line is 6 lb (unless big tench are anticipated, in which case step up to 8 lb straight through) to a size 10 or 8 hook. If you always sit next to the rods (within grabbing distance) this method works best fished with a closed bale arm, although some may consider this rather risky. After casting and dunking the rod-tip to lower the line along the bottom contours, support the rod in two rests, pointing it at the bait. Leave a slight bow between surface and rod tip before clipping on a bobbin or monkey climber half-way between butt ring and reel, hanging on a 12 in drop. This scaled-down fixed-lead rig then catches tench in the same way as it does a carp that happens along and sucks in the boilie or particle.

When the bait is gulped back to the pharnygeal teeth for chewing, the tench suddenly (provided the hook and bomb

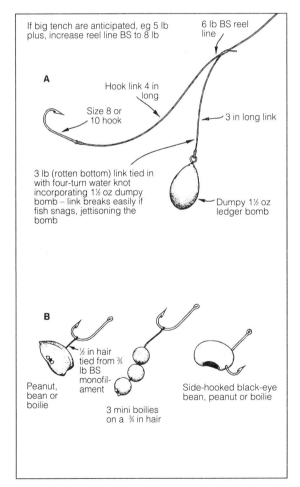

FIGURE 48 **A** Bolt-rig tenching and **B** Hooking and bait alternatives

links are not too long) feels the lead. It then quickly shuts its mouth and does a runner, forgetting the bait it was about to chew. Meanwhile, the hook is pulled down to the lips and jerked in by the fixed lead. When the line tightens a second later, with the tench 2 or 3 ft away and gaining speed, the hook is really banged home. While all this is happening (in a split second or so), the Optonic screeches a multiple bleep, followed by the rod trying to leave the rod rests. However, if the butt ring is jammed up against the Optonic, the rod will stay in place. You are then, without even having to strike, suddenly into a tench.

The bait may be side-hooked, or, if the tench are particularly wary, sleeved on to a fine (¼ lb) hair just ½ in long. Invariably a single bait produces a better hooking ratio to bites, while a mini-string of tiny boilies may induce more offers. Once the hook baits are positioned, loose feed, and an additional attractor bait such as hempseed, can be scattered accurately around the area with a catapult.

MULTI-PURPOSE CARP RIGS

For ledgering pieces of soft paste, cubes of meat, perhaps a couple of cockles, in diminutive waters where belt-off runs are neither expected nor desired, use a simple running link ledger as in fig. 49A.

Where a carp could go ploughing through weeds or snags, the ledger link, to which is attached a small bomb or swan shots, should be of a considerably lighter test than the reel line. Thus it creates a weak link which will break off when caught up in weeds, leaving the carp still connected to the main line.

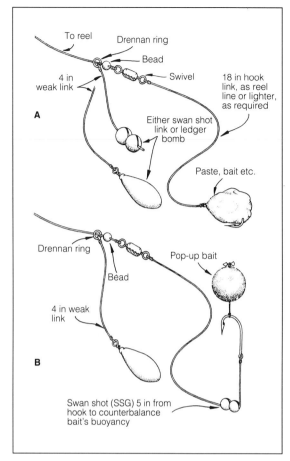

FIGURE 49 A multi-purpose rig – the running link ledger

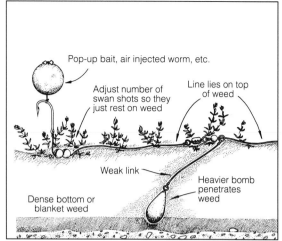

FIGURE 50 A heavier multi-purpose rig

For presenting pop-up baits, such as an air-injected lobworm or any of the floating baits (usually fished on the surface), fix on one or two swan shots 5 in from the hook to counterbalance the bait's buoyancy, as in fig. 49B.

When fishing over dense bottom or blanket weed simply extend the ledger link to compensate, and use a heavier bomb for penetration down to the bottom (fig. 50). Experiment in the margins where you can see the rig working until you are happy.

Scorching runs are sometimes experienced with this set up should the rig become hung up in weed. Generally, however, the indicator (monkey climber or coil) rises positively upwards, usually with enough time for an unhurried strike. Coupled to a buzzer the warning is quite adequate when sitting beside the rod. As I play fish from a pre-adjusted clutch, the anti-reverse is always on, enabling me at any point to grab the rod one-handed if necessary without the handle whizzing round.

THE SHOCK OR 'BOLT' RIG

Now we arrive at what in recent years has become the panacea to catching carp: the bolt or shock rig ledger. Sadly, some anglers use no other technique because it is so effective. I have left the bolt rig until last because I wish you to treat it as a deadly method for catching difficult carp – carp that are so wary they won't provide enough indications on other methods of

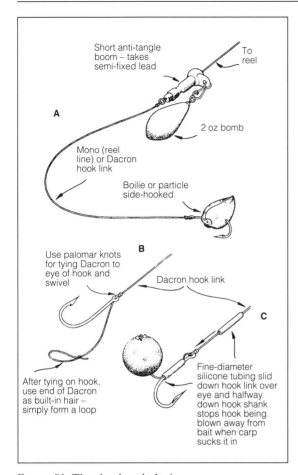

Short anti-tangle
boom – takes
semi-fixed lead

To
reel

A

2 oz bomb

Mono (reel
line) or Dacron
hook link

Boilie or particle
side-hooked

Use palomar knots
for tying Dacron to
eye of hook and
swivel

B

Dacron hook link

C

After tying on hook,
use end of Dacron
as built-in hair –
simply form a loop

Fine-diameter
silicone tubing slid
down hook link over
eye and halfway
down hook shank
stops hook being
blown away from
bait when carp
sucks it in

FIGURE 51 The shock or bolt rig

presentation for you to strike and hook them.

It's a fact that carp do not fall for the same tackle rig time after time. Bites that started out as slammers on simple ledger tackle soon become 'twitches', so imperceptible they are impossible to strike. And this is when the bolt rig comes into its own. Using a heavy lead (1½ to 2 oz), which is felt by the carp just as it sucks the bait from the bottom back to its throat teeth for chewing, shocks that carp into closing its lips and doing a runner. In

short it 'bolts off'. In the process it forgets about the bait and the hook is pulled home. The secret is in having exactly the right distance from lead to bait, which varies with different-sized carp.

A distance of somewhere between 6 to 10 in from hook to lead is favoured. The bait (boilies and hard particles such as beans or peanuts, etc., work best with this method) can simply be side-hooked (fig. 51A) or slid on to a 'hair' (fig. 51B), providing the carp with extra confidence when it sucks it in. In each case the hook link can be of monofilament (reel line), black or multi-coloured dacron or braid or of floss, which separates into numerous gossamer strands and becomes virtually invisible on the bottom.

With dacron hook lengths, after tying the hook on don't clip the end off short. Simply tie in a small loop and use it as a built-in hair.

To stop the hook being blown away from the bait when a carp sucks it in, sleeve a short length of fine-diameter clear or black silicone tubing down the hook link over the eye and onto the shank, thus shortening the hair length (fig. 51C). Note from fig. 51A that the (semi-fixed) 2 oz lead is attached to the clip of a short boom, which threads on to the reel line above the hook link swivel and stops the lead from tangling. Keep your terminal rig as simple as possible (fig. 52) The short hook link and reel line are both connected to the same end of a tiny size 10 swivel, so that should it break in half you are still playing the carp, while the weak bomb link is tied to the other end of the swivel. Lengths of both hook and bomb links can be varied to suit bottom or weed of varying types, but overall a hook link of 4 in and a bomb link of 3 in are ideal.

The beauty of this rig is that should a carp go belting off through heavy weed the weak link soon ditches the lead. It is also excellent for presenting pop-up baits on the hair rig above dense bottom weed (fig. 53). If the bottom weed is deeper than the 3 in lead link, simply alter it accordingly. Note the three AA shots pinched at 12 in intervals up the line from the swivels, which iron the reel line to the weed or hide it in soft silt so as not to scare carp as they approach the bait. To hide the reel line, dip the rod tip beneath the surface after casting, and with the left hand (assuming you are holding the rod in your right hand) gently pull the line until it is straight. Then allow a little slack from the reel and lift the rod horizontally on to the rests.

Contrary to popular belief, the line from bolt rig to rod does not necessarily need to be 'hauser' tight in order for the hook point to be driven home. The lead in conjunction with the speed at which a carp panics off are responsible for this. So wherever possible leave a slight bow in the line from rod tip to surface. This means the line close to the bolt rig will be lying along the bottom contours and not inhibiting carp in crystal-clear water from approaching the bait.

There is perhaps a better hooking rate once the carp has picked up the bait presented on a tight line from lead to rod. But if a proportion of runs do not happen because the carp sensed the bowstring line and depart, it does not help you catch more fish.

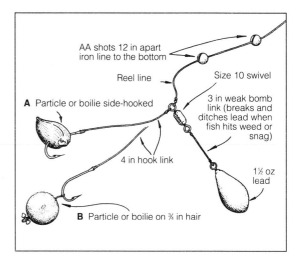

FIGURE 52 A simple bolt rig

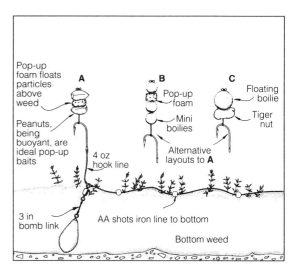

FIGURE 53 A pop-up bolt rig

Whenever there is a strong undertow in large waters, as in windy conditions, it is of course impossible to fish a gentle bow. Then it has to be a tight line 'clipped up' or nothing. At the reel end, after putting the line beneath the monkey, open the bale arm and neatly catch the line beneath a run clip fixed around the

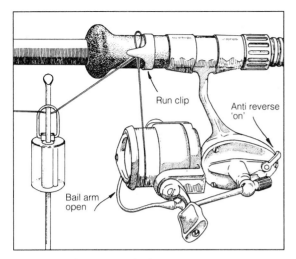

FIGURE 54 Clipping up the line

handle directly opposite the spool (fig. 54). When a carp grabs the bait and promptly does a runner, line spews from the open spool while the monkey body drops a couple of inches, held there through the sheer speed of line evaporating from the open spool, while the buzzer screams its head off.

If using a reel with a bait runner facility, the bale arm will, of course, already be closed while the spool itself revolves. For both situations, a hefty strike is not required; indeed it could even prove disastrous. Simply close the bale arm by winding forward (which also puts the bait runner reel back into gear with a pre-set clutch) and gently bend the rod back into the fish when all is nicely tight. It is a very stereotyped and easy method to master.

In confined overgrown fisheries where the erection of rod-rest set ups, buzzers and monkey climbers could ruin the chances of carp even patrolling close by, let alone picking up a bolt-rigged bait, I fish in a very basic, effective, if rather risky way. As I never leave the rod or rods (I occasionally use two rods, though for much of my carp fishing, because it is based on opportunity rather than patience, I use just one), after placing the bait accurately and ensuring the line is nicely sunk along the bottom I simply lay the rod down on the carpet of marginal plants. I use no rod-rests or alarms, but the anti-reverse is on and the clutch is set a shade lighter than I intend to play a fish with when the time comes.

One minute there is nothing. The very next there is a furrow on the surface (if fishing shallow water) as a carp panics off, easily setting the hook and jerking the rod across the marginal plants in the process.

LEDGERING IN RUNNING WATER

FOR MAHSEER

When I first set eyes on the unbelievably fast, rocky and swirling waters of an Indian mahseer river, I wondered how on earth it would be possible to keep a bait ledgered on the bottom. The current speed seemed just too excessive for even a 2 lb lead to hold position. The biggest mahseer of all, monsters in the 70–100 lb class, occupy the fastest, snaggiest water where the current speed can vary between 3 and as much as 10 knots. Their barbel-like shape allows them to hold station behind a boulder with minimal effort, while they grub about beneath the stones for small loach-like fish and the freshwater crabs that make up the bulk of their staple diet. It is imperative that the bait is anchored on the bottom among the rocks, right where the whoppers are. If big mahseer preferred a clear, sandy run beneath fast water, ledgering a bait, any bait, completely static on the bottom would prove impossible. Fortunately they prefer rocks, and it is into one of the countless crevices within the black bedrock covering much of the bottom of the river that the fisherman must deliberately snag his lead in order for the bait to stay in place.

I know it sounds crazy to snag up deliberately, but there is no alternative. You make a cast downstream and considerably further across than where you intend the bait to settle behind a poten-tial fish-holding cluster of rocks, and allow the current to bump the bait around until the lead snags. It is as simple as that. On really rocky stretches of river – if a mahseer doesn't grab the bait and do a runner, instantly yanking the lead free, each time to recast, you first have to work the lead and hook free of the bottom – which, incidentally, seems almost impossible.

It is rather a tricky operation that you must master for mahseer fishing, but one, incidentally, which could stand you in good stead for all future fishing in fast, rocky rivers, regardless of the species.

It is usually pointless pulling or yanking hard on the line with the rod held over in different positions, as if caught on a snag in a gravel pit at home. The lead, of course, needs to be pulled from a downstream direction, which is why the mahseer has no difficulty in belting away with the bait and simultaneously freeing the lead, treating you to the boldest, most arm-wrenching bite you are ever likely to experience. The secret is to pay out a good length of line, say 20, 30, even 40 or 50 yd, and wait for the current to bow it

Top right Watched by guide Suban, John exerts maximum pressure to stop a huge mahseer reaching the next set of rapids

Right Note the long barbels on this huge mahseer, which weighed only a few pounds less than Suban at 92 lb.

Far right Following a luckless two days, Andy Davison (centre) produced this superb mahseer.

81

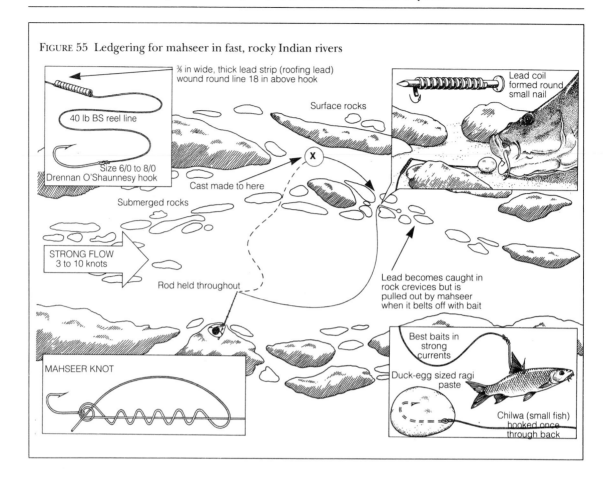

FIGURE 55 Ledgering for mahseer in fast, rocky Indian rivers

⅜ in wide, thick lead strip (roofing lead) wound round line 18 in above hook

40 lb BS reel line

Size 6/0 to 8/0 Drennan O'Shaunnesy hook

Lead coil formed round small nail

Surface rocks

Cast made to here

Submerged rocks

STRONG FLOW 3 to 10 knots

Rod held throughout

X

Lead becomes caught in rock crevices but is pulled out by mahseer when it belts off with bait

MAHSEER KNOT

Best baits in strong currents

Duck-egg sized ragi paste

Chilwa (small fish) hooked once through back

downstream in an enormous arc, as in fig. 56. You then hold the rod tip down close to the surface so all the line is being pulled by the current and suddenly swish the rod back as fast, as hard, and as high as you can. Because, for a few seconds at least (until you straighten the bow out), the line is actually pulling the lead from a downstream direction, the lead usually plinks out from its crevice among the rocks. More often than not, you are also rewarded with the bait still on the hook. Occasionally, perhaps once or twice a day, this ruse doesn't work, and neither does walking way downstream below the point

where the lead is snagged and having a few pulls from a different direction. So you simply pull for a break. I say 'simply' here, but trying to break 40 lb monofilament can prove unbelievably difficult, if not dangerous, when you are perched above the water among jagged rocks.

The best way is to put the rod down and grab the line across your back, wrapping it several times around your strongest arm, and slowly and steadily walk back sideways until it breaks. However, care must be taken.

When presenting a large deadbait or a huge ball of paste, an 8/0 hook is advisable. Otherwise, I find a 6/0 perfectly adequate. Such a hook seems huge for freshwater fish, but not when held beside the open mouth of a 10 lb mahseer. Having been let down by other patterns that straightened out or snapped during the powerful and long fight of a big mahseer, I tried Drennan's stainless steel O'Shaunnessey hooks, and now use them exclusively. The hook is tied direct to the 40 lb reel line with a knot first shown to me by my good friend and guide, Suban, which I have since named the 'mahseer knot' (fig. 55). It is easy and quick to tie, and thoroughly reliable. Hooks and knots are, to a large extent, rather taken for granted by a large proportion of anglers when fishing in the UK because only very seldom are they really tested. But believe me, mahseer fishing is completely different and tests every piece of your tackle to the full. When 70 lb of muscle heads off downriver at a speed you just cannot believe, ripping line from

a reel whose clutch is so tight you cannot pull line off by hand, then, and only then, do you realize the awesome power of this very special freshwater fish.

One very good reason for using a reel line of 40 lb test is that as a mahseer belts off it does not exactly play fair, but often takes a route along the bottom through huge groups of boulders, shredding the line as it goes. Most mahseer in excess of even 50 lb could be landed on a line of 20–25 lb test – but during the fight the line could be reduced to half its test or less through constant shredding. So I play safe with 40 lb straight through.

As far as reels are concerned, for virtually all mahseer fishing I have used, and been extremely pleased with, ABU's 9000c and 10,000c and the Ryobi S320. My rods, and I now have several variants (although I use only one rod at a time when fishing for mahseer) are made from the Fibatube 11 ft hollow-glass 132 blank, which has a test curve of close on 3 lb. The North Western 11 ft PK3 hollow-glass blank has also proved its durability. You may wonder why I use hollow glass and not carbon, and the answer is simply that being much thicker in the wall, glass is much less prone to being crushed or broken from the occasional knock during the rugged demands of mahseer fishing, which includes continual rock-hopping and long bumpy rides over boulder-strewn tracks in the back of a vehicle where everything

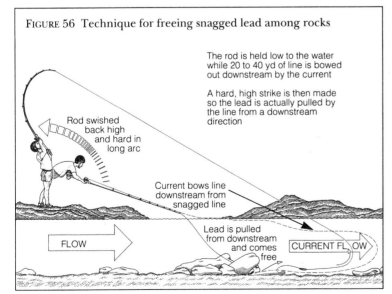

FIGURE 56 Technique for freeing snagged lead among rocks

The rod is held low to the water while 20 to 40 yd of line is bowed out downstream by the current

A hard, high strike is then made so the lead is actually pulled by the line from a downstream direction

Rod swished back high and hard in long arc

Current bows line downstream from snagged line

FLOW

Lead is pulled from downstream and comes free

CURRENT FLOW

Following a strength-sapping battle for over an hour, the first glimpse you have of a mahseer is when it surfaces belly up, exhausted – an unforgettable experience when the fish tops the 90 lb mark, like this monster.

Go Fishing cameraman, Tim Piper, and director, Paul Martingell, capture the end of an hour-long coracle chase when Suban and John landed this superb mahseer.

is liable to be dumped on top of the rods.

On my first mahseer trip, my guide must have thought I was crazy, loading up the business end with matt black lead bombs, swivels, beads and link ledgers. But Suban let me go through the learning process of losing, in the rocky bottom, enough sophisticated anti-tangle devices to start a tackle shop before producing from his pocket a 2 in long coil of hand-beaten lead strip. This he promptly wound around the line 18 in above the hook. To make it hold, he crunched each end in with his teeth.

I was to find out that the old methods

really are best as far as mahseer fishing is concerned, and I can well remember that before our first stay in India was over, Andy Davison and I were smelting down our entire stock of designer carp bombs to make good, old-fashioned lead strips. This we did in an old saucepan over an open fire, pouring the molten lead into shallow grooves made in the compacted river-bank sand with a twig. We then beat the knobbly strips flat with a hand-sized rock, and used them as mahseer weights. Talk about Bronze-Age fishing. Of course, I now make more than enough ready-wound strip weights in advance from a sheet of roofing lead, which is the perfect gauge and easily cut with a pair of large scissors.

Although mahseer are regularly caught on artificial lures and on the fly, among the swirling waters of the rocky Indian rivers many of the runs are often extremely confined and difficult to cover with any other method than bottom-fished baits, or a bait (deadbaits in particular) worked slowly along the bottom from one cluster of rocks to another.

There are, in fact, two baits that are more effective than all others. Small, barbel-like bottom-dwellers, or just about any 5–10 inch fish freshly caught from the shallow pools with a cast net, including baby mahseer, (all loosely referred to as chilwa), which make fine deadbaits. The other is *ragi* paste. To prepare *ragi* you add water to the fine, grey, local flour milled from millet, and mould it into paste balls the size of ducks' eggs. These are then immersed for 20 minutes in boiling water, which brings out the natural gluten of the flour and makes the paste

exceedingly rubbery. Once they have been allowed to cool, a light skin will have formed (boilies no less), so each then needs to be firmly reworked by hand. They are then moulded onto the size 6/0 hook, which must be completely covered. *Ragi* casts well, and when medium-sized nuisance species are not over-troublesome, will remain whole on the hook and completely thwart the attention of tiny nibblers for at least half an hour. If you are careful on the retrieve, it will still be there, to be remoulded for the next cast.

FREELINING IN STREAMS AND SMALL RIVERS

The art of freelining the bait in small rivers and clear-flowing streams to catch quality roach and the odd sizeable dace is based upon concealment, and is most effective during the summer months when fish are really active. You need to creep and crawl stealthily about in order to get close to the quarry, so that you can flick the bait out a few yards – or even feet. Make no mistake, it is possible to catch even specimen fish at such ridiculously close range so long as you do not expose your form above the skyline, or stumble along clumsily, sending unnatural vibrations from the bank through the water.

On open waters you can get away with using a 12 ft carbon float rod, but wherever the banks are heavily overgrown – and the most interesting and prolific diminutive rivers usually are – a long rod is an encumbrance. My choice is a 10–11 ft built-in quivertip ledger rod. While you are not always watching the rod tip for indications, but just the line (as the word 'freelining' implies), the bait does at times need to be anchored on the bottom with a swanshot or two. And this is when the sensitive quivertip comes into its own.

All the weight for casting (pinching on a shot 12 in above light baits such as maggots is permitted) is in the bait itself, which will easily peel line from the spool provided it is full to the brim with around 2½ lb test. Do not forget to adjust the slipping clutch, because free-lined large baits – and there is nothing better than a large lump of bread flake hiding a size 10 or 8 hook tied direct – really does sort out the better quality roach.

Groundbait is, of course, quite unnecessary. To get the fish interested, flick in a few hookbait samples every so often. Search all the likely looking spots where you would expect roach to be in residence.

After pinching the flake on, 'dunk' it momentarily at your feet to make sure it sinks (dunking also makes it heavier), then flick it downstream, and allow the current to trundle it along the bottom. Keep a bow in the line from the rod tip to the point where the line enters the water and watch it like a hawk. It is your resistance-free bite indicator.

Even bites from 10 oz roach will look like a shark run. As the fish senses no fear from the food it is swallowing, due to a complete lack of terminal gear, it will grab it confidently, the line straightening in a ridiculously positive manner. If the roach decides to turn around and swim to a position at the rear of the shoal, the rod tip will even pull round. And if it chews the flake on the spot the line may only jerk forward momentarily once or twice.

In order to add chub and barbel to the species that may be caught freelining during the summer and autumn from both diminutive and medium-sized, clear-flowing rivers, a step up in tackle is necessary. There is nothing to beat the versatility of an 11–12 ft, carbon Avon rod of 1¼ lb test with hooks tied direct. Such an outfit is capable of subduing a large barbel, yet permits enjoyment from smaller species such as roach and bream when they occasionally show up.

In trying to achieve maximum distance (to reach chub for instance, occupying a run on the opposite bank of a reasonably wide river) I occasionally punch the bait out with a double-handed cast. However, accuracy is more easily achieved by hooking the line over the ball of the forefinger (to 'feel' the bait's weight) and casting with an underhand swing and flip. Provided that the spool is filled to the very lip, even with 5–6 lb test, the bait will fly effortlessly and accurately through the air until you 'feather' it down to land over the desired spot with the same finger. It is an art worth practising.

If you find this one-handed technique awkward or unsuitable, use the same underhand swing and flip, but hold a loop of line in your left hand (assuming the rod is in your right) and do a couple of pendulum swings with the rod tip pointing at the target to build up momentum before letting go. The key is confidence, and using a bait which is heavy enough – a large slug, lobworm, cube of meat, a large piece of bread flake or cheese paste, and so on. All are perfect for freelining.

Because the bait appears to be untethered and behaves so naturally fish are not concerned by the diameter of a 6 lb line or its colour, or even by a large, visible hook.

Although freelining for chub and barbel is most effectively accomplished by careful stalking along overgrown banks and manoeuvering yourself into a position from which you can make a short cast to fish lying between or beneath vegetation features, there are certain situations where wading is necessary. In diminutive, shallow, overgrown streams and rivers, you could easily frighten the fish long before a cast is made by taking to the water. In larger, overgrown and weedy, reasonably shallow rivers, where thick floating beds of potomogeton or water crowfoot clog the surface during midsummer, or impenetrable bankside trees separate you from fish that are visible, wading permits several casts to be

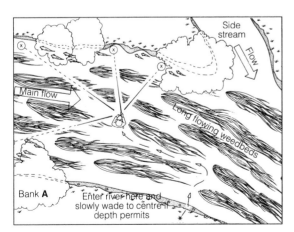

FIGURE 57 By carefully wading into the centre of gravel shallows between weedbeds, you can offer a freelined bait to barbel and chub that are unapproachable from bank **A**

made into spots that are completely unapproachable from the bank. Consider the situation, for instance, in fig. 57.

In these choice lies you will naturally have to wait for the bait to reach bottom before a barbel grabs hold, whereas chub will strike from the second the bait hits the surface. A common occurrence when freelining the bait directly upstream is for the line momentarily to fall slack. This is caused by the chub moving a few feet downstream, but then returning to its original position. This is just as 'positive' an indication as the rod tip going over, so strike immediately and strike hard, quickly levering the chub away from the sunken tree or bullrush bed behind which it is hiding and into which it will surely try to bury the hook. Chub are masters not only of ridding themselves of the hook, but also of transferring it into the closest snag. Keep the rod well up and in a full curve from the moment the hook goes home.

Should the line quite suddenly fall completely slack, this is because a chub is actually swimming downstream towards you with the bait. Quickly crank the reel a few times to pick up the loose line before slamming the hook home. These bites often occur instantly, within seconds of the bait hitting the surface, so you need to be watching that line like a hawk even before you close the bale arm. The most instant bites of all come to natural baits such as a large slug skipped or skate-cast across weed-beds to where cut weed or debris collects around the trailing branches of overhanging trees; down into the swirling cross-currents and eddies where a side stream enters the main

A bunch of quivertipped maggots proved the downfall of this double-figure barbel.

stream; into the gloom beneath the low, overhanging brickwork of a road or rail bridge.

ROD-TOP LEDGERING

A natural progression from freelining is to add weight to the bait, either for casting or for anchoring it down in a particular spot, or both, and watch the rod top for bite indication. Because of the water pressure in really fast runs, whether shallow or deep, in large powerful rivers such as the Severn or Wye, a 1 oz bomb or more may be required to nail the bait to the bottom. A similar situation exists in all rivers, even comparatively small ones such as the fast, swirling waters of weir-pools where, unless the bait stays put until the chub or barbel locate it, the force of the current will simply wash it downstream to an unproductive area.

As with freelining, the ideal rod is the standard-top Avon, which should be held during the summer months when bites are liable to be quick in coming. Whether standing or sitting, hold the rod firmly with two fingers either side of the reel stem and your entire forearm supporting the handle. After casting, and once the ledger has settled in the desired spot, make a habit of hooking your forefinger (at the first joint) around the line. Once adopted, you will find this a particularly sensitive and comfortable way of keeping the rod still. There is nothing to stop you from using a front rod-rest, which helps steady the tip, especially in windy conditions and extremely fast water. You will quickly come to recognize the line tightening across your forefinger as the rod tip knocks.

When you cast downstream, the rod tip will be pulled round if the fish moves downstream with the bait. If it simply moves across the current, however, the tip might suddenly relax or spring back immediately following a gentle knock.

When casting directly upstream use only enough weight to hold bottom so that when a fish sucks in the bait and turns around, the bomb is dislodged causing the line to fall slack immediately. These are great bites to hit, but remember that, as when freelining, you need to lift the rod back in a long, hard, sweeping strike to straighten the line and bang the hook home.

It is best to use the minimum amount of lead needed to hold bottom for ledgering downstream. It allows you to inch the bait down and across the bottom by raising the rod tip every so often in order to search the swim thoroughly (fig. 58). This imparts a certain amount of life to

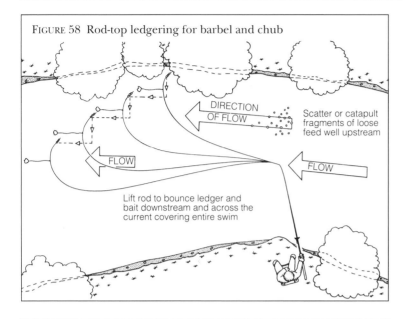

FIGURE 58 Rod-top ledgering for barbel and chub

DIRECTION OF FLOW

Scatter or catapult fragments of loose feed well upstream

FLOW

FLOW

Lift rod to bounce ledger and bait downstream and across the current covering entire swim

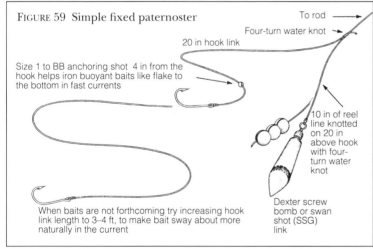

FIGURE 59 Simple fixed paternoster

To rod

Four-turn water knot

20 in hook link

Size 1 to BB anchoring shot 4 in from the hook helps iron buoyant baits like flake to the bottom in fast currents

10 in of reel line knotted on 20 in above hook with four-turn water knot

When baits are not forthcoming try increasing hook link length to 3–4 ft, to make bait sway about more naturally in the current

Dexter screw bomb or swan shot (SSG) link

pull the rod in, although a barbel just might.

For heavy water ledgering a 5 or 6 lb line is ideal. Resist the temptation to make up complicated ledger rigs. Running ledgers with swivels, split rings and non-tangle tubing may look accept-able on paper, but in reality work no better than a simple fixed pater-noster (fig. 59). 1 would in fact say that as all the various bits tend to collect weed, running ledgers are inferior to the fixed paternoster described.

Simply tie on a 10 in length of mono (reel line), using a four-turn water knot, 20 in above the hook. To this, fix either an Arlesey bomb or enough swan shots to just hold bottom. Swan shots are more practical because it takes seconds to add or subtract one for fine adjustment. For currents requiring in excess of five or six swan shots, bombs are advisable.

the bait and often promotes an instant bite. There are times when fish will only accept a completely static bait and times when, unless it is constantly on the move like the unattached offerings thrown in to attract fish, they will show not the slightest interest. So always be willing to experiment and to work the bait along. Don't sit there waiting for something to

The brass-screw design are good because they make a quick change of weight easy. Attention to little things such as continually changing the ledger weight to suit the current force of each swim as you move up or down river may seem unnecessary, but will be reflected by more fish in the net.

Buoyant bait like bread flake does not always settle on the bottom in really strong currents; it tends to flap about and look unnatural. Sometimes fish gobble it up for this very reason, and at such times an increase in the hook length to 3 or even 4 ft will encourage more confident bites. On other occasions it is refused for the same reason. Experiment by adding an anchoring shot just 4 in from the bait, which will ensure it settles statically.

Worms and hard baits such as cheese are ideal fast-water offerings. They stay on a large hook well, and withstand the attentions of unwanted nuisance species. Also worth trying, particularly during the autumn, is a small fish such as minnow, bleak, gudgeon or stone loach. Hook once only through the top lip or through both nostrils, and fish as any other bait. If little interest is shown when the fish is presented hard on the bottom, bump it downstream every so often by lifting the rod tip to dislodge the lead and lowering it again. And be ready for a really slamming take as you do so. Both barbel and chub grab small fish with considerably more force than they do paste baits. In weedy or particularly snaggy parts of the river don't bother to present the fish live. Tap it sharply on the head before casting and you won't have to worry about it hiding or swimming into snags. Alive or dead, it will be sucked in just the same.

So far we have looked at freelining and rod-top ledgering techniques, and the use of largish baits, where indications on the line or the rod tip are likely to be most positive during the summer and autumn months, but as the season progresses and much colder weather sets in, a different approach is required.

No longer will chub and barbel in- stantly respond to large 'moving' offer- ings. In low water temperatures especially, smaller baits will be the order of the day, which of course produces much smaller bite registrations. And to identify smaller indications the finely tapered tip of the Avon quivertip rod is the answer.

QUIVERTIPPING

There are two important points to re- member when using the quivertip in running water. Choose the most sensitive quivertip to match current strength in order that even tentative bites from small species will register. Secondly, use the minimum weight, whether swan shots, bomb or feeder, so that drop-back bites are always indicated. Smaller species do not have the strength to move a heavy bomb or feeder and indicate a drop-back bite on the quivertip, so make sure you anchor the bait with no more weight than necessary. I cannot stress the importance of this enough. Far too many anglers show a total disregard for the exact weight used in their ledger rigs and consequently sit there biteless because their quarry is unwiling to tolerate undue resistance.

Loose feeding/groundbait

You must also decide whether to in- troduce loose feed or groundbait or both, by feeder, or by hand. When fishing clear- flowing small rivers during the summer months, for instance, where swims and even the position of shoal species like dace, roach, bream and chub is clearly defined, the answer is to flick in a few fragments of hookbait every so often by hand or catapult – pieces of flake, stewed wheat, maggots and so on. Indeed, throw in too much free food and your sport might end prematurely, as it is easy to overfeed the fish unintentionally.

In clear water it is sometimes possible to see how many fish there are in the swim and to observe how they react to free food. You can then regulate the feed exactly to match their mood and appetite. There is a problem of course, when ledgering in coloured water or into distant, clear-water swims, where the size of the shoal cannot be seen – which, let us face it, is most of the time.

In large rivers where shoals of roach or bream, for instance, might number several hundreds rather than dozens, and competition for food is high, loose feed or groundbait deposited by a swimfeeder with the hookbait on each cast is imperative for constant sport. See fig. 60 for the various rig options.

Incidentally, when ledgering into deep water or for casting a feeder out 30 to 40 yd plus, generally speaking I prefer the safety margin provided by a 4 lb reel line. When barbel and chub are the quarry a 5–6 lb reel line makes more sense, while quivertipping slow-moving or small rivers for dace, roach and perhaps the odd chub or bream, a 3 lb reel line is quite sufficient. To keep a massive shoal of roach feeding in the fast, deep waters of Norfolk's tidal rivers Bure, Yare and Waveney, or the River Bann in Northern Ireland, you have the option of using a cage or open-end feeder packed with maggot- or caster-laced breadcrumbs, or a blockend feeder holding maggots or casters only. On some days roach will respond better to the addition of cereals,

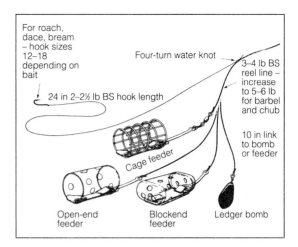

FIGURE 60 Basic quivertip ledger rig for river fishing

some days they will not. If in doubt, stick to a blockend and loose feed only.

For attracting the roach, bream and chub living on the bottom of a fast and deep weir-pool into a given area, the blockend certainly reigns supreme. The cereal/open-end or cage feeder combination is more likely to scatter fish all over the swim because the crumb particles are so light that they disperse a long way. And in winter conditions, when you need to really concentrate the shoal into a small area, this could prove disastrous. Unless your casting is consistently accurate, the same thing will happen.

For dace and roach that inhabit really fast shallow swims, the blockend and maggot or caster combination is certainly more productive (use a small blockend for dace). It is worth remembering that in strong currents the blockend's load (even casters) will wash out much quicker than in slow currents. For fast water, therefore, choose a blockend with a limited amount of small holes for slow dispersal of the bait. This of course

When Norfolk's River Wensum runs fast and with a tinge of 'winter green', quality-sized chub fall to mashed bread in conjunction with bread flake on the hook; something that John Watson of Kent quickly latched on to.

applies whatever the species. In slow swims, go for the reverse – a feeder well punched with large holes.

Incidentally, the 'spring tip' indicator is great in really gentle currents for shy-biting fish, especially dace, when you need to step down to really fine hook lengths and tiny hooks. Use it in exactly the same way as the quivertip. In really cold conditions when bites are hard to spot, use a target board.

Some feeder manufacturers offer different weights for their feeders. The Drennan Feederlink (a great blockend for slow-moving water), for example, has a plastic spigot at the bottom to which different weights of between ⅛ and ½ oz can be clipped. It is handy to have a supply of fold-over or strap leads in varying sizes from ½ to 2 oz so that any make of cage, open-end or blockend feeder, can be doctored to hold bottom regardless of current strength (fig. 61).

Rod positioning

Many anglers are unsure about which position the rod should be placed in

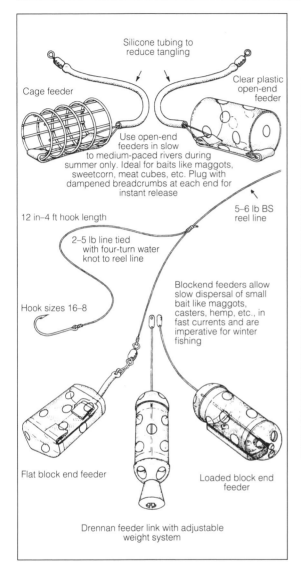

Silicone tubing to
reduce tangling

Cage feeder

Clear plastic
open-end
feeder

Use open-end
feeders in slow
to medium-paced rivers during
summer only. Ideal for baits like maggots,
sweetcorn, meat cubes, etc. Plug with
dampened breadcrumbs at each end for
instant release

12 in–4 ft hook length

5–6 lb BS
reel line

2–5 lb line tied
with four-turn water
knot to reel line

Blockend feeders allow
slow dispersal of small
bait like maggots,
casters, hemp, etc., in
fast currents and are
imperative for winter
fishing

Hook sizes 16–8

Flat block end feeder

Loaded block end
feeder

Drennan feeder link with adjustable
weight system

FIGURE 61 Fixed paternoster feeder rigs

Eleven of the best, weighing between 3 and 4 lb. They were all taken quivertipping in a two-hour stint.

when quivertipping in flowing water, and the best positions are illustrated over the page in fig. 62.

More drop backs will occur when you are casting way out across the flow in big rivers such as the Thames or Severn to distant swims, and the further out you fish directly across the flow, the greater is the bow in the line (created by current pressure) between bait and quivertip.

When casting across river to swims beyond the accurate range of the catapult, the best way to introduce loose feed to attract species like chub, and particularly barbel, is with the aid of a large blockend swimfeeder. Five or ten minutes spent casting and recasting to lay a thick carpet of hempseed (including a few hookbait samples) on the bottom of the swim at the start of a session is time well spent. Do not forget to enlarge the holes

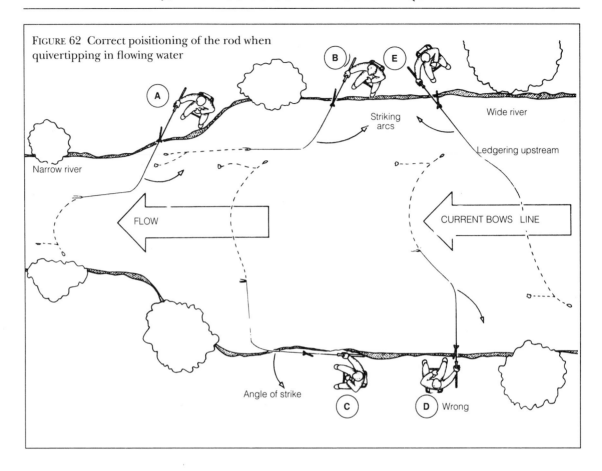

FIGURE 62 Correct poisitioning of the rod when quivertipping in flowing water

Narrow river

Striking arcs

Wide river

Ledgering upstream

FLOW

CURRENT BOWS LINE

Angle of strike

Wrong

of the (pre-baiting) feeder with a pair of scissors so that its load washes out within a second or two of it hitting bottom. And do not worry about the splash it makes as it goes in. On most well-fished chub and barbel rivers, the occupants of the swim might even be rooting about among the seeds before you have finished the pre-baiting. But then again, well-educated chub and barbel may make you wait an hour or so before they move up into the swim and over the seeds. If bites do not materialize within a few minutes, do not be tempted into introducing more loose feed.

When upstream ledgering, sit facing the river with the rod angled slightly upstream, as in fig. 62D.

Quivertipping upstream

The advantage of quivertipping upstream is that on most rivers there will always be a percentage of swims that can only be tackled successfully by casting directly upstream against the flow, using just enough weight to hold bottom so that species like barbel and chub feel minimal resistance when moving off with the bait. Bites are sudden, dramatic drop-backs, the quivertip flipping backwards as the line falls completely slack.

Generally, a long, sweeping strike will

drive the hook home, but odd occasions arise when you need to wind like mad in order to recover most of the line as the fish swims several yards towards you before you can make a successful strike.

Swims with excellent potential are ignored by many anglers because they cannot cast the bait downstream and across in the accepted manner, and loose feed is taken down by the current. Fig. 63 illustrates an example of a river in which barbel and chub occupy runs behind the tree-line features and in runs between bullrush beds. However, three of the five swims can be fished effectively only by ledgering upstream. Moreover, loose feeding with either a particle attractor such as hempseed or fragments of the hook bait, or both, is not as difficult as it may at first seem. In most instances, the problem is solved by quietly walking upstream, parallel with the head of the swim, and catapulting the bait out a little upstream of the shoal.

If overhanging trees or tall beds of dense bullrushes prevent you catapulting in loose feed upstream, use a blockend feeder for depositing baits like hemp, casters or maggots; or make up a PVA (plastic vinyl acetate) dissolving stringer and tie it to the bomb swivel, when presenting large offerings such as meat cubes or cheese paste.

Quivertipping for bream

Used in conjunction with an open-ended swimfeeder filled with dampened bread-crumbs, quivertipping is the most deadly and versatile method of ledgering for bream in running water, all season through.

For many fishermen, it has completely taken over from the swingtip in recent years due to the wonderful choice of specialist, built-in quivertip rods now available. For close in work there are super-sensitive, 7–9 ft wands. At the opposite end of the scale, powerful 11–12

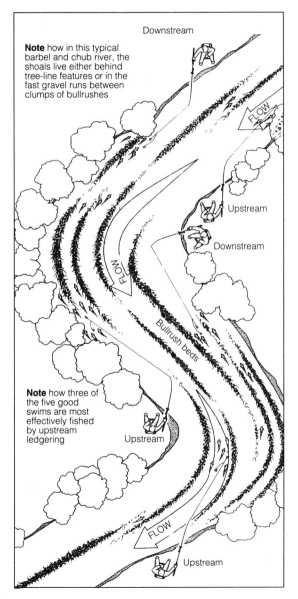

FIGURE 63 Upstream ledgering

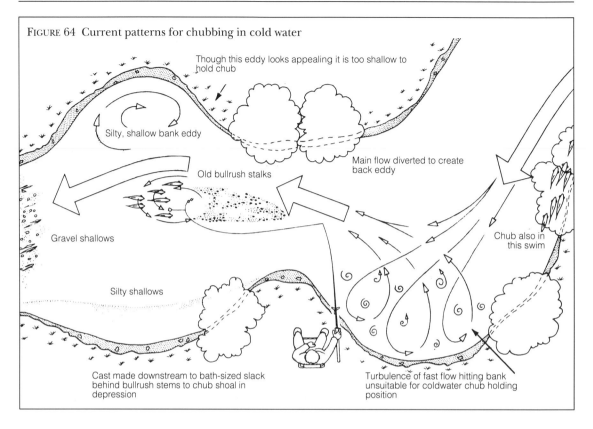

FIGURE 64 Current patterns for chubbing in cold water

Though this eddy looks appealing it is too shallow to hold chub

Silty, shallow bank eddy

Old bullrush stalks

Main flow diverted to create back eddy

Gravel shallows

Chub also in this swim

Silty shallows

Cast made downstream to bath-sized slack behind bullrush stems to chub shoal in depression

Turbulence of fast flow hitting bank unsuitable for coldwater chub holding position

ft feeder rods are available. These are capable of detecting the tiniest bite on a finely tapered tip from the swirling waters of a weir-pool, but have enough backbone to subdue any size of bream – and even a barbel should you hook one. If you do not wish to own lots of specialist rods, a 10 ft multi-tip quiver rod with a choice of three or four interchangeable tips (kept in the handle) is the answer. However, whatever you decide upon, it is the very tip that you must keep your eyes concentrated on, and you must learn to interpret its every movement so that you can distinguish the difference between weed on the line, line bites, current pull and, of course, a genuine bite.

The main difference to consider between quivertipping in still and in flowing water is the influence of pressure on the line. In really fast currents, unless you support the rod in two rests with the tip up in the air to keep most of the line above the surface, the tip will be pulled right round by current pressure alone. This completely defeats the object of having a finely tapered tip in the first place. Moreover, when current pressure becomes just too great, the bomb or feeder will bounce off downstream and in towards the bank along the bottom, dragging the bait well away from the intended swim.

Coldwater chubbing

Use of the quivertip to catch winter chub is all about understanding the river, and deciding where the fish are most likely to be shoaled up (fig. 64). For instance, when the level is up and the water coloured, large areas of particularly shallow water, unlikely to hold chub, (except in full flood) are not immediately apparent to those unfamiliar with the river. Those who know it well, of course, don't bother with these barren swims because they remember how the river was during the summer. And those who observe surface currents wherever they fish will, from the action of surface displacements, be able to distinguish between shallows and deeps. Tiny vortexes of water are sent upwards when hitting the dying stalks of bullrushes sprouting from the gravel shallows, and the same spiralling and displacement occurs when fast currents hit the tiniest of pebbles. Thus gravel shallows are easily identified on the surface from completely 'broken' water despite the fact that through heavily coloured water the bottom cannot be seen.

Having said all this, for part of the day chub may very well choose to occupy the fastest, shallowest part of the swim, but on a 24-hour basis their requirements are consistent. They prefer to hold station in a quiet slack out of the main current force, but not so far away that they cannot nip out and suck in a juicy tit bit every so often. Maximum food for minimum effort aptly sums up the chub's outlook towards life. Of course, in mild winter conditions chub are renowned for being continually on the move and will follow a food source (the anglers loose feed) from a considerable way downstream. But in the coldest of sub-zero weather and freezing winds the shoal will huddle together,

loathe to move very far. And when you decide to fish in these conditions, pinpoint accuracy is essential for success.

Low temperatures

Much depends on the daytime temperature and whether it increases a few notches or not. Some days chub might move several yards to a bait when the light values increase at around midday. On another they will not budge an inch until dusk sets in. And then one solitary knock on the quivertip is all you will get. Sometimes the bait has to be bumped on their noses for baits to materialize.

QUIVERTIPPING AT NIGHT

Quivertipping is as effective throughout the hours of darkness in flowing water, as float fishing is in stillwaters. It is often the best way of coming to grips with specimen roach, chub, bream and barbel inhabiting rivers that run very clear. I illuminate the quivertip with a narrow-beam torch set on the ground downstream of the rod, pointing upwards and out, so it shines only on

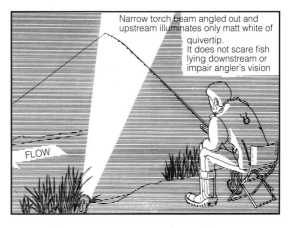

FIGURE 65 Quivertipping at night

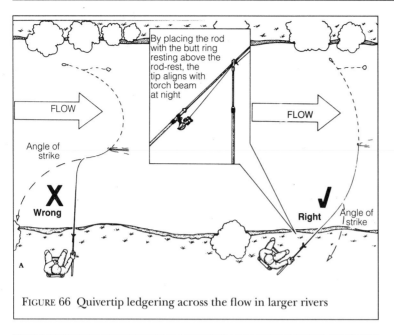

FIGURE 66 Quivertip ledgering across the flow in larger rivers

Within figure 66:
By placing the rod with the butt ring resting above the rod-rest, the tip aligns with torch beam at night

FLOW

FLOW

Angle of strike

X Wrong

✔ **Right** Angle of strike

A

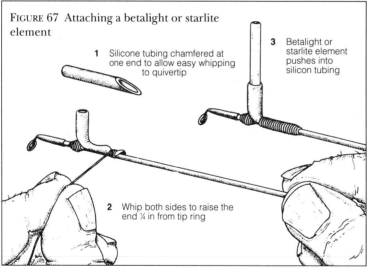

FIGURE 67 Attaching a betalight or starlite element

1 Silicone tubing chamfered at one end to allow easy whipping to quivertip

3 Betalight or starlite element pushes into silicon tubing

2 Whip both sides to raise the end ¼ in from tip ring

easy to watch, even for hours at a time, and also improves daytime concentration on the quivertip in poor light conditions and against a broken background. If the rod is firmly set on two telescopic rests with the butt ring hung up against the curve in the front rest (fig. 66), before the torch is positioned, the quivertip will then settle right in the middle of the torch beam every cast without further ado. As I keep a second, small torch in my jacket pocket, there is no need to move the one carefully positioned on the ground.

A second, and I think less effective, method of visual indication at night is provided by whipping a ¾ in section of silicone tubing on to the very end of the quivertip and pushing in a powerful betalight element (600 microlamberts), or a mini starlight chemical element, which is considerably brighter but lasts for only 6–8 hours (fig. 67). When fish are biting regularly, a luminous element on the end of the quivertip is quite sufficient. However, considering that there will inevitably be long periods of inactivity, coupled with those occasions when bits of weed and other debris continually hit the line and register false bites, I find the

the tip and not into my eyes or on the water (fig. 65). This is most important, because in clear water the fish might easily become scared.

All my quivertip rods are painted matt white (two coats) along the last 16–20 in to catch every bit of light. This makes them torch-illuminated tip far easier to concentrate on.

At night always tighten up to the bait a little more than you would during daylight, so the tip has a definable curve.

Drop-back bites then become apparent immediately.

When fishing new swims, it is well worth doing some pre-baiting to ensure that you do not waste a night's sleep.

PREDATOR RIGS

SLOW-MODE TRAILING FOR PIKE

To the best of my knowledge, this fascinating method of catching pike, which also occasionally works for both perch and zander when conditions suit, originated during the 1970s on Norfolk's tidal River Bure between Wroxham and Horning.

As trolling from a boat powered by an engine is illegal throughout Broadland's interconnecting maze of overcrowded tidal waterways (and rightly so), pike fishermen evolved the next best thing, 'trailing' their livebaits or mounted dead-baits, or both, behind the boat while regulating the boat's speed and direction with the oars. By slowing up on the bends where depth is greatest, so that the line from float to bait is angled vertically down, and then speeding up over the shallows and over known snags with the line at a 45-degree angle from float to bait, you can overcome the ever-changing bottom contours of rivers. In really thick water the baits are worked as slowly as possible, with an increase in oar speed commensurate with that of visibility, or water clarity, as it improves. The baits are trailed close beside all the obvious pike-holding features, such as overhanging willows, boat-dyke entrances, entrances to a broad or lagoon, permanently moored

Opposite A sabre-toothed tiger fish from Zimbabwe's fabulous Lake Kariba, where game viewing at close quarters and fishing go hand in hand.

cruisers or houseboats, and a mental note is made of the most productive spots for future sessions.

On arrival at those mega hotspots, it is often worth putting an anchor out from the bows (if fishing alone), or a mud-weight down at each end when sharing a boat. Provided that the current has sufficient force, you can then trot livebaits downstream tight up against the feature where pike might be lying.

Trailing has much to offer and can be an extremely versatile technique, allowing you to work a pair of rods comfortably, even while rowing. Two anglers can work a pair of rods apiece. However, you need to be well organized and equipped with specialized rod-rests that support the rod on both sides of the reel in a shepherd's crook U. These angle the line out well, making possible a wide search of the area behind the boat (fig. 68).

Obviously, an echo sounder/fish finder with a sizeable display screen showing bottom contours, depth, and fish lying beneath the boat, is invaluable, particularly when trying to locate pike in large stillwaters. In recent years, in fact, since trout fishery reservoirs have opened their doors to pike enthusiasts once the trout season is over, 'trailing' has become the accepted method for catching pike that have grown to monstrous proportions on a supplemented diet of rich trout flesh.

On some of these vast reservoirs (Rutland Water, for example, Europe's

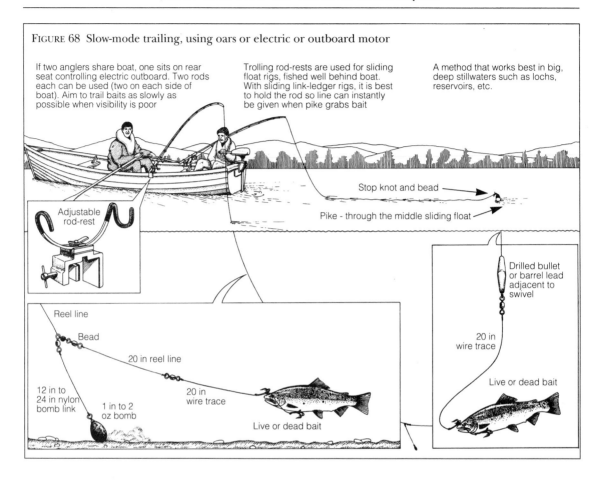

FIGURE 68 Slow-mode trailing, using oars or electric or outboard motor

If two anglers share boat, one sits on rear seat controlling electric outboard. Two rods each can be used (two on each side of boat). Aim to trail baits as slowly as possible when visibility is poor

Trolling rod-rests are used for sliding float rigs, fished well behind boat. With sliding link-ledger rigs, it is best to hold the rod so line can instantly be given when pike grabs bait

A method that works best in big, deep stillwaters such as lochs, reservoirs, etc.

Stop knot and bead

Pike - through the middle sliding float

Adjustable rod-rest

Drilled bullet or barrel lead adjacent to swivel

20 in wire trace

Live or dead bait

Reel line

Bead

20 in reel line

12 in to 24 in nylon bomb link

1 in to 2 oz bomb

20 in wire trace

Live or dead bait

largest man-made lake with a perimeter of 27 miles and a storage capacity of 27 thousand million gallons), where depths shelve to 50 feet plus, trailing scores because of the sheer amount of water it is possible to cover in just one day. Moreover, some fishery managers also permit the use of environmentally friendly electric outboard engines (rowing against the wind all day can prove extremely tiring in open water), which permit the slowest of speeds and are completely silent. Those in the American, Minn Kota range are regarded by most enthusiasts to be ideal for trailing (because they can be worked at really slow speeds). Like all electric outboards, they work from a 12-volt car battery supply. In addition, an electric motor, as opposed to oars, makes it possible for the angler who is steering to hold his second rod if he is bouncing a bait along the bottom.

Suitable tackle for 'big-water trailing' consists of 12 ft carbon, 2–2¼ lb test curve rods of a medium tip action, and small multiplying reels such as Ryobi T2 or T20s or the ABU 6500 loaded with 12 lb test. Step up to 15 lb test for reservoirs where real monsters are on the cards, or if loch fishing over a boulder-strewn bottom. I prefer multipliers because either the reel can be left in gear with the ratchet on and a light clutch setting, permitting line to be taken without undue resistance; or, in really calm conditions, it can be left out of gear with the ratchet on. If you prefer a fixed-spool reel, use only models equipped with a 'baitrunner' or with a similar device, so that the spool can be completely disengaged and line can be taken by a running pike. Now for the terminal end, which consists of standard pike rigs (fig. 68). Reasonably close behind the boat (although it can be worked someway back, too) is a running bomb ledger on a 12–24 in mono-link, stopped with a bead and swivel against the size 10 swivel used on the reel line. Note there is a 20 in section of reel line separating the top swivel from the swivel on the 20 in 15–20 lb wire trace holding a brace of size 8 or 6 (depending on bait size) semi-barbed trebles.

This has the marvellous effect of alleviating most would-be tangles. Try it and see. And with this rig you can bounce a 1–2 oz bomb along the bottom (beware of snags, though) in the knowledge that your livebait or deadbait is following along behind just 2–3 ft above bottom, right where the pike are. You can bump the bait along at engine speed or oar speed, and every now and then allow it to remain static on the bottom for, say, 20–30 seconds, while paying out line, before working it back towards the boat again, slightly faster than the troll. Naturally, you must hold the rod all the time.

The float rig can also present a deadbait or a livebait, which is kept down at the desired depth by a bullet or barrel weight stopped with a bead against the trace swivel. Use a reasonably large (through the middle) sliding float stopped by a tiny bead and sliding stop knot. In really cold or thick water conditions, pike will be lying close to or actually on the bottom, so present the bait really low down. Conversely, in mild, clear water conditions, expect action at virtually any depth. This, of course, is the beauty of two anglers each fishing two rods. On the bounce ledger rig one can fish a deadbait while the other fishes a livebait at different distances behind the boat. Deadbaits or livebaits can be presented on the float rigs at varying depths until a common denominator for the day is found. You need plenty of room to work four outfits, so give other boats a wide berth, and try to make every turn as slow and as smooth as possible, or tangles will result.

WOBBLED DEADBAITS

The technique of retrieving a small dead fish mounted head first on the trace so that pike assume it is alive and grab hold, is extremely effective and exciting, and is guaranteed to keep you casting and thinking all day long, just as when lure fishing.

This method is invariably a more effective way of catching pike than lure fishing, particularly when fishing in clear water; a dead fish feels exactly like the real thing and will not be ejected post-haste as with an artificial lure.

It is also a very versatile, mobile method that provides total coverage of any given area. For instance, if you like to fish with a two-rod set up to increase your chances in big stillwaters, but nothing is coming to the static deadbaits being presented on

Slow-mode 'trailing', using oars or an electric outboard motor, is the method for keeping livebaits and deadbaits well down; jumbo-sized pike can lurk in depths of up to 50 ft in trout reservoirs.

each, reel one in and cover the area in more depth by wobbling a deadbait in a grid-searching pattern. A total blank, when pike are not moving around and hunting out your static baits, can be turned into an exciting session by taking the bait to the fish by continually searching with a wobbled bait. This situation occurs most commonly in deep, coloured lakes and pits during long periods of low light values, such as day upon day of overcast weather. Unless you almost hit a pike on the head with a wobbled deadbait they simply do not move about much. The situation can, of course, change instantly if the weather changes, when the strong rays of the sun penetrate deep, dark water. Suddenly pike are on the move, and in a short feeding burst they might make several runs to a previously untouched

static deadbait in as many minutes. Such feeding sprees, however, rarely last more than a couple of hours, and a switch to the wobbled deadbait (still leaving one static on the bottom) could well keep pike coming to the net throughout the rest of the day.

To mount deadbaits for wobbling, fix the trebles so they are just 3 in apart by wrapping the wire around the shank of the upper treble, and firmly embed two of its prongs into the bait's eye socket. The bottom treble is nicked with the barbed prong only into the bait's flank along the lateral line (fig. 69). The deadbait is now firmly rigged for casting and when retrieved will wobble attractively. When the top hook eventually pulls through the socket, re-rig on the other side.

For fishing over thick weed or in shallow water do not add any weight to the trace. However, to keep the bait down close to the bottom where pike lie during the colder months you will need somewhere between two and four swan shot pinched on to the trace immediately below the swivel. It all depends on the depth and the rate at which you retrieve.

Where the bottom contours vary due to weed-beds, shallow bars, snags and so on, you need to retrieve the bait well up lest it catches – say, 3 or 4 ft above where you imagine the bottom to be. In lakes and pits of even depth where the bottom is clear, however, you can twitch the bait along, almost bumping pike on the nose. To do this, allow the bait to reach bottom before starting the retrieve. Then wind erratically, but very slowly; try to 'feel' what is happening down below. Keep the rod tip at an angle to the bait and watch it for any indication of a taking fish. Every so often give the tip a jerk or a twitch, followed by a couple of fast turns on the reel handle. Then pause, allowing the bait

to nose-dive for a couple of feet before twitching it back up again (fig 70). Remember that the swan shots hit bottom ahead of the bait, so if you lift it quickly upwards you will not pick up much bottom debris. In the past this technique was called 'sink and draw' because you allowed the bait to sink before drawing it up again.

Now for the strike. Do not wait for the pike to grab and then turn the bait in its jaws by giving it free line when you feel a 'take'. Pike react completely differently when snatching at a wobbled deadbait than they do when sucking up a resistance-free static from the bottom, when time is given. So unless you want the pike to drop the bait, whack it immediately by winding quickly down until you feel its full weight, and follow through with a long, powerful strike to put the hooks home, striking a second time to make doubly sure. At this point the pike tries to eject the bait by opening its jaws and shaking its head, so keep a good bend in the rod or the hooks will literally drop out.

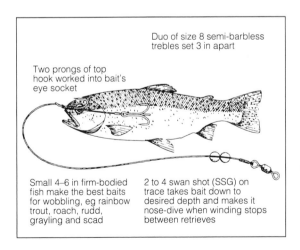

FIGURE 69 Hooking a deadbait for wobbling

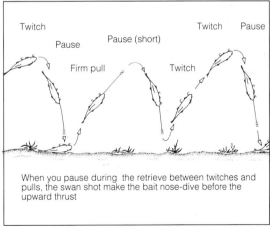

FIGURE 70 Make your wobbled deadbait come to life on the retrieve by pulling and jerking it erratically

Wobbling in running water

In slow-moving water, the wobbled deadbait is mounted and retrieved in exactly the same as on stillwater. It is great fun to work the bait purposefully alongside regular pike hideouts such as overhanging or sunken willows and have it taken at the very place you imagine a pike to be lying. This is reading the water at its very best, and provides a mobile method of fishing whereby, with a pocketful of fresh baits, miles of winding river can be searched, wobbling beside all the 'feature' swims.

In deep, cold, fast rivers, however, where pike keep close to the bottom, a slightly different approach is called for, in the form of a 3 ft nylon kink joined to the reel line 1 ft above the trace (fig. 71). A small bomb goes on the business end to bounce the bait along the bottom. A snap swivel allows for a quick change of bombs.

This rig ensures that the bait works just above the pike's immediate field of vision, which is so important, especially in coloured water. It can be great fun to bump the bait systematically across the bottom of a deep-weir pool, for instance, and results in some thunderous takes. And apart from ledgering the bait, no other method ensures that the bait is actively presented just off bottom where the vast majority of cold-water pike will be lying.

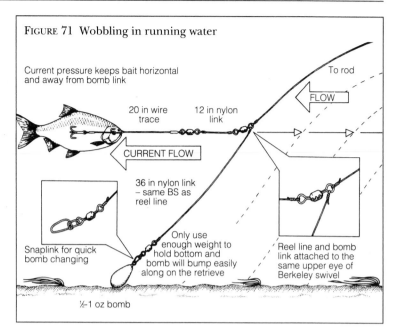

FIGURE 71 Wobbling in running water

Current pressure keeps bait horizontal and away from bomb link

To rod

FLOW

20 in wire trace

12 in nylon link

CURRENT FLOW

36 in nylon link – same BS as reel line

Snaplink for quick bomb changing

Only use enough weight to hold bottom and bomb will bump easily along on the retrieve

Reel line and bomb link attached to the same upper eye of Berkeley swivel

½-1 oz bomb

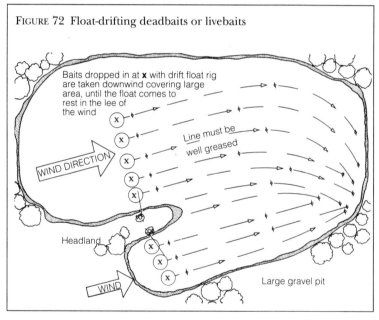

FIGURE 72 Float-drifting deadbaits or livebaits

Baits dropped in at **x** with drift float rig are taken downwind covering large area, until the float comes to rest in the lee of the wind

Line must be well greased

WIND DIRECTION

Headland

WIND

Large gravel pit

106

As when wobbling in the usual manner, strike the minute the pike grabs hold with a long, hard, sweeping strike, taking a step or two backwards to keep the rod fully bent, lest the fish manages to create some slack and ejects the bait.

FLOAT-DRIFTING DEADBAITS AND LIVEBAITS FOR PIKE

Float-drifting deadbaits is a method that really works best and covers the maximum area from an anchored boat (see 'Boat-fishing' p. 116), but may be used to good effect in large stillwaters fished from a headland when there is a strong wind coming from behind (see fig. 72). The line must be greased so that it floats well. Note how, by allowing a belly to form between rod tip and float, the same line can be held as the rig is taken down the lake (line must be given during this time from an open spool) until it comes to rest in the lee of the wind, having covered and possibly shown the bait to pike lying over an enormous area. Start by casting a short way out, and once the bait comes to rest downwind retrieve slowly (in case a pike takes the bait on the way in). Then recast a little further out each time. Using the wind and waves to bounce about the bait attractively is a fascinating way of presenting a deadbait to pike, which in many cases assume the bait to be alive due to its erratic action.

There are numerous sail-like drift floats now available, like the original ET Drifter shown in fig. 73. Note how the bait is presented horizontally to simulate the position of a live fish. It can be set to fish at any depth from within 2 ft of the bottom upwards, and in coloured water it is best presented closer to the bottom. In reality, however, taking into account a large area of water where, during the drift on a particular line or arc, depths of 10 to 18 ft of water may be encountered, my advice would be to set the float (easily rigged as a slider with bead and stop knot above) to fish the deadbait at 9 ft. It will then not foul bottom, and has a chance of attracting pike from almost any depth if the water is not too coloured. The beauty of drift-fishing is that as so much water is covered, action can come at any time

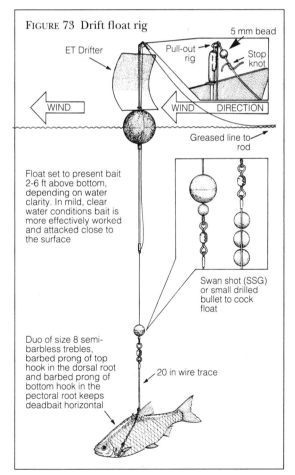

FIGURE 73 Drift float rig

5 mm bead

ET Drifter

Pull-out rig

Stop knot

WIND

WIND DIRECTION

Greased line to rod

Float set to present bait 2-6 ft above bottom, depending on water clarity. In mild, clear water conditions bait is more effectively worked and attacked close to the surface

Swan shot (SSG) or small drilled bullet to cock float

Duo of size 8 semi-barbless trebles, barbed prong of top hook in the dorsal root and bottom hook in the pectoral root keeps deadbait horizontal

20 in wire trace

from the moment when the bait is first plopped in to over 100 yd away. It is imperative when drift fishing to use a long, powerful rod and to have the spool of your reel full to the brim with fresh line, otherwise the distance that you can cover will definitely be limited.

The best way of rigging the ET Drifter is with the line passing through the small, detachable ring on top of the stem and then through the swivel at the bottom of the stem, so the greased line floats easily on the surface throughout the drift. A sharp pull at the end of the drift, or indeed when a run occurs and the pike is struck, will release the line from the top ring, instantly converting the drifter to a waggler (bottom end only) for easy retrieval.

Drifting livebaits

The only difference is in swapping the deadbait for a small livebait. Fix the hooks as described in the livebaiting section (p. 127), with one barbed prong of the top treble through the bait's top lip and one prong of the bottom treble nicked into its pectoral root – semi-barbless size 8s, of course.

Striking

When the float suddenly sinks to a pike that has grabbed the bait (alive or dead) 80 to over 100 yd away, it is not enough simply to wind down until the line is tight, and then strike. The amount of stretch in even 50 yd of 10 lb monofilament is enormous, and to set the hooks successfully with twice as much line out, a new approach is required. In fact, there is no way of striking the hooks home when distance fishing. You simply point the rod

Marketing Manager of Ryobi Masterline, Chris Leibbrandt, prepares a float-drifted deadbait rig to tempt the pike of the Norfolk Broads.

In calm conditions, the float-fished static deadbait is a deadly method that has produced numerous 20 lb plus pike for John from his local venues.

at the pike, tighten up the clutch on your reel (so it does not slip under pressure and cause line twist) and keep winding like a person possessed until you feel the weight of the fish. And you keep on winding, and dragging the pike towards you, until it senses danger and opens its jaws to eject the bait. At this point, so long as the line is kept tight, the hooks should catch hold. A really big fish just may swim off in the opposite direction and help to pull the hooks home, but most pike will be led towards the rod for quite some distance. Once the pike's head-shaking routine has been transmitted up the line and the hooks are obviously well in, readjust the reel's clutch, keep the rod in a full curve and enjoy the fight. Remember to slacken the clutch immediately, prior to netting as a safety precaution

THE FLOAT-FISHED STATIC DEADBAIT

Big, fat, old female pike in the majority of waters are far more susceptible to sucking up a static deadbait from the bottom than they are to chasing about after livebaits, particularly in heavily coloured waters where the pike's senses are geared decidedly more towards smelling out their food than sighting and chasing it. And so, presenting the easily located and taken 'static' deadbait has become the big-fish method in the majority of fisheries; except, perhaps, those clear-flowing rivers where the pike invariably show a preference for a moving bait.

In stillwater

The most enjoyable and effective way of presenting the static deadbait is beneath a

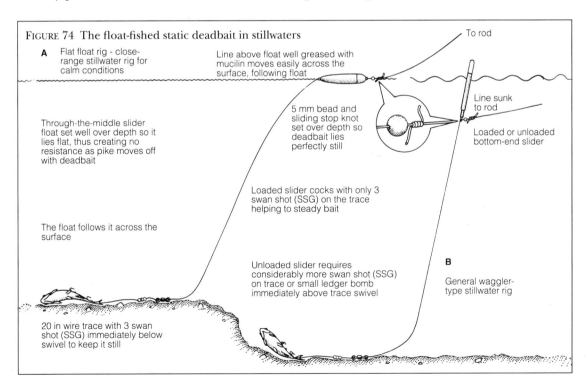

FIGURE 74 The float-fished static deadbait in stillwaters

A Flat float rig - close-range stillwater rig for calm conditions

Line above float well greased with mucilin moves easily across the surface, following float

To rod

Line sunk to rod

5 mm bead and sliding stop knot set over depth so deadbait lies perfectly still

Loaded or unloaded bottom-end slider

Through-the-middle slider float set well over depth so it lies flat, thus creating no resistance as pike moves off with deadbait

Loaded slider cocks with only 3 swan shot (SSG) on the trace helping to steady bait

The float follows it across the surface

Unloaded slider requires considerably more swan shot (SSG) on trace or small ledger bomb immediately above trace swivel

B

General waggler-type stillwater rig

20 in wire trace with 3 swan shot (SSG) immediately below swivel to keep it still

float, because apart from minimizing resistance to a pike taking the bait (compared, say, to ledgering with a heavy bomb) a float also gives you something nice to watch. There really is nothing quite like observing the drunken antics of a deadbait float. It is almost possible to imagine what is going on down below by relating it to the movements of the float.

I prefer a sliding float with the line (greased above the float) passing through the centre for close-range work in still-waters, where it won't get blown about and thus move the bait, as in the flat float rig (fig. 74A). For general fishing and most other situations, including really windy weather, consider the waggler-type rig in fig. 74B, where the line passes through the bottom eye and is sunk from float to rod tip just as in waggler fishing for other species in stillwaters.

The secret of presenting a deadbait beneath a float lies in ensuring that it remains absolutely static. Pike will then confidently suck it up, but not if the float is set too shallow, causing the bait's tail to be monotonously lifted up each time the float bobs up and down with the waves. This is why I like to set the sliding float well over depth, whether it fishes flat or upright; it should be at least twice as deep as the swim, so that at least 2 ft of line lie along the bottom in addition to the trace and bait. The pike will then not feel any degree of buoyancy from the float as it engulfs the bait in its jaws, and you will experience very few dropped runs using static deadbaits. Although when fishing for pike you use larger floats and thicker lines, the principles involved with the float-fished static deadbait are always the same.

THE FLOAT-FISHED STATIC BAIT IN RUNNING WATER

In really slow-moving rivers use the general waggler rig in fig. 74B with a small bomb on the line above the trace to ensure the bait lies static. But for fast-running water, because it lies flat and cannot be submerged by the flow, the close-range flat float rig (fig. 74A, p.109) is ideal so long as the cast is made directly downstream and the rod tip angled upwards to keep the line off the surface. Those who like to stret peg for roach or chub during the winter months will know all about the mechanics of presenting a static bait with this method.

With both of these float rigs, after tightening up and positioning the rod on two rests set horizontally, open the bale arm and clip a loop of line beneath an elastic band or run-clip fixed around the handle. This is a safety measure against the occasional suicidal pike that really belts off with the bait, and of course

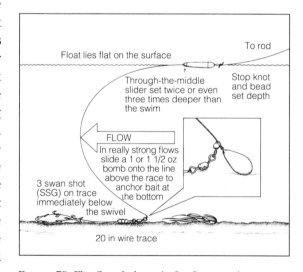

FIGURE 75 Flat float-ledger rig for fast running water

against those unforgivable occasions when you failed to notice the float trundling away. We are all human, and there is no point in losing a rod and reel from the rests through sloppiness

As when livebaiting, I prefer to strike straight away when presenting static deadbaits, on the basis that if it comes off it was probably a small pike anyway.

Half baits

I only ever use relatively small whole baits, say up to 7–8 in long – smelt, herrings and the like. In fact, for most static deadbait situations these days I much prefer to use half baits. I am certain that when cut in half the freshness and oily attractiveness of a deadbait permeates considerably more quickly through stillwater, and a half mackerel is nothing compared to the size of the jaws of a 10 lb pike.

The best way of presentation is to cut the bait in half diagonally and mount it as in fig. 76, using the standard duo (snap-tackle) of semi-barbless size 8 trebles.

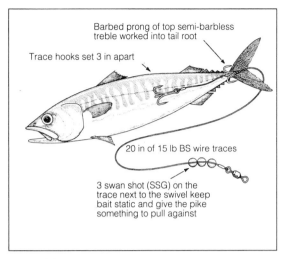

FIGURE 77 Presenting a whole, static deadbait 1

FIGURE 78 Presenting a whole, static deadbait 2

Whole baits

When offering whole baits, fix the duo of trebles firmly into the tail root and along the flank as in fig. 77, with a distance of around 3 in between hooks. This allows the pike to swallow a good half of the bait before the hooks enter its throat tissue,

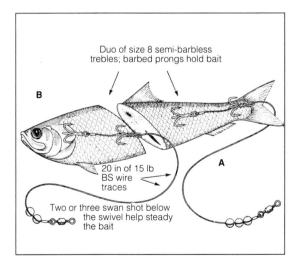

FIGURE 76 Mounting half baits

and will result in few deeply hooked pike. Pike do occasionally become suspicious of the static deadbait lying flat on the bottom (after being caught on them several times), and if the bait's head is buoyed upwards by air injected into it or a foam strip inserted into it, it can produce runs from spooky fish (fig. 78).

FREELINING AND LEDGERING FOR PIKE

When weather conditions, especially high winds, render float fishing impossible, or the deadbait needs to be cast distances that are too far for the float, say 50 yd plus, use a simple freeline or ledger rig.

I dislike using any appreciable amount of weight on the line (apart from three swan shot on the trace) when presenting static deadbaits, unless absolutely necessary. Heavy bombs lessen the sensitivity of the static bait, and because the line passes through while the bomb stays put (often creating a right angle in the line between bait and rod tip) striking could also be impaired (fig. 79A), whereas with a freelined bait the line simply follows the route of the pike and is easy to straighten for a quick, positive strike (fig. 79B). Provided the bait (with just three, or a maximum of four swan shot on the trace) can be cast to the desired spot (and a mackerel tail can easily be pushed 60 yd out), a freelined bait is best. If not, then rig up a simple ledger with the bomb attached to a 4 in anti-tangle boom sliding above the trace (fig. 80). Small, firm-bodied whole fish of between 4 and 5 in cast well and are not likely to break up.

Whether freelining or ledgering the static deadbait, bites are best registered

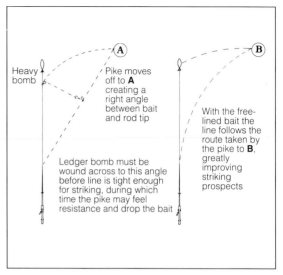

FIGURE 79 The effectiveness of a simple, freelined static deadbait

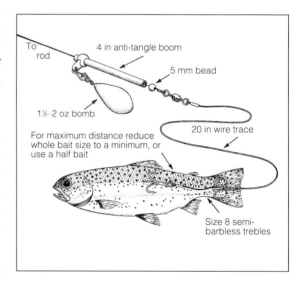

FIGURE 80 Simple static deadbait rig for distance

on drop-off/arm indicators, which fit on the rear rod-rests and clip to the line once the bale arm has been opened. As a precaution against deeply hooked pike, strike any indication of a bite immediately when ledgering or freelining.

In clear and weedy stillwater fisheries, ledgering with a sunken-float paternoster rig provides minimum resistance to big, crafty old pike.

Ledgering, again using the drop arm as bite indicator, is an effective way of presenting the static deadbait in running water. To minimize water pressure against the line, set the rod on two rests with the tip angled up high. Very often a definite 'knock' is seen on the rod tip (just as when ledgering for chub) as the pike sucks the bait up before moving off, at which point the line should be released from the indicator and the rod held. There then comes an eerie sensation as the line slips positively through the fingers in response to the run of the pike. But don't let it run too far. Close the bale arm and as soon as the fish's weight plus the current pulls the rod over into a full bend, whack the hooks home hard.

FISHING AT NIGHT FOR PIKE

Static deadbaits presented during darkness is something worth trying on clear-watered rivers, lakes or pits which receive regular attention from pike fishermen during the day time.

Pike are certainly no different to all other species in that they become far less suspicious of baits offered to them under the cloak of darkness. Pre-bait two separate areas so that, should the first fail to produce for any reason, after an hour you can move and try the next. In fact, if fishing at night starts to catch on, there is nothing to stop you pre-baiting and keeping several swims going.

Take along just two rods and start by placing one bait really close into the bank, with the second further out or deliberately next to a particular feature. Use simple freeline tactics with two or three swan shot on the trace next to the swivel, adding a bomb above the trace only to counteract a strong flow when river fishing.

For bite indication use drop arms or monkey climbers that incorporate luminous betalight elements, or simply illuminate the indicators with a wide-beam, low-powered torch laid on the ground away from the water and your line of vision.

BOAT DRIFTING

In rather similar fashion to loch-style trout fishing, drifting in a boat across stillwaters or wide river systems is one of the most effective ways of exploring large areas of the bottom when in pursuit of freshwater predators. And it is a method that works as effectively for pike on my local waters, the Norfolk Broads, as it does on foreign stillwaters like fabulous Lake Kariba in Zimbabwe, where huge catfish and the sabre-toothed tiger fish are the most likely customers. Back home, zander and perch can be added to the list of species that respond to this mobile technique.

With boat drifting you must use the wind to your advantage by first studying its strength and direction, and then selecting drifts along certain routes that will maximize on shoreline features (fig. 81). It makes sense to put the boat side on to the wind so that one angler can search alongside or cast to features like promontories, sunken trees and reed-lines, in shallow water, with artificial lures or a mounted deadbait on one rod, while in deeper water his sleeper rod utilizes the backdrift and slowly trundles a deadbait low down some 50 to 100 ft back along the bottom, or just above it, if the bottom is littered with debris or snags. This really does maximize on potential, providing the boat drifts steadily and slowly along, keeping parallel to the shoreline.

To really slow the boat down in strong winds, put out a drogue tied to the rowlocks. These sub-surface parachutes (for that is exactly what they are) might have been designed for the loch-style trout fisherman, but drogues also help the predator specialist with equal effectiveness. Incidentally, an old keepnet dragged behind the boat will create a similar effect and slow it down noticeably, but custom-built drogues are far superior and much less hassle.

The second angler also fishes a lure or wobbled deadbait out to one side, and a deeper rod presenting a deadbait on the backdrift behind the boat using a 15 lb test wire brace to 12–15 lb reel line if after pike or zander. If oddball tropical predators are on the cards, like the legendary vundu catfish of Zimbabwe, there is no finer bait than a lump of blue soap the size of a hen's egg moulded around a size 5/0 hook. It doesn't matter if the soap is blue or not, I am sure any soap will do. The bait may very well account for catfish in other parts of the world, because it creates such an attractive 'cloud' and oozes oil in the water.

As nothing else (apart from small species of catfish called barbel) is liable to suck up blue soap within the Zambezi system, which includes Lake Kariba a wire trace is not necessary for these monster pussies, which average 30–70 lb – simply 3 ft of 30 lb mono with a swivel and small bomb stopped above, on the 20–25 lb reel line. Incidentally, a small multiplier is the best reel to use when backdrifting the bait. You have the option of leaving the reel in gear with the ratchet on and the clutch on a light setting, or (light baits only) the reel completely out of gear with the ratchet on. Either way, you are treated to a resounding scream when a fish motors off with the bait.

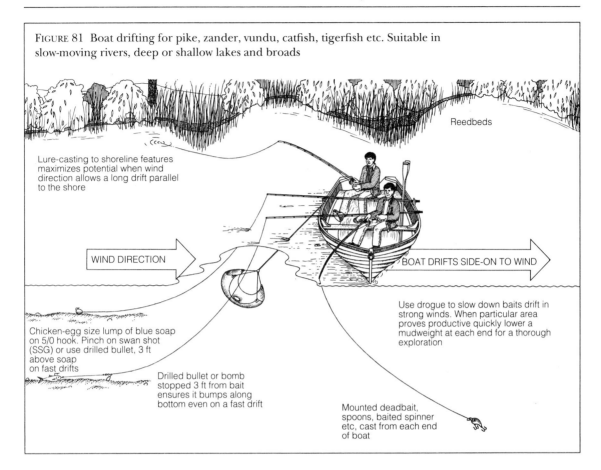

FIGURE 81 Boat drifting for pike, zander, vundu, catfish, tigerfish etc. Suitable in slow-moving rivers, deep or shallow lakes and broads

Reedbeds

Lure-casting to shoreline features maximizes potential when wind direction allows a long drift parallel to the shore

WIND DIRECTION

BOAT DRIFTS SIDE-ON TO WIND

Use drogue to slow down baits drift in strong winds. When particular area proves productive quickly lower a mudweight at each end for a thorough exploration

Chicken-egg size lump of blue soap on 5/0 hook. Pinch on swan shot (SSG) or use drilled bullet, 3 ft above soap on fast drifts

Drilled bullet or bomb stopped 3 ft from bait ensures it bumps along bottom even on a fast drift

Mounted deadbait, spoons, baited spinner etc, cast from each end of boat

As with pike and zander, if seeking the sabre-toothed tiger fish, which makes even a pirahna look friendly, a wire trace is imperative, whether presenting a mounted deadbait or a bunch of kapenta, which is a 2–3 in long freshwater sardine, and the most commonly used bait when fishing on Lake Kariba.

Of course, there is nothing to stop a vundu catfish from sucking up a bunch of kapenta intended for tiger fish, as indeed one did during the filming of our *Go Fishing* programmes made along the Zambezi Valley in 1991

That 60-pounder, which broke my 1¾ lb test curve carp rod in no less than three places before my boat partner, Buckley Hunt, finally heaved it on board (in a sea trout net hardly big enough for its head), following a dramatic 1¼ hour battle, provided one of the most hilarious and dramatic sequences ever filmed during our travels.

It is the one programme that viewers always mention when chatting at tackle shows and various other functions. And, would you believe, when I visited the very same, remote spot along the northern shoreline of Lake Kariba in the Sanyati Gorge during a holiday in Zimbabwe almost one year later to the very day, I hooked into and boated a vundu some 15 lb larger. This monster, however, succumbed to blue soap on the drift, and came out somewhat quicker, following a powerful 15 minute scrap on 25 lb line.

As to exactly what proportions these fascinating catfish reach, no-one really seems to know for sure. While my friend, Colin Froude, was playing a huge fish that finally went 90 lb after an hour's struggle, a group of South Africans who watched the fight from their boat told us of a 200-pounder they had taken the previous year, though the official Zimbabwe record for vundu is little over 100 lb.

While British freshwater fishermen might hold big pussies like the vundu in high esteem, in Zimbabwe it is, unfortunately, the very much smaller tiger fish that attracts everyone's attention. Come to think of it, in my experience the poor old catfish, whatever the species, is not that highly regarded the whole world over. And they say that looks don't count!

When a particular area turns up action more or less in the same spot on each drift, have an anchor or a mudweight ready at each end of the boat to lower down. Then give the area a really thorough search. Fish are very rarely spread around like currants in a well-baked cake, and in large waters, especially, hotspots containing numerous predators and their prey, are worth exploring exhaustively.

An echo-sounder/fish-finder like a humminbird or lowrance, which provides an accurate outline of bottom contours, can prove invaluable when drifting. When you are over areas of particularly rough ground, or, in the case of man-made reservoirs, where entire valleys were flooded, covering the stumps, or even complete trees, hedges and the like, you can raise the back-drifted baits so that you don't snag up.

Top *Ron Smith keeps an eye on Colin Froude's rod tip as a big vundu catfish heads off into deep water on Lake Kariba.*

Above *Hooked on blue soap in Kariba's Sanyati Gorge, a 70 lb vundu is about to be netted for John by Colin Froude.*

BOAT-FISHING FOR PIKE

Echo-sounders are a great addition for locating the deepest areas of waters both large and small, but are not a prerequisite for catching pike. Their use can come later, when you have learnt the funda-

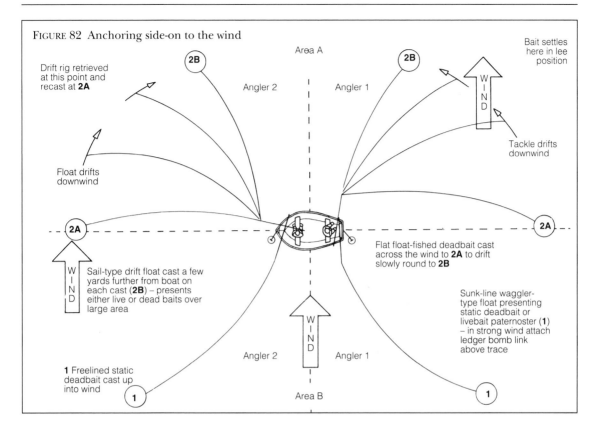

FIGURE 82 Anchoring side-on to the wind

Area A

2B

Drift rig retrieved at this point and recast at **2A**

Angler 2

2B

Angler 1

Bait settles here in lee position

WIND

Float drifts downwind

Tackle drifts downwind

2A

2A

WIND

Sail-type drift float cast a few yards further from boat on each cast (**2B**) – presents either live or dead baits over large area

Flat float-fished deadbait cast across the wind to **2A** to drift slowly round to **2B**

Sunk-line waggler-type float presenting static deadbait or livebait paternoster (**1**) – in strong wind attach ledger bomb link above trace

WIND

Angler 2

Angler 1

1 Freelined static deadbait cast up into wind

1

1

Area B

mentals of boat-fishing. The same can be said of outboard engines. Huge waters apart, you will learn to understand and be at one with pike fishing from an open dinghy far better by rowing quietly and positively, not aimlessly flitting from one area to another simply because getting there is easy with an engine.

It helps to divide the boat up mentally into two equal parts so that each angler has his own area of water to fish, assuming that the weather permits an ideal mooring side on to the wind. This takes a little extra time and concentration, but the results are so much better than rowing out and lowering the mudweights over the side, as fig. 82 illustrates.

Both anglers have an equal area to work and search, regardless of methods used, with an invisible line drawn down the middle of the boat and water. When the wind is too uncomfortable for a side-on anchorage, or when even the heaviest weights will not hold, it is advisable to anchor bows into the wind (fig. 83). Start by lowering the bows mudweight and pay out at least twice the depth of rope so that whenever wave action lifts the bows, it does not bounce the mudweight (fig. 84A). Get it wrong (fig. 84B) and the boat will not hold position in strong winds. Once the long bows rope and mudweight are holding, put down the stern mudweight on a relatively short (steadying) rope. The imaginary dividing line between the anglers then runs down the

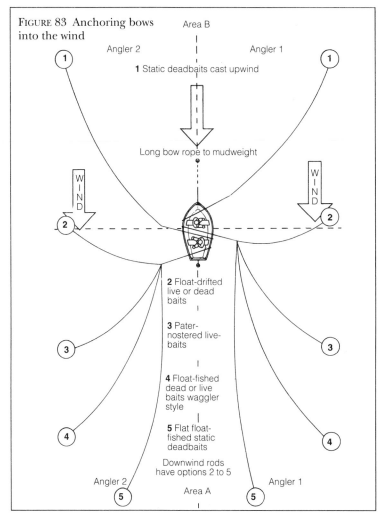

FIGURE 83 Anchoring bows into the wind

Area B

Angler 2   Angler 1

1 Static deadbaits cast upwind

Long bow rope to mudweight

WIND   WIND

2 Float-drifted live or dead baits

3 Pater-nostered live-baits

4 Float-fished dead or live baits waggler style

5 Flat float-fished static deadbaits

Downwind rods have options 2 to 5

Angler 2   Angler 1

Area A

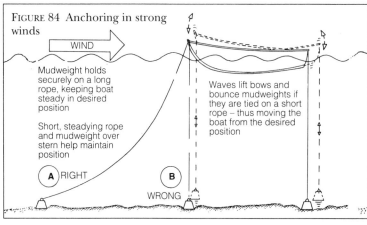

FIGURE 84 Anchoring in strong winds

WIND

Mudweight holds securely on a long rope, keeping boat steady in desired position

Short, steadying rope and mudweight over stern help maintain position

Waves lift bows and bounce mudweights if they are tied on a short rope – thus moving the boat from the desired position

A RIGHT

B WRONG

length of the boat, from bows to stern, so each can fish out from his own side with a full 180 degrees to cover.

You will see from the diagrams (assuming two rods are used by each angler) that each also fishes across the water without affecting the other so long as the invisible line is adhered to. This is important because it maximizes the potential pike areas around the boat in a 360 degree circle, and provides a mental picture of the divisions within the area for experimenting with various techniques.

Remember that when you are afloat on a huge expanse of stillwater (unless you are fishing towards the shoreline right up against obvious pike-holding features like reed-beds and overhanging or sunken trees) there is generally little indication of where the bait should best be placed other than depth. If the bottom is of even depth over much of the fishery, it pays to think in terms of taking a grid-searching approach with the emphasis on downwind, across wind and upwind areas in relation to the boat's anchorage. This permits the use of

118

virtually any method from the free-lined static deadbait to drift-fished livebaits or deadbaits. You simply use the most likely method on the day, or indeed a whole variety of methods throughout the day, until one is successful, considering weather and water conditions as you would if bank-fishing.

For instance, consider area A in fig. 82, part of which, being in the lee of the wind, can be fished effectively by Angler 1 with a greased line and 'sliding flat float rig' presenting a static deadbait on the bottom. What is more, by casting slightly across the wind and flicking off a belly of line downwind, the bait can even be drifted along the bottom for a while and worked into lee positions far in excess of distances that can be cast. Angler 2 could fish likewise or work his part of area A with either live or dead baits beneath a sail-type drift float (p. 107), starting with short casts and working progressively further out after each drift. Both anglers could also wobble deadbaits or lure fish as alternative 'active' methods within area A.

Area B, which incorporates both across the wind and upwind options, is rarely used to full advantage by most pike fishermen because, unless the line is well sunk below the waves when float fishing, the bait is whisked away far too quickly downwind, resulting in both baits being ridiculously close to each other. This is hardly conducive to searching the entire area effectively. In this instance a waggler-type (bottom end) 'loaded slider rig' is perfect for presenting a static, bottom bait across the wind. In really gusty weather use an unloaded slider and add a

bomb above the trace to nail the bait to the bottom. Angler 2 could fish his B area with a freelined static deadbait by casting it directly upwind. It is worth remembering always to pinch three or four swan shot on the trace immediately below the swivel so that drop-back runs can easily be detected. Without a float to create valuable slack the pike must feel a certain amount of resistance when sucking up a freelined static deadbait, steadied with swan shot, which is why they invariably belt off at speed directly away from the boat. Then again, it could be that the pike just happens to be working an upwind course when it locates the bait and simply carries on in that direction. Certainly this can be verified on those really windy days when most runs come to the upwind rod. Strangely, such occasions are far from uncommon, which prompts me to suggest that there is far more to the upwind phenomenon than meets the eye.

In really choppy weather with white horses topping the waves for instance, when it becomes pertinent to anchor bows into the wind, I become more optimistic about the upwind baits being taken, even when casting range is greatly reduced. Incidentally, for maximum distance when pushing baits into a strong wind, the mackerel tail, due to its density, is hard to beat. Half an eel (the head end) casts well too.

There is no doubt that, once anchored, it pays dividends to present baits with varying methods within a grid and wind division basis. Think of the boat as your very own piece of bank in the middle of the lake, with the advantage of also

Boat fishing is a prerequisite for pike on John's local fisheries, the Norfolk Broads. This 25-pounder sucked up a freelined deadbait.

way for drifting at an acceptably slow rate tie a keepnet behind the boat at each end to act as drogues.

Special boat drogues are available for fly-fishing trout reservoirs where drifting is a popular technique because it covers so much water. So if you intend doing any amount of drift fishing, invest in a specialized drogue.

When a hot area is located, quickly lower the mudweights and explore the area exhaustively before continuing the drift. It is a wonderfully effective way of locating pike in vast areas of water that are completely bare of visible features. Obviously you can only wobble deadbaits or work artificial lures with the one rod, but there is nothing to stop you using a second, 'sleeping' outfit by trailing a deadbait behind the boat. This often takes pike that follow lures in but shy away at the last moment. Try it and see.

River boat-fishing

Boat-fishing in running water is virtually the same as in stillwater, except that current pace and direction must be taken into account. Rivers invariably contain very definite habitats and pike-holding features or areas, and because they are easier to read, you can quietly anchor to full advantage, spending say an hour or so in each likely spot before pulling the mudweights and drifting with the flow downstream to the next likely area.

So that each angler enjoys both up and downstream lies, consider the set up in fig. 85, where the boat has been anchored bows-on to the flow, a rod's length out from one bank. Anchoring right in the middle is not only dangerous

having water behind in which to search.

When searching huge, even-depthed lakes, broads, meres or pits there are days when, in complete contrast to anchoring, fishing on the drift will produce numbers of pike. I much prefer mild weather for drifting because pike are generally more active and respond well to baits on the move, either wobbled deadbaits or artificial lures. The secret is to row well upwind to the very top of the fishery and to work back with the wind, working baits on both sides of the boat as it drifts slowly along. Manoeuvre the boat so it starts side-on to the wind, and to ensure it remains that

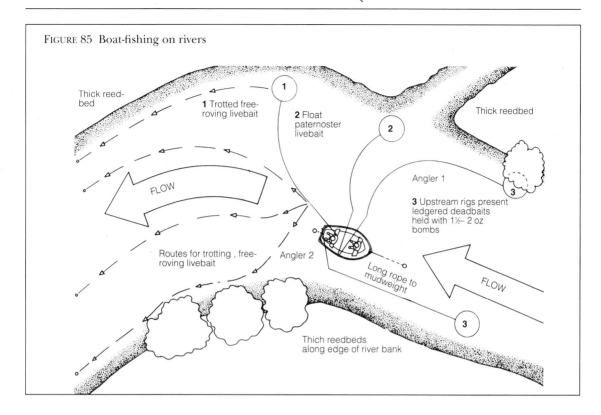

FIGURE 85 Boat-fishing on rivers

Thick reed-bed

1 Trotted free-roving livebait

2 Float paternoster livebait

Thick reedbed

FLOW

Angler 1

3 Upstream rigs present ledgered deadbaits held with 1½– 2 oz bombs

Routes for trotting , free-roving livebait

Angler 2

Long rope to mudweight

FLOW

Thich reedbeds along edge of river bank

if other craft use the river regularly, it is invariably against the local river by-laws. Note that Angler I presents a ledgered deadbait on his upstream rod and a paternostered livebait on the downstream outfit, fished across the flow into the mouth of a confluence.

Angler 2 also fishes a ledgered deadbait on his 'sleeping' outfit, presented with the bale arm open and a loop of line trapped beneath a strong run clip or elastic band over the handle, so only the pull of a pike and not the current can initiate a run. His downstream rod presents a float-fished, free-roaming livebait trotted 2 ft off bottom, along different lines, searching across the river thoroughly. As change methods, both anglers could swap their livebait rigs for wobbled baits, artificial lures, or even static deadbaits when the river colours up after heavy rain and pike switch to hunting more by smell than a combination of vibration and sight. Playing the waiting game with four static deadbaits from the one boat is then the best approach.

ARTIFICIAL LURE FISHING FOR PIKE

I say this quite without reservation: if you can catch pike (and any other predator) regularly from a wide spectrum of waters by fooling them into munching artificial lures constructed from quite alien materials such as plastic, copper, aluminium, steel, brass or wood, then by comparison every other technique should prove delightfully easy.

Without question, catching regularly on lures demands an optimum level of skill, and you need to have a fair idea of each fishery's character: the depths, the snags (otherwise it is costly for obvious reasons), the visible and non-visible sub-surface habitats preferred by pike and so on. In other words, by pulling lures you enjoy a complete involvement with your quarry.

On a poor day when pike are unco-operative, the session could be put to good use by clipping on a heavy spoon and plummeting the depths all around the lake or pit for future occasions. By leaving the bale arm open after casting and using the countdown method (applicable to any sinking lure) of allowing roughly 1 ft in descent for every second counted, it is a simple matter to plummet the water to obtain an accurate idea of the depth, plus the exact whereabouts of shallow bars, plateaux, holes, gullies and so on (fig. 86). I favour heavy spoons for this wandering technique because they can be cast long distances, and flutter down to the bottom in an attractive way. Pike have grabbed hold so many times after just one turn of the handle to lift the spoon from the bottom at the start of the retrieve, that it cannot be coincidence.

Pike hear the spoon's arrival on the surface, and in clear water visually follow its route all the way down to the bottom, as they do with sinking lures. Throughout the retrieve hold the rod with the tip pointing at the lure, with just the slightest sideways deviation for twitching and jerking, If you hold the rod to one side, the hooks may not be driven home on the strike because of the incredible amount of stretch in monofilament. There is no chance of the line snapping with the rod pointing directly at the pike. Besides, when the hooks are felt to bite, you can raise the rod into its full curve and rely on the pre-set clutch to give line whenever the pike runs.

Occasionally, and this is more noticeable when you are fishing on a short line, pike will hit the artificial really hard and belt off all in one lovely, arm-wrenching movement, banging the hooks in hard as they turn. To facilitate hooking I doctor the trebles on most lures by gently flattening all the barbs down, then hone each prong to a needlepoint with a file. This indispensable item I keep in the back pocket of my waistcoat so it is always at the ready. Lure trebles soon blunt from being continually retrieved through thick weeds, hitting the bottom and, of course, biting into the bone of a pike's jaw. And for the price of a good-quality file (which costs little more than just one lure), to fish with anything less than really sharp hooks is foolhardy.

A spoon is just one way of depth finding; an echo-sounder is the most effective but costly method. If you already fish a particular pike water for other species, you will no doubt already have a reasonable idea of its topography. The point is that many artificial lures have been designed not only to wiggle or dive or vibrate in a particular way due to their shape or weight, but to work in a particular depth band.

Take plugs, for instance, which fall into three basic categories: floaters, floating divers and sinking divers. It is pointless working a floating surface popper across

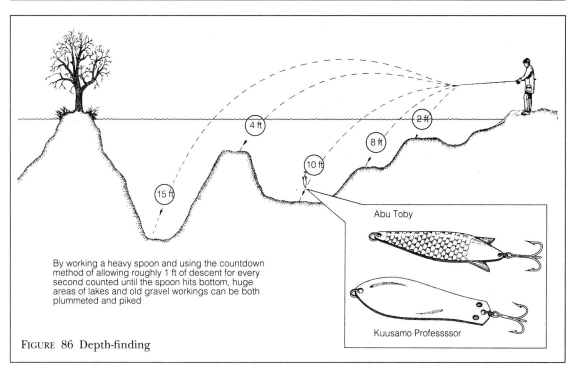

By working a heavy spoon and using the countdown method of allowing roughly 1 ft of descent for every second counted until the spoon hits bottom, huge areas of lakes and old gravel workings can be both plummeted and piked

Abu Toby

Kuusamo Professsssor

FIGURE 86 Depth-finding

FIGURE 87 Working a floating/diving plug above irregular bottom contours

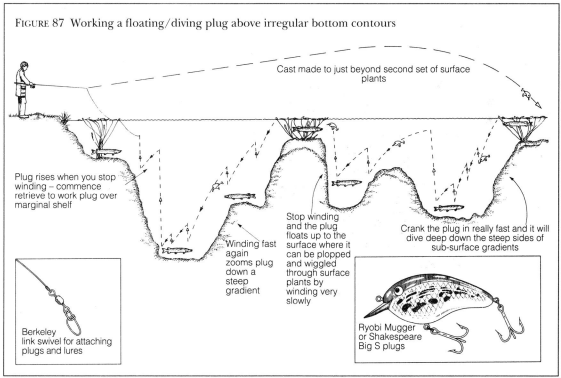

Cast made to just beyond second set of surface plants

Plug rises when you stop winding – commence retrieve to work plug over marginal shelf

Winding fast again zooms plug down a steep gradient

Stop winding and the plug floats up to the surface where it can be plopped and wiggled through surface plants by winding very slowly

Crank the plug in really fast and it will dive deep down the steep sides of sub-surface gradients

Berkeley link swivel for attaching plugs and lures

Ryobi Mugger or Shakespeare Big S plugs

14 ft of cold water. In no way will the pike lying on the bottom shoot up and grab hold (fig. 87). By the same token, a sinking diver tossed into dense lily-pads, where it will become immobile after one crank of the reel handle, is equally useless. You really need to know the capabilities of each and every artificial in your lure box, whether it floats, sinks or dives, and the respective depths to which each will dive on the retrieve; and, of course, their action.

It is then a case of selecting a suitable artificial for the type of water or habitat at hand and making it come alive. For instance, and this applies particularly to clear water conditions, when a pike is following but will not hit, suddenly start speeding up the retrieve, making it faster and faster until you completely run out of water. It may well seem that time has run out, but then right at the last second the pike will make a lunge and grab hold

Pike will attack all kinds of artificials, even coloured, plastic worms. And on a light rod/multiplier combination, pike of all sizes are great fun.

with unbelievable speed. Do not chicken out and slow up over the last few yards or the pike will do the same and swim off disgruntled.

Conversely, when working lures deep down in coloured water the retrieve needs to be slow in order to allow the pike time to home in on it and grab hold.

Summer plugging

For imparting the most life-like action to surface plugs and sub-surface lures the best rod for the job is one with a snappy tip action. This is why the short, single handed American bait-casting rods are so effective. Every single jerk and twitch is transferred to the artificial instead of being absorbed by the rod, as happens with soft actioned, two-piece spinning rods.

With a surface lure, from the moment it touches the surface the retrieve should be as varied and as unusual as you can make it. Encourage it to gurgle by slamming the rod tip down to the surface. Jerk it, pause, twitch, gurgle again. Leave it static for a few seconds, jerk, twitch, pop, pause and so on. The variety of movements is as endless as the types of lures you can try. But be forever ready for that sudden hit by immediately whacking the rod back high to set the hooks and keep it high in a powerful curve, lest the pike's antics shake out the hooks. And for this it requires slack line. So play pike hard on artificials, giving line on demand, but begrudgingly.

Chub, perch and zander

Much that I have written about fishing for pike also applies to catching chub, perch and zander on artificials, because they behave in a similar way. My favourite outfit is a 5½ ft, single-handed, American bait-casting rod coupled to a baby multiplier well heeled with 8 lb test. This may seem heavy line, but it is an insurance against the odd big pike that might happen along and against the rigours of working lures through heavy weed. For the same reasons I connect the lure to a 10 lb, 6 in alast-icum wire trace.

Any light-action spinning rod and small fixed-spool reel will suffice. However, on the baby American combo all chub seem like whoppers.

If worked erratically enough, any surface popper will persuade a chub into having a go. You impart the action by twitching it, popping, jerking, skipping it across the surface and so on.

Having said this, on numerous occasions when working artificials I have experienced chub coming up to grab hold of a plug that is simply being trotted downstream on the surface of a long run prior to being retrieved.

BAITING ARTIFICIAL LURES

Because 90 per cent of the freshwater fishing in North America revolves around working artificial lures, which is the opposite of the UK – indeed, probably less than 10 per cent of us use artificial lures with any kind of regularity – we have a lot to learn from fishermen on the other side of the Atlantic.

The addition of bait (real or synthetic) to a spoon or spinner is a common and popular technique with North Americans, who add all manner of attractors to their

Stuart Shaw admires the fantastic colours of a Robustus bream, a predatory species from the Zambesi River that readily falls for worm-baited spinners.

artificials, in addition to worms and small fish: bacon rind, strips of fish gut, a sliver cut from the fish's silvery white belly, rubber and plastic worms in an unbelievable range of fluorescent colours, plus crawfish tails, newts, salamanders, etc.

American lure catalogues are quite an education in themselves, and each new year sees yet more outrageous, synthetic, imitative creations on the market. They are all designed to encourage predators like trout, small and large-mouth bass, and over a dozen more lure-grabbing members of the sunbass family, plus saugers and walleyes (almost identical species to the zander) and, of course, pike and muskelunge to hit that lure harder!

I must admit that until visiting the Zambezi River in Zimbabwe to do battle with the legendary and high-jumping tiger fish, I had no idea of the devastating effect that bait on an artificial lure can have on predatory fish. I naturally (and wrongly) assumed that a lure's worth lay solely in its particular action, be it a gurgle, wobble, vibratory pulse, or a mixture of all three. But not so. As I was to discover with tigers and numerous tropical freshwater oddities from the warm, flowing rivers of India and Africa, especially the predatory breams and members of the perch family, if the treble hook is swopped for a large single and loaded with a bunch of worms, the chances of getting a hit are doubled, compared with when using an unbaited spinner.

Fish strip worked well, too. For tiger fish it proved even more effective than worms. And so it has since proved for me with predatory fish in British freshwater. The addition of worms, for instance a bunch of brandlings, especially to a small spinner, drives chub and perch so wild that they lunge at it with real venom. Every so often you need to top up the bunch of worms as they can fly off during casting, but this can be remedied to some extent by casting gently, and by sleeving the point of the single (fine-wire) hook through and along the body of each worm, rather than once only through its middle.

A bait-holder hook, a single with tiny barbs on the back, also helps retain the worms, as does slipping on a small section cut from a wide elastic band over the point and barb of the hook once the worms have been threaded on carefully.

Chub, perch and zander also love what the Americans call spinning jigs, which have a vibrating blade on top and below, a lead-headed single hook onto which is sleeved a synthetic worm or grubtail, or the real thing – a big juicy lobworm or two. Alternatively, how about a small, freshly killed fish like a minnow, or a sliver of silvery belly flesh. Just use your imagination. A 6 lb test line coupled to a light-actioned spinning rod of 7–9 ft is perfect for working these baited artificials, allowing you maximum enjoyment from the smaller predators, with enough in reserve should a double-figure pike happen along, and they usually do just when least expected. To be safe, always use a short, 10 lb test wire trace if pike are on the cards.

Large, simple baited spoons can often produce pike that, in clear water, can repeatedly be seen following but not taking the line. If you can remember to take along a few slivers of fresh, silvery-white belly flesh (that cut from a mackerel is ideal), try a strip every so often to see if it encourages hits. Or simply keep them handy in a poly bag in your jacket pocket, and sleeve one on quickly immediately after a visible refusal, or even a missed strike.

Fish strips work very much better on large, single hooks than trebles. Simply exchange the treble for a single of at least two sizes larger and ensure that the strip of flesh is supported along the shank of the hook without impairing the point and barb.

THE FLOAT-FISHED 'FREE-ROAMING' LIVEBAIT

There is a good reason why livebait are so effective at catching pike. Because you are offering the pike a part of its daily diet of live fish, the presentation arouses far less suspicion and caution on the part of the pike when it grabs hold of the bait, compared to something alien and metallic such as an artificial lure, or even a wobbled deadbait that does not try to get away. The pike is therefore more likely to keep hold of a live bait.

Close-range rig

As can be seen from fig. 88A, my float rig for close-range, free-roaming livebaiting is simplicity itself, incorporating one or two swan shot on the trace to keep the bait down, and a 1 in diameter pilot float plugged to the line with a thin, 2 in stem of peacock quill. It is well worth taking time to grease the line above the float for 20–30 yd with solid mucilin (available in tins complete with felt applicator pad), to stop the line from sinking between rod tip and float. Otherwise, the bait's movements are hampered and it immediately becomes far less attractive. Apart from which, striking becomes impaired when the line is heavily sunk. But with the line floating nicely on the surface film, even small (5–7 in) livebaits can be encouraged to work long distances, and thus present themselves to pike over a greater area in either still or running water.

Because free-roaming livebaiting is a truly roving technique, I usually prefer to hold the rod in order to 'work' the bait, encouraging it to swim wherever I suspect pike might be lying. For instance, gentle pressure against the bait invariably encourages it to swim off in the opposite direction, so I leave the bale arm open and apply gentle pressure against the spool with the forefinger. Whenever the line forms into a huge bow due to the bait's movement, current or wind direction, it is a simple matter (because it is well greased) to lift the line from the water without affecting the bait's direction and to straighten it.

Consider the typical pike river in fig. 89, for instance, where, due to careful use of the flow pattern to trot the bait down-

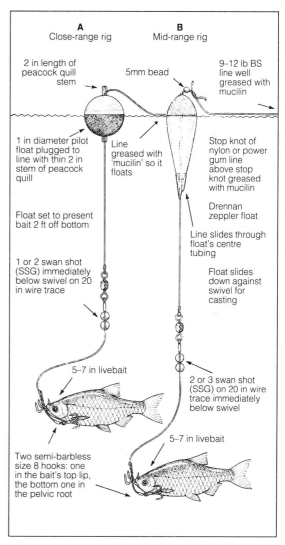

FIGURE 88 Float-fished free-roaming livebaits for still or running water

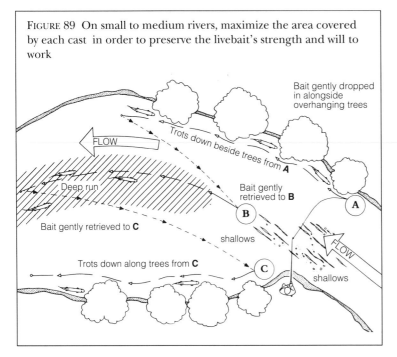

FIGURE 89 On small to medium rivers, maximize the area covered by each cast in order to preserve the livebait's strength and will to work

and show the pike equal respect. It is no less sensitive than other species even though it owns a mouthful of sharp teeth.

Striking

A few lines are in order at this stage about that age-old problem, the best time to strike a pike that has taken a livebait, because they do tend to hang on tightly, even to relatively small baits. With static dead-baits, on the other hand, the pike seems to know that the bait is not going to put up a fight and it invariably sucks it straight back for swallowing.

stream over choice lies, and delicate float control to veer it across the flow before retrieving slowly and trotting down again, every pike has an opportunity to see the bait. Only one actual cast has been made, minimizing disturbance and maximizing the bait's freshness and strength, whereas continual casting would soon sap the bait's capacity to work.

In small to medium-sized rivers, pike (especially the larger, craftier ones) often succumb during that first all-important cast and trot through, provided the bait is set at an acceptable depth beneath the float, say 2 ft off bottom. When pike have learnt to associate the disturbance caused by an angler with danger, the chance of success diminishes with each successive cast.

It goes without saying, of course, that a careful approach up to the water is very important. Pretend you are chub fishing

With artificial lures you are compelled to strike immediately, quicker than the pike can eject it. But with livebaits a decision has to be made, and I am of the view that it is always better to strike early than late. To miss a small pike through striking prematurely is infinitely better than to hook deeply a big pike that has totally gorged the bait. And there is no way of telling what size of predator has grabbed your livebait. Adopt the view that if the hook comes unstuck on the strike or on the way in, the fish probably was not worth catching anyway. You will then suffer few deeply hooked fish.

The beauty of presenting relatively small livebaits is that as soon as the float goes positively under and away (often accompanied by a glorious swirl in shallow swims), you can close the bale arm and tighten down until you feel the weight of the fish, and then lean the rod back powerfully into a full bend and firm strike. Don't allow the rod tip to straighten at any time because when the pike senses danger it will open its jaws and shake its head from side to side in an effort to ditch the bait. Keep the rod well bent and continue winding so that when the bait does move, the hooks will be pulled home. Bear in mind that until the pike opens its jaws it is impossible for the hooks to catch hold, so tightly does it hold the bait.

When temperatures are low take along a small, fine-meshed aquarium net so that you do not have to search with your hands for a fresh livebait in freezing cold water. Its price more than compensates for the alternative of painfully cold hands.

Medium-range rig

For presenting the bait at greater depths or distances in stillwaters, or deep down close to the bottom of medium-paced rivers, an additional swan shot or two must be added to the trace, and this necessitates a larger float such as a Drennan Zeppler, which is available in various sizes, or a pike ten-pin No. 2.

RUNNING PATERNOSTER LIVEBAIT RIG

Occasions will arise when the free-roaming livebait has less effect and you need to keep the bait in one spot. This happens when the water is well coloured, as in poor visibility the pike needs more than the usual amount of time to home in on the livebait. Free-roaming livebaits can even outrun a pike in heavily coloured water, and so the running paternoster rig

is used (fig. 90). This rig is also effective during extremely low water temperatures, when pike are liable to be considerably more lethargic. Again, presentation of the bait in one spot allows the pike time to investigate its movements. Alternatively, you may wish to anchor the bait in the middle of a deep hole on the bend of a river where continually trotting a free-

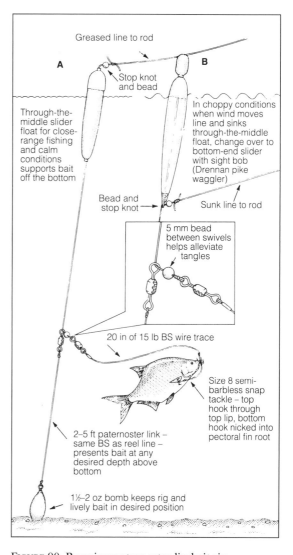

FIGURE 90 Running paternoster livebait rig

roaming bait proves unsuccessful; or to present it during windy conditions at various points along a deep gully in a gravel pit or lake without continually having to recast, as you would a free-roaming livebait.

As you can see from fig. 90A, the running paternoster is simple to construct, using the sliding float as a built-in plummet. For instance, if after casting out and tightening up gently the float lies flat, it has been set too deep. And if it is taken beneath the surface it has been set too shallow. Ideally it should be set slightly deeper than the swim so that after tightening it remains upright and gently 'knocking' to the movements of the livebait. In case a violent, long run develops I like to fish with the bale arm open and a loop of line lightly clipped beneath a run clip or an elastic band situated around the handle immediately above the reel. A pike can then pull the loop free and take line from the open spool, but the livebait cannot. It is a simple yet effective ruse that works best with the rod set on two rests with the tip pointing at the float and angled upwards.

When fishing at distance or in strong winds, it is impossible to present a float-paternostered livebait with a greased line and through-the-middle slider. The wind bows the line and eventually pulls the rig away from the desired position. So you simply exchange the 'through-the-middle slider' for a bottom-only slider (such as the Drennan waggler pike float, which has an easily visible sight bob on the tip) and sink the line after casting – just as though you were roach fishing using a waggler float (fig. 72B), because exactly the same principles are involved. To ensure the line sinks quickly, keep a small bottle of neat washing-up liquid handy and dab a fingerful around the spool prior to casting. The bait can be presented at any depth from 2 ft off bottom upwards, depending upon the length of the paternoster bomb link; you should allow for dense bottom weed or snags, and take into account pike that may be feeding among fry shoals, for instance, at mid-water. So increase or decrease the bomb link accordingly.

Before making each new cast and re-positioning the bait, always make a point of inspecting the wire trace to ensure that constant bait movement has not kinked the wire. Badly kinked traces could easily fracture at the wrong moment, possibly leaving a set of trebles in the pike's throat. If in doubt, replace the trace with a new one. The cost of 20 in of wire to those who make their own traces is not worth thinking about.

FLAT-LINE TROLLING IN FRESHWATER

Flat-line trolling consists of pulling or 'trolling' an artificial lure (or mounted deadbait) on a flat line (as opposed to one clipped into a downrigger) behind a boat powered by an outboard engine. In many river and lakeland systems within the British Isles, such as my local waters, the Norfolk Broads, this method is actually illegal. Whereas in other waters, most of the Irish and Scottish lochs, for instance, flat-line trolling is considered to be one of the most effective methods of catching specimen brown trout, pike and salmon. It is, nevertheless, always advis-

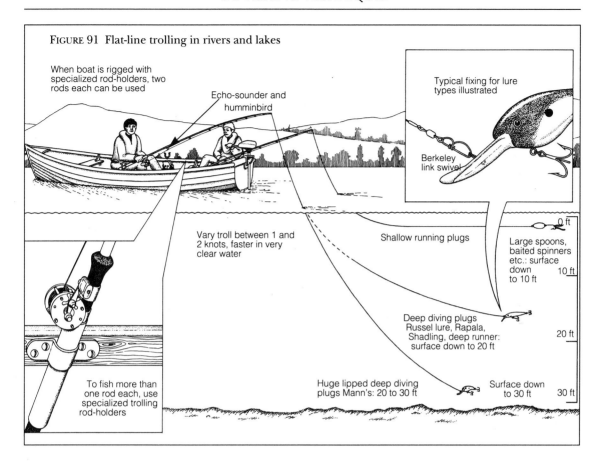

FIGURE 91 Flat-line trolling in rivers and lakes

When boat is rigged with specialized rod-holders, two rods each can be used

Echo-sounder and humminbird

Typical fixing for lure types illustrated

Berkeley link swivel

Vary troll between 1 and 2 knots, faster in very clear water

Shallow running plugs

0 ft

Large spoons, baited spinners etc.: surface down to 10 ft

10 ft

To fish more than one rod each, use specialized trolling rod-holders

Deep diving plugs Russel lure, Rapala, Shadling, deep runner: surface down to 20 ft

20 ft

Huge lipped deep diving plugs Mann's: 20 to 30 ft

Surface down to 30 ft

30 ft

able to check with the National Rivers Authority about the ruling in your particular area.

Trolling is so devastatingly effective because of the amount of water covered and, consequently, the numbers of fish that get to see the bait, compared to being anchored in just one spot. However, you can always drop down an anchor or mudweight at each end of the boat and search a particularly bountiful area more thoroughly once fish have been located by trolling. Or you can keep working through the same area time and time again, trying a selection of different lures at varying depths until a winning formula is found. It is a wonderfully mobile, explorative, often relaxing way of searching out large, featureless expanses of stillwater and wide river systems. There is no way you should ever feel bored, and if you do it is because you have stopped thinking. So reappraise the situation and consider varying your trolling speed perhaps, or trying previously uncharted areas, known snaggy areas, or even extreme shallows.

Unless you have intimate and exact knowledge of the depths and bottom contours of the water being fished, you will be at a distinct disadvantage without the use of a sonar/fish finder. This is not so helpful for its fish-locating powers,

Top *The rivers and lakes of Canada's North-West Territories contain prolific numbers of lake trout in excess of 20 lb that succumb to trolled spoons and plugs.*

Left *A trolled spinner baited with fish strip provided some hectic off-camera tiger fishing for Paul Martingell.*

Above *Having expertly netted this magnificent 14 lb tiger fish, guide, Stuart Shaw, shares in John's happiness.*

because when trolling through shallow or clear water especially, fish tend to move away from a moving boat as it approaches, and so will not be picked up by the sonar's transducer and registered on the display screen. However, what does continually show up on the screen is an accurate outline of the bottom – its actual structure with regard to snags and features such as sudden drop-offs, peaks, gullies, rock formations, etc. and, of course, the depth.

The best way to tackle the depth down to 30 ft, – beyond this, flatline trolling becomes ineffective – is to think of the lake in cross section and divide it into three distinct segments: 0–10 ft; 10–20 ft; and 20–30 ft. As can be seen from fig. 91, big spoons, shallow running plugs and spinners on their own or baited with worms or a strip of fish belly, are all most

effectively presented in depths from the surface down to 10 ft. In clear water, especially where the deepest point is around 10 ft and the bottom shelving up to as little as just 5 or 6 ft in places, all

Top *On their first day at Rusinga Island on Kenya's Lake Victoria, John and Andy Davidson talk lures with Anthony Dodds before doing battle with the Nile perch.*

Left *After a deep-down battle, John was surprised at the way which Nile perch tail-walk when they surface.*

Above *Paul Martingell grabs a camera to record John's expression during the powerful fight given by a 50 lb Nile perch.*

these lures will be seen regardless of what depth fish are lying at.

For fish situated in the second layer 10 – 20 ft down, especially if they are holding station close to the bottom, deep, floating/diving and sinking/diving plugs are the order of the day: lures with large lips or diving vanes that quickly angle down to 10 ft and more, such as the Rapala range, Shadling deep diver, or the unusually shaped Russelure made from sheet aluminium. These American lures come fitted with a choice of three trolling positions to which the snap swivel (always buy those of renowned quality) may be connected, so that the lure can be worked anywhere between 5 and 20 ft.

The unique sideways, throbbing action is absolutely irresistible to the huge Nile perch of Kenya's Lake Victoria, the second-largest lake in the world. When trolling out from Rusinga Island with my old mate, Andy Davison, and skipper, Anthony Dodds, during the filming of *Go Fishing* on Lake Victoria, we tried just about our entire armoury of huge diving plugs on those perch, but they really did show an unusual preference for the action of the Russelure. And the two 'taking' colours proved to be metallic green and gold.

Nile perch do not have powerful, piercing teeth but huge bristle pads containing thousands of tiny rasp-like teeth just inside the mouth, and exceedingly rough gill plates. A wire trace is not, therefore, essential, but a 4 ft shock leader of 100 lb test mono added to the 40 lb reel line via a strong swivel is imperative for absorbing the inevitable abrasions that take place during a long fight. For the record, and

because I personally rate these jumbo perch among the most exciting of freshwater trolling adversaries, our tackle consisted of ABU 10,000 and the rugged Ryobi S320 multiplying reels matched to 9 ft trolling rods that I constructed specifically for the job from Fibatube 132 hollow-glass blanks, fitted with trolling gimble butt pads to stop the rods swivelling round in the rod holders.

While I am on the subject of rod holders, if you intend doing any amount of trolling using your own boat, invest in a pair of the 'tube-type', which are securely clamped and screwed to the inside of the boat at a slight forward angle, and thus support the entire butt below the reel. Fit two on each side of the boat, so four rods can be fished comfortably between two anglers, with a shallow-running and a deep diving artificial working from each side. You can even make them quite easily and cheaply yourself from the thick-wall plastic piping used in the plumbing trade. An inside diameter of around 1¼ –1½ in should accommodate most rod butts. Otherwise, sooner or later you will experience the sickening sight of a rod you put down for just a few seconds flying overboard.

For trolling a lure in depths below 20 ft, there are few models from which to choose. I put the outrageously lipped Mann's 20+ and 30+ in the 'depth plus' series at the top of the list, but they must be trolled a long way behind the boat. Provided the 30+ is trolled with around 75 yd of line out, the makers claim this incredible lure will actually reach depths of over 40 ft and maintain stability without flipping over at speeds of several knots.

Talking of actual trolling speed, there is, I am afraid, no general rule of thumb, other than to start off slowly at around 1 knot and step up the speed slowly until 'hits' materialize. Some fish like a chase, others want that lure bumped on their noses. Naturally, it makes good sense to troll more slowly when the water is thick and visibility low, and considerably faster in really clear water when a predator might well pick up the sight of your lure from 20 to 30 ft away in addition to its vibratory pulses.

If you cannot grab the rod immediately when the lure is taken (have the clutch on a firm but 'forgiving' setting should a monster happen along), and whack it back to set the hooks, rev up the motor and double your speed for a few yards to eliminate any slack line. In some circles, use of the engine to set the hooks is considered to be cheating, and is known as 'drowning your fish'. I have never been able to see the objection, and in certain situations I have found that unless I accelerate the motor when the rod tip buckles over, very little ends up in the boat.

Trolling for the big tiger fish of the Zambezi River above Victoria Falls is one such situation. During the filming of *Go Fishing* along the lush, tropical valley, where huge crocodiles, elephant herds and hippos are everyday sights, those crazy tiger fish hit the baited spinner trolled 2 ft below the surface at around 2 knots with unbelievable aggression, leaping high into the air and shaking the hook clear all in one frustrating movement. And this repeatedly happened while I was holding the rod and expecting a hit at any moment.

The tiger fish's unbelievable jaw structure, containing a row of large, sabre-shaped teeth both top and bottom, means that setting a barb behind them using treble hooks is virtually impossible. Even when the treble has been replaced by a large single and made more attractive with a bunch of worms or fish strip to encourage the tiger to hold on longer, you are still lucky if you boat one tiger from half a dozen hits. If accelerating by a few extra knots on the strike increases the odds of the fish staying on, that's wonderful.

A ruse always worth trying when trolling spinners, and particularly big spoons, whether baited or not, is to suddenly drop the lure back by knocking the reel out of gear (this is why multipliers are imperative for trolling) and pay out several yards of line. This can prove to be an awkward and laborious task if you are using a fixed-spool reel; with extra torque loaded around the bale arm there is much more chance of a break-off occurring to any sudden, savage hit.

What happens is that, being quite weighty, the spoon not only stops, but flutters enticingly downwards for a second or two, until it suddenly jerks into motion again as you put the reel back into gear – something that the giant, char-like lake trout of Canada cannot resist. Pike fall for it, too. In the crystal-clear waters of the deep Canadian lakes in Manitoba and the North-West Territories, I have encouraged numerous lake trout into following the spoon fished short behind the boat (so I can see what happens), often for several minutes at a

distance of 2–3 ft. Every now and then they have the audacity to swim alongside the spoon and head-butt it, but show not the slightest inclination to grab hold.

These sudden bangs are often felt on the rod tip when flatline trolling for big lakers, but in this case with the spoon way back behind the boat, it obviously cannot be seen. If nothing materializes, small trout, trying to take on more than they can chew, can be mistaken as the culprits. However, if you suddenly drop the spoon back, it is often hit powerfully before it can jerk upwards again. This is well worth remembering wherever you are flatline trolling, regardless of the species, in freshwater and in salt.

LEDGERED LIVEBAIT RIGS

Although livebaits usually work best when presented beneath floats, and simultaneously provide immense visual enjoyment, there are situations that demand a ledgered bait because floats are impractical: for presenting the bait to pike on the bottom of deep, swirling weirpools, for instance, or pike occupying deep gullies far out in lakes or gravel pits, or during gale-force conditions when any sort of float fishing is impossible.

Make up a simple running ledger as in fig. 92 with a 1–2 oz bomb clipped on to a 3 in anti-tangle boom stopped with a bead against the swivel of the 20 in snap-tackle trace. This gives an effective rig that casts well and presents the bait close

Opposite Nile perch grow so large that catching one is often very much easier than trying to lift it out. Andy Davidson hoists an 80-pounder for the cameras.

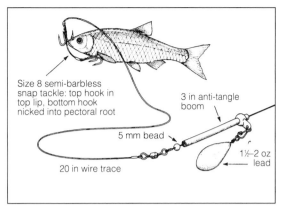

FIGURE 92 Ledgered livebait rigs 1

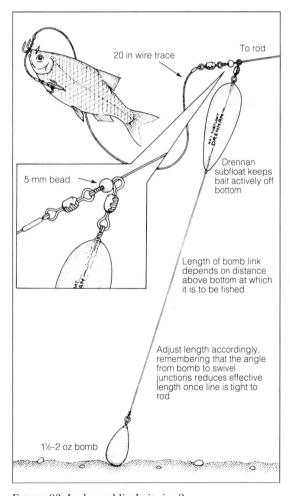

FIGURE 93 Ledgered livebait rigs 2

to the bottom. To present the bait well off bottom to pike working the upper water layers, or to avoid the bait tangling with dense bottom weeds or snags, consider the benefits of the sunken float rig in fig. 93. Again the set up is kept simple, and is rather like the bottom end of the running float paternoster. Use a long bomb link with a Drennan clear plastic subfloat running free on the line. This rises and supports the livebait at the desired depth once the line has been tightened from reel to rig.

For bite indication when using these rigs, the drop-arm indicator is recommended because tension can be applied at the line clip to allow for constant pulling from the bait.

FREE-ROAMING MINI LIVEBAIT RIGS FOR PERCH AND CHUB

Small livebaits worked beneath a float are a most productive and exciting method of catching perch and chub in both still and running water. When exploring rivers, trotting tiny fish like minnows or the fry of any small shoal fish beneath a float, a 2 to 3 swan shot chubber fixed to a 5 to 6 lb line both top and bottom should suffice. Set it to present the bait 1 to 2 ft above the bottom with the bulk shot set 1 ft above the hook.

For larger fish, such as a 2 to 4 in bleak, gudgeon, bullhead, small dace or lamprey, use a ⅞ in diameter pilot float plugged to the line with 2 in of fine peacock quill (fig. 94).

Use a size 6 hook for minnows and a 4 for larger baits, hooking them once only through the top lip or through both

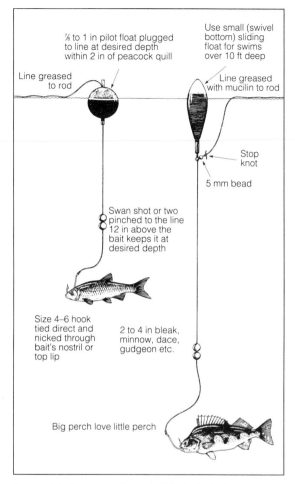

FIGURE 94 Free-roaming mini livebait rig for perch of chub – for use in still running water

nostrils. Trot steadily downstream holding back every so often to waver the bait tantalizingly up and away from the bottom.

Summer live-baiting can produce hectic results, especially at the tail end of large weir-pools and in the back eddies where perch and chub gather in large shoals. Trot the bait beside all the usual habitats along the opposite bank, remembering to let it swing across the current at the very end of the run so it finishes up in the margins along your own bank. Then retrieve it gently in slow pulls plus the occasional twitch, ready for a take at any moment.

Generally speaking that first run through the swim offers the most likely chance, so move on after giving each spot two or three casts. With this wandering, searching way of fishing, the opportunist always catches more fish.

When the float does suddenly shoot under and the line tightens, you are on your own. If you strike immediately you will pull the hook from a percentage of fish, and if you leave the run to develop you could still pull it out or have the bait returned minus its lower half. In short, there is no set formula guaranteed to hook chub and perch on livebaits, which is why nowadays I strike with a long sweep of the rod as soon as the float goes. I keep it fully bent as the fish shakes its head, hoping the hook will find a purchase. If anything, winter livebaiting has the edge, and is particularly effective in very cold, clear-water conditions when Jack Frost has painted everything white and most other methods are less effective.

Sometimes small jack pike become a nuisance and every so often bite the hook off, which might just sway you into using a wire trace, but resist the temptation. Far fewer perch or chub will suck in the livebait as a result, and pike rid themselves of a large single hook unbelievably easily.

To present the bait in really deep water, say swims in excess of 10 ft, where the fixed pilot float inhibits casting, switch over to a small swivel-bottom sliding float (fig. 88, p.127), and remem-

ber to grease the line for several yards above the sliding stop knot to help control the bait. Remember also to wet the line with saliva before moving the sliding stop knot either up or down to accommodate a depth change.

Stillwater

The sliding float rig is, overall, a better option for presentation in stillwaters. For instance, if the depth is not known, you can use the rig (without bait) to plummet large areas prior to fishing, so that you can always work the bait in that all-important layer of water a couple of feet above the bottom. As only a small percentage of stillwater fisheries contain chub, it is larger-than-average sized perch (1½ lb upwards) that are attracted by small, free-roaming fish close to the bottom. It is my favourite method for big perch throughout the summer and autumn, and in reasonably mild periods in winter. It works especially well whenever a good chop on the surface permits a large area to be explored. In extremely cold weather, however, I prefer to anchor the bait down in one place, and for this the perch paternoster livebait rig (fig. 95, p.141) is recommended.

LIVEBAITING AND DEADBAITING IN STILLWATERS FOR CHUB

There is no doubt that chub become significantly harder to catch once introduced into stillwaters. However, where they can be seen charging into the fry shoals during the summer months, the usually enigmatic stillwater chub is at its most vulnerable to a freelined or float-

size 4 hook is tied. He does suffer wonderful catches of pike in an effort to locate these nomadic specimen chub, including the occasional whopper, but every so often a group of chub passes through the swim and one of them succumbs to the bleak deadbait on offer.

Specimen perch like this 2½-pounder are more suspicious of resistance than any other freshwater predator, and will quickly drop the bait if it is presented beneath an over-large float.

fished livebait. They will take deadbaits too. Numbers of really huge specimen chub have fallen for large deadbaits such as whole herrings and half mackerel intended for a pike. A friend who regularly chub fishes some of the large, deep gravel pits adjacent to the River Thames near Oxford actually pre-baits for chub during the winter months with whitebait or freshly killed bleak.

A dozen or so free offerings are introduced close into the margins along a gradual drop-off every other night (grebes and cormorants clean them up if put in during daylight) for a week or more, followed by several consecutive sessions during darkness, fishing two rods with a freelined dead bleak on each. To ensure the 6 lb line is not bitten through by the chub's pharyngeal teeth, the hook length is made from 10 lb test dacron to which a

PERCH PATERNOSTER LIVEBAIT RIG

In very deep, cold water, when perch do not respond immediately, and may take their time approaching even a particularly lively bait, the most effective way of locating them is to anchor the bait close to the bottom in a selected area using the paternostered livebait rig (fig. 95). By employing a two-rod set up and continually repositioning each bait every half hour or so until the action is initiated, you can explore a large expanse of water during a day's fishing. Remember to pinch a small shot onto the line a couple of feet above the end rig for the sliding float to rest against prior to casting, or tangles could result.

I find the bait works most attractively, and for considerably longer, if the single-eyed hook (tied direct) is gently slipped through the nostrils or once only through its top lip, provided that the cast is an unhurried, gentle lob. Fierce casting encourages the livebait to fly off the hook, or become damaged by the time it arrives in the swim. As for bait preference, that old adage, 'the best way of catching a big perch, is by using a little perch', could not be more true. I also have much faith in gudgeon, which work attractively for hour after hour. Small roach, rudd and dace are good too.

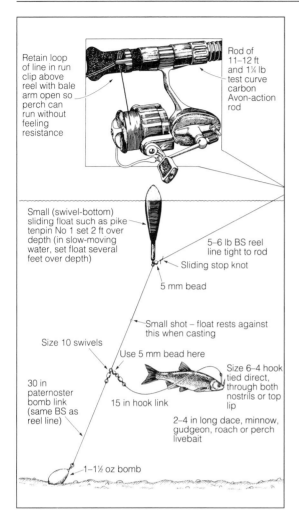

Retain loop of line in run clip above reel with bale arm open so perch can run without feeling resistance

Rod of 11–12 ft and 1¼ lb test curve carbon Avon-action rod

Small (swivel-bottom) sliding float such as pike tenpin No 1 set 2 ft over depth (in slow-moving water, set float several feet over depth)

5–6 lb BS reel line tight to rod

Sliding stop knot

5 mm bead

Small shot – float rests against this when casting

Size 10 swivels

Use 5 mm bead here

Size 6–4 hook tied direct, through both nostrils or top lip

30 in paternoster bomb link (same BS as reel line)

15 in hook link

2–4 in long dace, minnow, gudgeon, roach or perch livebait

1–1½ oz bomb

FIGURE 95 Perch paternoster livebait rig

A 1–1½ oz bomb tied to the 30 in link ensures that the bait works only in the lower water layers close to the bottom, and makes this rig perfect for snaggy or weeded spots in both still and running water during the summer, when a lively, free-roaming bait may either work away from the desired area, or become caught up in weed. It is particularly effective for exploring deep eddies, or beneath the main flush in weir-pools and in deep holes on the bends, because the bait stays exactly where you put it and works continually at the desired distance off bottom. To present the bait over a bottom covered in cabbages or thick weed, simply lengthen the bomb link to suit.

When fishing in stillwater, ensure that all the line from float to rod-tip is well sunk, or the float will be dragged under by the surface tow alone. When river fishing, however, the situation reverses, and to stop the float from being pulled under by the current, set it well over depth and angle the rod-tip well up on a front rest so that most of the line clears the surface. As perch are quite liable to eject the bait upon feeling undue resistance, once the rig is in position tighten up the float and slip a loop of line beneath a run clip or an elastic band on the handle immediately above the reel, with the bale arm left open. This allows a perch to run with the bait and peel line from the spool. However, do not wait too long before striking, or it may gorge the bait.

There is no golden rule as to exactly when the strike should be made. When water temperatures are extremely low, perch invariably take time in approaching, grabbing hold of and finally swallowing the bait. Indeed, the float may sink slowly, no more than a few inches beneath the surface. During mild spells, however, perch could work the bait down within seconds. So if the hook fails to catch hold on the first strike, wait a little longer on each successive run before winding down and striking. Adopt a philosophical attitude in that it is more desirable to miss than to net a deeply hooked perch!

PERCH AND ZANDER LEDGERED LIVEBAIT/ DEADBAIT RIG

Zander

Zander spend the greater part of their life feeding close to the bottom, and ledgering is by far the most effective method of catching them in both still and running water. As can be seen from fig. 96, to enjoy sport with zander of all sizes, an 11–12 ft heavy Avon-action ledger rod is perfect, used in conjunction with a reel line of 6–9 lb test, depending on the presence of snags and so on. Where possible, endeavour to fish lighter rather than heavier, because more runs will result. If you are fishing waters where, in addition to zander, a really large pike is more than just an outside possibility, then a compromise of an 8–9 lb test line is the wise choice.

To minimize resistance to a biting zander, the rod should be set in two telescopic rod-rests with the tip pointing downwards and directly at the bait. As there will inevitably be long periods of inactivity, it is comforting to employ an electronic bite alarm as the front rest, plus a visual indicator such as a greased monkey climber with a clear body. A betalight luminous element or a luminous 'starlight' can then be slipped into the clear body for those long night-fishing sessions. And on the majority of zander fisheries, night fishing greatly increases the chances of success with this predatory enigma, particularly the larger specimens, which are incredibly wary and shy in clear water conditions during daylight, unless the surface is broken by strong winds.

Even with the indicator set to hang on a drop of around 2 ft, zander bites are often extremely tentative and consist of little more than slight jerks on the line that raise the monkey climber no more than a few inches at a time. These initial twitches do, at least, allow you time to anticipate further, more positive action. Nevertheless, only a small percentage of runs will eventually peel line from a free spool, as a pike does when making off with a live or dead bait, and my advice is to strike in a long, positive, backwards sweep of the rod as soon as the indicator hits the tip of the needle. This is one reason why I usually fish for zander with the bale arm closed. Again, if a big pike is more than likely, fish with an open bale arm and a loop of line in a run-clip on the rod handle, just in case.

When offering livebaits, I suggest you fix a tiny run-clip or an elastic band over the rod blank between butt-ring and indicator, which eradicates the annoying bleep-bleep from the bite alarm that is caused by the intermittent movements of an active bait, not zander. Obviously there is no need to do this when presenting deadbaits, unless river fishing against a strong flow.

For fishing in heavily coloured water, small freshly killed deadbaits (with the emphasis on 'freshly killed') are more effective than livebaits – my favourite zander baits being gudgeon, small roach and rudd, or a 3 in long eel section. Make a few slits with a knife along the flank on both sides to allow the bait's aroma to permeate the water, and mount it on a 15 in alasticum trace of no more than 10 lb test, holding a duo of size 10 trebles set 2 in apart.

As can be seen from fig. 96, immediately above the trace swivel is a 15 in length of reel line with a running bomb (1–2 oz) link ledger above the second swivel, and a 'cushioning' bead between them. This set up rarely tangles and is most sensitive to the tentative bites for which zander are justly renowned.

When zander are biting in a particularly finicky way, a good method of instigating action is to ease the bait (live or dead) gently along the bottom every few minutes by slowly cranking the reel handle a couple of times and resetting the indicator.

If using a two-rod set up (most advisable when after zander, because only very rarely is sport fast and furious), a large expanse of water can be grid-searched by casting out both baits to a particular spot, and inching each back every few minutes, then repeating the procedure along a slightly different tack with each successive cast. Alternatively, plan to keep one bait static-fished at short to medium range (10–30 yd) while searching long-range areas with the 'retrieved' bait technique. However, it is also true that there are times when zander reinforce the fishermen's belief that 'patience is a virtue'. The puzzle is in sorting out which plan of action will work on the day.

Ledgering live and dead baits for perch

Much of what has already been said about ledgering for zander with live and dead

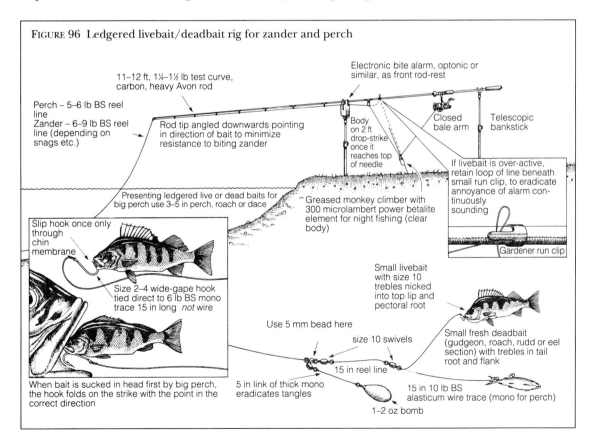

FIGURE 96 Ledgered livebait/deadbait rig for zander and perch

11–12 ft, 1¼–1½ lb test curve, carbon, heavy Avon rod

Electronic bite alarm, optonic or similar, as front rod-rest

Perch – 5–6 lb BS reel line
Zander – 6–9 lb BS reel line (depending on snags etc.)

Rod tip angled downwards pointing in direction of bait to minimize resistance to biting zander

Body on 2 ft drop-strike once it reaches top of needle

Closed bale arm

Telescopic bankstick

If livebait is over-active, retain loop of line beneath small run clip, to eradicate annoyance of alarm continuously sounding

Gardener run clip

Presenting ledgered live or dead baits for big perch use 3–5 in perch, roach or dace

Greased monkey climber with 300 microlambert power betalite element for night fishing (clear body)

Slip hook once only through chin membrane

Size 2–4 wide-gape hook tied direct to 6 lb BS mono trace 15 in long *not* wire

Small livebait with size 10 trebles nicked into top lip and pectoral root

Use 5 mm bead here

size 10 swivels

Small fresh deadbait (gudgeon, roach, rudd or eel section) with trebles in tail root and flank

15 in reel line

When bait is sucked in head first by big perch, the hook folds on the strike with the point in the correct direction

5 in link of thick mono eradicates tangles

15 in 10 lb BS alasticum wire trace (mono for perch)

1–2 oz bomb

baits also applies to perch, especially the common denominator of water clarity. In fact, I have only ever enjoyed good results with a ledgered deadbait in the deep and permanently coloured waters of old clay or marle pits, where the sediment is held in suspension, or in meres so rich in green or brown plankton that visibility is too bad for the perch to hunt by sight alone. And I am talking of inches here, not feet. When a perch can see its prey from 2 or 3 ft away, my confidence in deadbaits is much reduced and my thoughts switch immediately to presenting livebaits.

However, when offering a completely static deadbait, there is nothing better than a small, freshly killed little perch, which really does sort out the bigger perch of 2 lb and over. What is more, I

To catch jumbo-sized zander, ensure that your rig is resistance-free and that the bait is small, using no larger than size 10 trebles to a 10 lb alasticum wire trace.

find perch of between 5 and 6 in long weighing perhaps 2 oz the perfect bait. If big perch are the quarry, do not mess about with minnows or gudgeon, which any perch of 6 oz upwards can manage with ease. Go straight for the very largest perch (and the odd pike, of course), which feel confident in sucking up a comparatively large deadbait from the bottom. Concentrate only on the very deepest swims, and from late autumn onwards throughout the winter months.

At this point we arrive at whether to use a wire trace or not, and from fig. 96 you can see that my preference is for a mono trace of around 15 in long made from the same 6 lb test reel line. In over 30 years of pike fishing using wire traces, I can only recall a handful of big perch that have been stupid enough to accept the bait, both live and dead. I am sure, on numerous occasions, perch have momentarily picked up static pike deadbaits from the bottom, only to reject them, resulting in dropped run after dropped run (while pike fishing) with seemingly little explanation. The truth is that any form of compromise means missing out on big perch in the net.

As can be seen from the perch/zander ledger rig, a run is registered by the monkey climber body rising slowly to the top of the needle. At this point resist all temptation to strike anywhere near as hard as you would for pike. Merely wind down to the perch until all is solid and bend the rod back into a full curve. This usually results in much head-shaking as the perch endeavours to eject the bait, so keep the line tight, which allows the hook to find a purchase – or the bait will simply pop out. It is that simple. Fancy multi-hook rigs are simply not worth the bother. A single, wide-gape size 2–4 eyed hook tied direct to the 6 lb mono trace and nicked through the chin will fold on the strike and be pointing in the right direction for the best chance of penetration, whether you are offering a live or dead bait.

BASIC RUNNING LEDGER RIG FOR EELS AND CATFISH

The rig I employ when ledgering for eels and wels catfish is, in format, little different from my zander rig, except that I increase the reel line to 11–15 lb test

(depending upon existing snags and the size of fish expected), and the rod's test curve to 2–2½ lb.

As can be seen from fig. 97, there is a 15 in section of mono above the trace with a swivel at each end, which stops the running bomb (¼–1oz) ledger from tangling and possibly causing a fish to eject the bait. Incidentally, if actually fishing close to snags, construct the bomb link from much lighter mono than the reel line (a rotten bottom) so it quickly parts company and ditches the bomb if it becomes snagged.

With catfish in mind (though, of course, in waters where they co-exist, eels are regularly caught when seeking whiskers

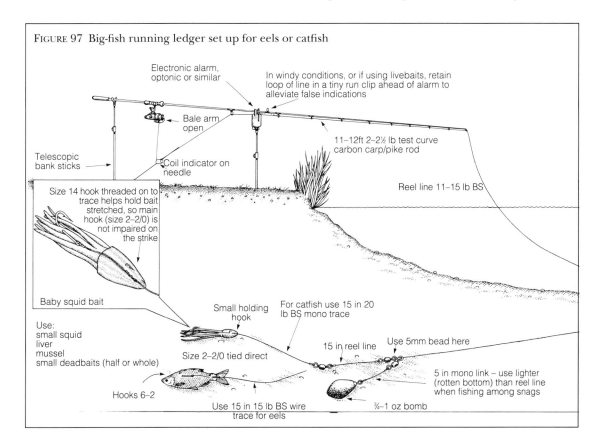

FIGURE 97 Big-fish running ledger set up for eels or catfish

Electronic alarm, optonic or similar

In windy conditions, or if using livebaits, retain loop of line in a tiny run clip ahead of alarm to alleviate false indications

Bale arm open

Telescopic bank sticks

Coil indicator on needle

11–12ft 2–2½ lb test curve carbon carp/pike rod

Reel line 11–15 lb BS

Size 14 hook threaded on to trace helps hold bait stretched, so main hook (size 2–2/0) is not impaired on the strike

Baby squid bait

Use:
small squid
liver
mussel
small deadbaits (half or whole)

Small holding hook

For catfish use 15 in 20 lb BS mono trace

15 in reel line

Use 5mm bead here

Size 2–2/0 tied direct

5 in mono link – use lighter (rotten bottom) than reel line when fishing among snags

Hooks 6–2

Use 15 in 15 lb BS wire trace for eels

¾–1 oz bomb

because they are attracted to identical baits) a 15 in bottom trace of 20 lb test mono is quite sufficient to withstand the abrasive action of numerous bristle-like teeth. The same might also be said of eels, except that every so often an eel will twist and squirm so violently that a mono trace becomes chaffed and eventually chewed through by the eel's teeth, which, in truth, are no more formidable than those of the wels catfish.

To be sure rather than sorry, construct your eel traces from 15 in of 15 lb test alasticum wire. You may well suffer the occasional refusal from a particularly choosy eel when contemplating making a meal of your bait mounted on wire, but at least you won't lose many once hooked. To complete the trace (whether wire or mono) thread on a tiny size 14 eyed hook before adding the wide-gape, strong, forged, straight-eyed hook. Select sizes 6–2 for eels, depending on bait size, and sizes 2–2/0 for catfish.

There is a very good and important reason for this additional tiny hook sliding on the trace, because without it the bait will either shift position during the cast and mask the hook point when you strike, or wedge down over the gape the second you bend into the fish. It is there simply as a holding device for keeping the bait straight or stretched, and thus attractively presented. To hold the small hook in the desired position, simply wrap the trace around its shank a few times (as you would the top treble on a pike trace) before pushing the point and bending it firmly into one end of the bait. The main hook can now be lightly nicked into the flesh of the bait with the entire gap and point clear for perfect penetration on the strike.

As most sessions in search of eels and catfish are planned 'all-nighters' (and should be, if you want the best possible chance of connecting with either), an electronic bite alarm as the front rod-rests is imperative, as there will be long periods of inactivity. Always present the bait with the bale arm open, allowing a long, resistance-free run to develop with the line retained beneath a lightweight coil or silver foil indicator slipped onto a needle to stop it moving about in the wind.

Also advisable when fishing in blustery conditions, and especially if presenting livebaits, is to retain a loop of line beneath a narrow-profile plastic run-clip or an elastic band fixed tightly around the rod in front of the bite alarm. This totally alleviates the nuisance of false indications, enabling you to relax until a genuine run occurs.

Invariably, lightweight indicators fall off as the line zooms upwards and starts to peel from the open spool. Now at this point, no amount of planning or advice can possibly prepare you for, or indeed have any bearing on, what happens next. One night you will close the bale arm while the line peels off in the most positive of runs, wait for all to tighten firmly, and promptly set the hook perfectly into an eel or catfish on the strike. On another session you are just as likely to miss screaming runs of a similar nature one after another.

In truth, there is no easy explanation. At times the culprits are, of course, either immature eels, baby catfish or even carp, each of which is liable to pick up a small squid or whole mussel, for instance, and do a runner. So do not despair. You can experiment by reducing bait and even hook size and try striking early the very second the indicator rises to the top of the needle. And this does definitely work, producing some very large and wary specimen fish in the process. On other occasions, you can allow the eel or catfish to run until it would seem to bury itself in the opposite bank, yet still fail to connect on the strike.

To enhance the chances of runs from eels and catfish, try pre-baiting the chosen swim with hookbait samples, such as chunks of raw liver, cockles, the insides of swan mussels or small, freshly killed fish, etc., every other evening for a week prior to fishing. However, I advise you not to pre-bait waters that are prolific in carp, pike or small eels, or you could experience rather more action than you bargained for.

FRESHWATER GAME FISHING TECHNIQUES

FLYFISHING FOR COARSE FISH

Setting out to catch coarse species on a fly-fishing outfit opens up a whole new and exciting world of technique and challenge. Fly fishing even allows you to approach and subsequently catch species like grayling and roach living in ridiculously shallow or overgrown streams, for instance, where no other method could possibly be employed.

Although not an accepted method (as yet), I have in recent years enjoyed hooking and landing on a super-light fly outfit numerous carp running into double figures after spectacular fights – fish that I could perhaps have more easily hooked on a simple floating controller rig. I reasoned that as they were rising so freely to small floating biscuits, and sucking in all manner of items floating on the surface, why not offer them a mayfly. Like all the cyprinids, carp consume a quantity of emerging aquatic insects, so why not present them with artificial imitations.

I also pursue pike with the fly rod by offering large, gaudy streamer flies and jigs presented on 4 in of 10 lb test alasticum (otherwise bite-offs are inevitable) tied to a 6 ft, 10 lb leader. Double-taper fly lines are useless when casting heavy flies and lures. I even cut down the front end of a weight-forward line by 3 or 4 ft so the thickest, heaviest part is as close as possible to the artificial. If you can obtain one, an American bass-bug taper floating line greatly improves casting accuracy and distance.

With perch in mind, I revert to standard tackle using a weight-forward line for easy casting, because perch go absolutely mad over the jigging action of lead-headed lures such as the dog nobbler. By reducing the leader length to just 4 or 5 ft, and by cast-

Mullet spend much of their life in freshwater and are easily caught with the fly rod, as John proved during the Go Fishing *programme on the River Ebro.*

Opposite Brian Gerahty of the Irish Tourist Board hoists a fine wild brown trout from the peaty water of the lovely River Liffey near Dublin.

149

ing carefully, the very tiniest of spinners or fly spoons may be worked close into the bank around pilings, beneath bridges and beside wooden stagings.

In European freshwater rivers and lakes the coarse species most likely to provide enjoyment with the fly rod on a regular basis throughout the warmer months are dace, grayling, chub, roach and rudd.

DACE

Dace are forever willing to suck in artificials, and because they rise to the dry fly so quickly, they are actually more difficult to catch than trout. This provides a wonderful challenge on a lightweight dry-fly outfit requiring a leader point of no more than 2 lb. In fact, when presenting tiny size 18 dry flies, I taper the leader down to a 1½ lb point.

The splashy surface movements of dace are easily seen at the tail end of shallow runs and pools, where several fish might all hit the surface together during a prolific hatch.

You can match the hatch of natural insects or present any small patterns

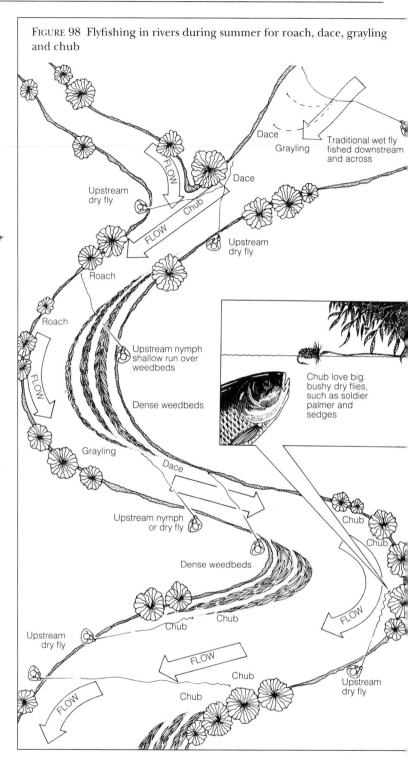

FIGURE 98 Flyfishing in rivers during summer for roach, dace, grayling and chub

Dace
Grayling
Traditional wet fly fished downstream and across
Dace
Upstream dry fly
FLOW
Chub
FLOW
Upstream dry fly
Roach
Roach
Upstream nymph shallow run over weedbeds
Dense weedbeds
Chub love big, bushy dry flies, such as soldier palmer and sedges
Grayling
Dace
Upstream nymph or dry fly
Dense weedbeds
Chub
Chub
Upstream dry fly
Chub
Chub
FLOW
FLOW
Chub
Upstream dry fly
FLOW
Chub
FLOW

and expect to see some action, so long as the fly is gently put down just up-stream of the shoal on a snaky line so it does not drag. Remember to grease the cast well, and make use of any available bankside cover to creep into a casting position a little downstream of the rising shoal. You cannot wait a second or two, as you must with trout, for the fish to get its head well down. Dace rise to and eject that fly like greased lightning. So you must strike and pull into them with equal speed.

DACE AND GRAYLING

Presentation of the dry fly is a super way of tempting really big dace and grayling inhabiting clear, shallow streamy runs where they repeatedly refuse baits on float tackle because presentation is difficult due to the extreme shallowness of the water. And this is the real beauty of using the fly rod to catch coarse species because they can be extracted from spots where no other method will work (fig. 98).

Wherever dace and grayling are not interested in accepting the dry fly on the surface, try them on a slowly sinking nymph. Grease all but the last 2 or 3 ft of the cast and offer a size 16 leaded shrimp or pheasant tail. Cast it upstream to the head of the run, watching the ungreased line sink as the flow brings the nymph downstream towards you. Any sudden twitch, jerk or obvious slow pull should be instantly met with a firm pull on the line with your left hand (assuming you hold the rod in your right) and a lift of the rod. Both dace and grayling also take the wet fly when it is presented in the traditional manner downstream and

across on a sunk line, but they are far more sporting and challenging to catch on a dry-line outfit.

CHUB

The chub may well be regarded by some as the poor man's trout, but in many small rivers and streams, the fly rod adds another string to your bow. The saying, there's more than one way of skinning a cat, could not be more true of chub.

On the dry fly – big sedges, mayflies, craneflies (daddy long legs) – the chub offers wonderful sport, particularly at dusk and even during the heat of a summer's day when numbers of them forage between long flowing beds of weed in search of tit bits brought down by the current. When shoaled up in reasonable numbers they are not so selective as a lone brown trout, so provided your casting is accurate and you cast the fly from a downstream position so it alights gently at the head of the run, it won't be there long (fig. 98). Chub also respond to buoyant patterns like deer hair sedges, and muddler minnows skated deliberately across the surface as the light is failing and at dawn.

In really streamy, broken water where heavy beds of rock or gravel are almost completely clear of weeds, the traditional wet fly cast downstream and allowed to swing across the current will take chub. Use flies with silver bodies imitative of tiny fish fry, such as the butcher or dunkeld in sizes 12, 10 and 8 on a 3 lb cast.

For some extra fun try a large, heavily weighted nymph such as a Montana stone fly or the mayfly patterns, cast well upstream and twitched slowly along the bottom as it is brought back down by the current. As long as your approach is stealthy, chub will gobble up almost any large, weighted nymph pattern presented in the clearest water. I particularly like to tempt chub that are lying beneath floating canopies with lead-headed lures like the dog nobbler.

ROACH

Roach lack the agility of the dace and grayling but are wily. They are also most partial to a slowly sinking nymph. Grease the cast to within 2 or 3 ft of a slightly weighted nymph if fishing a shallow river (4 to 6 ft for stillwaters), and watch like a hawk as the tip of the cast descends, striking at any unnatural movement.

Where possible, try to identify what is actually being taken and match it with something from your box. Alternatively, where roach are known to inhabit a certain spot but are not actually moving up to intercept pupas prior to hatching, offer a small leaded shrimp or pheasant tail nymph, sizes 14 and 16, to stimulate their interest.

In deep, steady pools a much larger artificial, such as a heavily leaded mayfly nymph, will attract roach. Size 12 and 10 are not too large, and remember to use a leader point of no less than 2 ½ lb.

RUDD

During those really warm, sultry days of summer, rudd are readily fooled at the surface with small dry flies. And as the artificial could be floating for some time

in stillwaters, I prefer the extra buoyancy of winged patterns like the coachman, alder and small red sedge, on size 14 and 16 hooks tied to a 2 lb point, well rubbed in mucilin.

Where rudd exist in numbers, the disturbance they cause at the surface, swirling after hatching aquatic flies, can be relied upon as the sun starts to set. And this, incidentally, is when specimen rudd move close in to the margins in large lakes and pits.

Rudd might also rise at any time of the day, even in bright sunshine, whenever there is a hatch, but they are more likely to be located basking around the trailing branches of overhanging willows and beneath large lily patches (fig. 99). A dry fly delicately presented close by is rarely refused, but even more deadly is a slowly sinking nymph. As rudd obtain most of their natural food during the summer months from the upper water layers, a pheasant tail, shrimp, sedge pupa or corixa plopped deliberately beside a lily-pad or overhanging branches, and allowed to sink slowly, promotes really positive takes. The cast shoots dramatically across the surface as a rudd inhales the artificial and darts immediately away lest other shoal members attempt to get in on the act.

A favourite oddball method that I favour and practise regularly in the summer, when rudd and roach are visible through clear water of estate lakes, pits and weedy, slow-moving rivers, but are not rising, is to put the shoal into a feeding mood by creating my own hatch and regularly catapulting out maggots. Once the fish are freely accepting each maggot as it descends (you can, with practice, even work

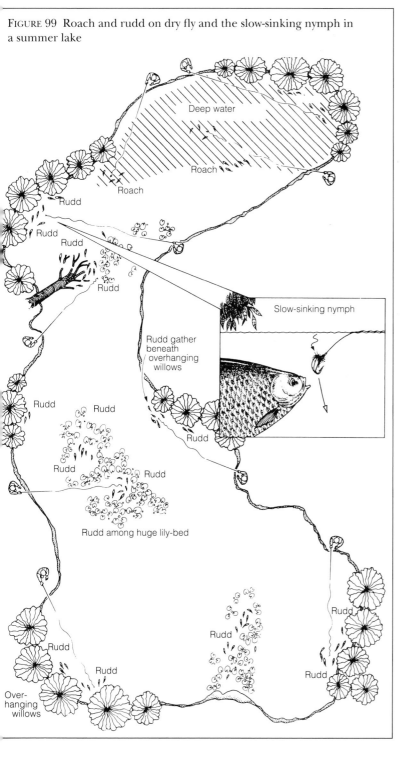

FIGURE 99 Roach and rudd on dry fly and the slow-sinking nymph in a summer lake

Deep water

Roach

Roach

Roach

Rudd

Rudd

Rudd

Rudd

Slow-sinking nymph

Rudd gather beneath overhanging willows

Rudd

Rudd

Rudd

Rudd

Rudd

Rudd

Rudd among huge lily-bed

Rudd

Rudd

Rudd

Rudd

Rudd

Rudd

Over-hanging willows

the shoal into a feeding frenzy on the surface), I tie a size 16 or 14 hook to the end of the cast and nick a couple of maggots on firmly. Provided that the casting is not fierce, only occasionally does one come off (hence the reason for putting two on), you have the option of watching the maggot slowly sink or the cast for indications of a take – or both. Give it a try; it is also a fun technique for chub, dace and even grayling.

INDUCED-TAKE NYMPHING FOR STILLWATER TROUT

In many of today's man-made put-and-take fisheries (for want of a better expression), especially those in southern England where the water runs through chalk and is subsequently crystal clear, it is often possible to track the descent of a weighted nymph from the moment it hits the surface, all the way down to the bottom through 10 ft of water or more. Such situations offer the opportunist fly fisherman induced-take sport at its very finest, the ultimate prize being a jumbo-sized double-figure rainbow, or even a brown. Such monsters up to and even over the

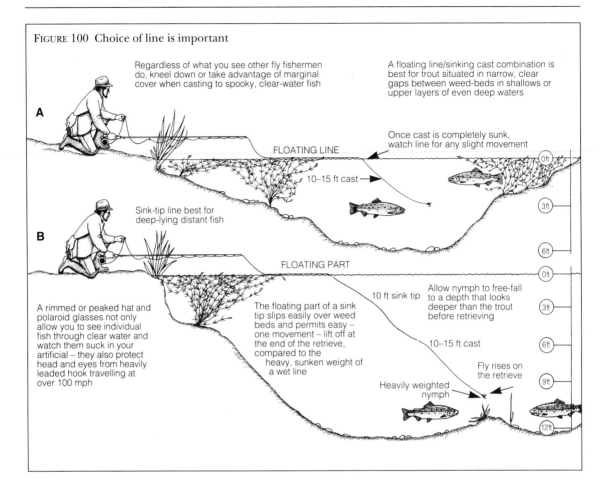

FIGURE 100 Choice of line is important

A

Regardless of what you see other fly fishermen do, kneel down or take advantage of marginal cover when casting to spooky, clear-water fish

A floating line/sinking cast combination is best for trout situated in narrow, clear gaps between weed-beds in shallows or upper layers of even deep waters

Once cast is completely sunk, watch line for any slight movement

FLOATING LINE

10–15 ft cast ➤

0ft

3ft

6ft

B

Sink-tip line best for deep-lying distant fish

FLOATING PART

0ft

A rimmed or peaked hat and polaroid glasses not only allow you to see individual fish through clear water and watch them suck in your artificial – they also protect head and eyes from heavily leaded hook travelling at over 100 mph

The floating part of a sink tip slips easily over weed beds and permits easy – one movement – lift off at the end of the retrieve, compared to the heavy, sunken weight of a wet line

10 ft sink tip

Allow nymph to free-fall to a depth that looks deeper than the trout before retrieving

3ft

10–15 ft cast

6ft

Fly rises on the retrieve

Heavily weighted nymph

9ft

12ft

20 lb mark are now an everyday prospect from certain southern fisheries, whether you agree with the instant 'specimen' and trophy fish syndrome or not. I love the excitement of induced-take nymphing, which usually revolves around first sighting and then stalking individual fish by taking into account their speed, the casting distance involved, weed-beds, etc., and the depth at which you have guessed the trout to be holding. This is the most important and critical factor of all, because in the blue- clear visibility of chalk- fed lakes especially, you can so easily judge the trout to be lying very much shallower than it in fact is. And if your nymph falls short by 3 or 4 ft, only the most aggressive fish are liable to zoom upwards and take – provided, of course, they caught sight of it in the first place. It is far better to cast way in front of a moving fish or just to the side of a stationary fish, allowing enough time for the nymph to free-fall slightly deeper than the trout (and with moving fish this takes no small measure of judgement). Then start an erratic retrieve and watch intently through polaroid glasses as the nymph makes its upwards journey. Get it right, and you'll see the trout's tail waggle as it moves to intercept the nymph, fol-

lowed by the white flash of the inside of its mouth as it sucks it in. Such a sight is wonderfully rewarding and I have to compare it with the sense of anticipation that I always experience when a carp sucks a floater off the surface.

Apart from using a heavy enough nymph of an appealing colour and shape, on a long cast, the fly line itself is of paramount importance. For instance, as can be seen in fig. 100, if you are fishing over surface weed into relatively shallow water, say 3–6 ft, to trout moving through a clear channel, whether at close or long range, use a floating line and degrease the 10–15 ft cast, enabling the nymph to free fall easily down to and slightly below the trout.

For fish lying in considerably deeper water, use a sink-tip line. Because of its 10 ft fast-sinking tip, plus the 10–15 ft cast, it allows the nymph to be presented to fish holding in depths down to at least 12 ft. The nymph does not sink on a vertical line. The cast and sink tip descend at an angle of about 45 degrees. This means that trout lying as deep as 12 ft get to see it, as the combined length of cast and sink tip is somewhere between 20–25 ft.

A peaked cap or hat with a wide brim to shield your eyes from the sun, plus polaroid glasses are imperative for induced-take fishing. I find that Polaroids with yellow lenses are preferable because they do not reduce the transmission of light in the way that grey lenses do. Polaroids will also protect your eyes from fluke accidents that may occur when, for example, a heavily leaded nymph is travelling through the air at over 100 miles an hour.

The beauty of induced-take nymphing is that you have the opportunity to watch how trout respond to your artificial, and to either speed up or slow down the retrieve accordingly. And the knowledge gained can be put to good use when you are trying to make the nymph come alive in other fisheries where the water is not so clear.

You will also appreciate that stillwater trout like to work a certain beat or route in their search for natural food. Observation of the goings-on in one particular area of the lake will soon reveal this, and when you can expect a certain whopper to come round again – hopefully within casting distance. Don't be in a hurry to chase fish.

TRADITIONAL WET FLY
(Presented downstream and across)

The wet fly offered downstream and across in more or less the traditional manner is the most common game-fishing technique that viewers have seen me use on television. It has accounted for huge lake trout and grayling in the North-West Territories and in the province of Manitoba in Canada. And again in Canada, over on the fabulous west coast in river systems of British Colombia that empty into the Pacific Ocean, I eventually managed to catch on an outlandish American wet-fly pattern called a green-buck skunk, the legendary steelhead trout.

This superbly contoured and athletic game fish is really a sea-running rainbow

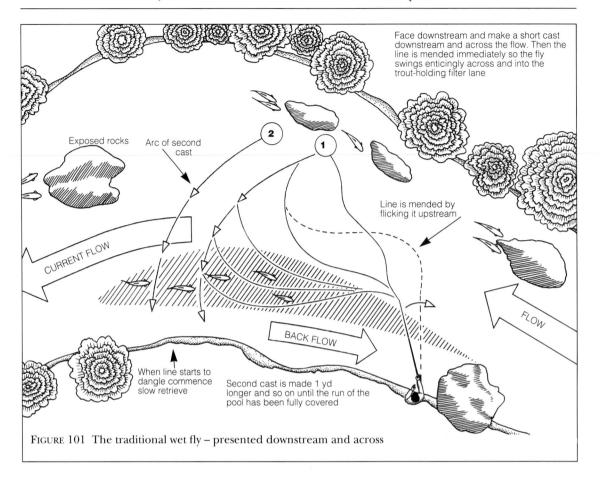

Face downstream and make a short cast downstream and across the flow. Then the line is mended immediately so the fly swings enticingly across and into the trout-holding filter lane

Exposed rocks

Arc of second cast

2

1

Line is mended by flicking it upstream

CURRENT FLOW

BACK FLOW

FLOW

When line starts to dangle commence slow retrieve

Second cast is made 1 yd longer and so on until the run of the pool has been fully covered

FIGURE 101 The traditional wet fly – presented downstream and across

trout that fights with incredible power after a few acrobatic leaps. It has extraordinary endurance when fresh run, perhaps more so than even a salmon of the same size.

In Northern Ireland the traditional wet fly (a shrimp pattern tied by Bert Atkins) was once again responsible for producing several nice grilse from the fast, bubbly weir at Carn Roe on the River Bann during the fourth series of *Go Fishing*.

The tube flies used in Sweden for sea trout would, to say the least, be considered rather on the large size by British standards, but then Swedish sea trout do

average very much larger. Those in the River Mörrum and Em, for instance, average over 10 lb at certain times of the season, and are not uncommon over 25 lb. So if the river's height or condition dictates a 3 in brass tube fly, use one. After all, it can still be presented on a sporting outfit.

During our Swedish sea-trout shoot, and after freezing while a biting snow blizzard swept down the valley, I eventually gave up the spey outfit – firstly because I am not the best of spey casters; and secondly, because much of the River Mörrum is so over-grown along the margins, with low-

Hooked on a tube fly known locally as the 'woollen sock', this splendid sea trout provided John and the cameras with some wonderful action for Go Fishing's *Swedish programme on the River Mörrum in 1992.*

hanging branches overhead, and many pools are far too deep for wading. A single-handed rod allows you to cover more of the water, albeit in unorthodox fashion. Incidentally, when the fly rod is completely ruled out, the Scandinavian-style spin-fly technique really comes into its own.

Returning to our Mörrum trip, however, as far as fly fishing was concerned, I felt very much happier making use of the delightful wooden-slatted platforms the Swedes construct. They reach from the bank well out over the river for a distance of several yards. The end is supported on one of the countless huge, black rocks projecting above the surface, so that even with just a 9½–10 ft rod, you are right out there, able to cover even quite large, boulder-strewn pools with a sink-tip or fast-sinking line.

At the start of April, with the water colder than it should have been at just above 40 degrees, and the sea trout really hugging the bottom, I found that a fast-sinking line and 2 in tube fly (a local pattern called 'woollen sock') worked deep down through most of the fast runs. And, of course, this is the essence of wet-fly fishing wherever you fish throughout the world, especially in very cold water, because the fish are not liable to give chase. That fly needs to come around slowly, right in front of their noses to fish whose bellies, for much of the time, will be scraping the gravel bottom. However, it isn't going to do this no matter how competently you cast and let it swing round, if your line fails to sink the fly fast enough to the correct level.

You come to appreciate whether you are using a heavy enough line on the day if every so often the fly catches bottom at the end of the swing round, especially if you leave it too long on the dangle before starting the retrieve. In fact, as a guideline, I would say that if you cannot make the fly catch bottom on the dangle, then your line is nowhere near heavy enough.

Fish will also not grab the fly if the current works it along much too fast – something guaranteed to occur if you do not quickly flick a loop upstream and across in order to mend the line as soon as the fly hits the surface. As can be seen from fig. 101, once mended, and this technique should be adopted for all cold and deep water fishing except when casting directly downstream in special circumstances, the current grips the line and swings the cast and fly invitingly across the river into the downstream filter lane rather like a tiny fish would behave when swimming in that characteristic darting fashion against a strong push of water.

Though trout love to use bridge supports, boulders and acute depressions in the river-bed as current breaks before moving out to feed, or while resting during their upriver migrations, some rivers also contain a wealth of classic holding pools. Wherever the flow is diverted or broken by a feature, for instance, leaving a distinct filter lane of noticeably slower water on the inside, as in fig. 101, fish might be present in real numbers. Wet-fly fishing is about being able to read the water and study the surface flow patterns to establish the possible whereabouts of fish, because in no way do you want to scare them by standing directly opposite their lie. It is far better to cast from well upstream and work down the pool, starting short and increasing each successive cast by a couple of yards. Once you reach your full casting potential, take a few paces downstream and start again.

The cast, of course, should always be made downstream and across, with one exception, and this is when seeking grayling. These swift-moving fish often respond instantly to a fly, that has been cast directly across the flow. They are definitely switched on by that sudden movement when the fly is 'zoomed' unnaturally around and downstream across the flow in a sweeping ark by the current catching the cast and line fully sideways on.

THE SPIN-FLY RIG

If you are a salmon fisherman who loves feature-packed, rocky rivers and the diversity of spinning, trundling a bunch of worms along, or dibbing about with prawns, then there is no doubt that the art of spin-fly fishing will add another weapon to your armoury, and not only for salmon and sea trout.

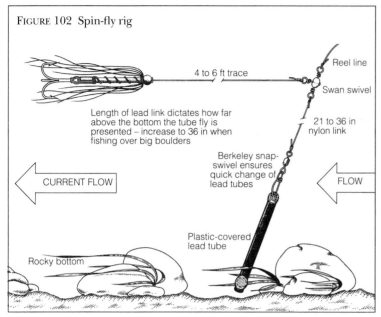

FIGURE 102 Spin-fly rig

Reel line

4 to 6 ft trace

Swan swivel

Length of lead link dictates how far above the bottom the tube fly is presented – increase to 36 in when fishing over big boulders

21 to 36 in nylon link

Berkeley snap-swivel ensures quick change of lead tubes

CURRENT FLOW

FLOW

Plastic-covered lead tube

Rocky bottom

This Scandinavian method of presenting a tube fly (you can, of course, use any type of fly or even a small spinner) in conjunction with a tubed weight (fig. 102), ensures that it fishes at exactly the level above bottom you want it to, and that it has less chance of snagging among rocks than a bomb or bullet ledger rig. I first used this, and to good effect, on the famous River Mörrum in Southern Sweden. This was when we

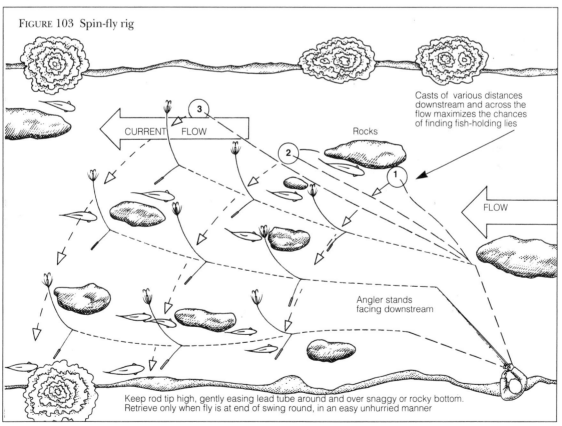

FIGURE 103 Spin-fly rig

CURRENT FLOW

Casts of various distances downstream and across the flow maximizes the chances of finding fish-holding lies

Rocks

FLOW

Angler stands facing downstream

Keep rod tip high, gently easing lead tube around and over snaggy or rocky bottom. Retrieve only when fly is at end of swing round, in an easy unhurried manner

159

Above *This tempting sea-trout pool in the River Mörrum can be fished with the wet fly downstream and across, or with a versatile spin-fly rig.*

Right *A superb Swedish sea trout for John, taken on a light spinning outfit and the most effective spin-fly rig (Fig. 102).*

were filming sea-trout action for the *Go Fishing* 1992 series. Although there were only a few fish in the river at that time, I was able to search each run thoroughly, regardless of current speed and despite the presence of enormous hidden rock formations littering the river-bed in many of the pools.

The rig is simple to make and requires just three items of terminal tackle. Your choice of tube fly tied to a trace of 4–6 ft long and a three-way swivel. To the top of

160

the swivel goes your reel line (8–12 lb) and to the bottom, a plastic-covered lead tube on a nylon link of about 18–36 in. The length of the link will, of course, depend on how far above bottom you wish the fly to be presented. If the water is very deep and perhaps the bottom strewn with great car-sized boulders, there is nothing to stop you increasing the lead link to as much as 4 or even 5 ft long.

As can be seen from fig. 103, the cast is always made downstream and across (a fixed-spool reel is preferable) well beyond where you expect fish to be lying. With the rod held high, the current then swings the rig across each lie, with the lead tube bumping over rocks and gravel. It presents the tube fly (or spinner) low down close to the bottom exactly where and how you want it, and in a manner no fly line ever can.

Once the tackle has swung in along your own bank and the tube fly starts to dangle, retrieve it in an unhurried, slightly erratic way, and expect a take at any moment. Cover the near lies on your first throw, and make each new cast 1–2 yd progressively further downstream and across, in this way covering all the potential fish-holding lies. Gently ease the tubed weight over boulders by lifting the rod tip whenever you feel the rig catch and the line feels heavy. Do not expect all fish to be resting behind and immediately downstream of large boulders; they won't necessarily. Sea trout in particular, often hold station a little upstream and directly in front of feature boulders.

Spin-fly fishing is one of the most devastating cold-water techniques I have ever used for game fish in tricky situations, and it also works effectively for several other species besides salmon and sea trout.

Whether you use a tube fly, gaudy reservoir lure, small spinner, spinning jig and worm, or even a small, mounted dead fish like a minnow or loach, species like perch, grayling, chub, brown trout and pike all respond eagerly. It has since become a favourite method whenever I find myself on the banks of swirling waters; weir-pools in particular. You don't need to fork out the extortionate fee of a Scottish salmon beat (not that you would be allowed to spin-fly fish anyway) to give it a try.

FLY-RODDING WITH SPINNERS AND JIGS

If you are a purist and derive pleasure only from tempting trout in the traditional manner from off the surface with a dry fly, and occasionally the upstream nymph, then I won't be offended if you skip this particular technique and move on to the next. Some may call me heathen but for me, fly fishing, or rather 'fly-rodding' is a matter of making full use of a lightweight tool to enjoy the fight of any species that can be fooled into taking artificial lures – and these artificials do not necessarily have to be made from fur and feathers and called a fly.

For instance, using the spring of a fly rod to propel small spinners or tiny leaded jigs to catch perch, grayling, pike, zander, chub, and trout is wonderful fun. It demands a rather specialized, well-matched outfit naturally, especially if you wish to enjoy long, trouble-free casting without danger to your self. Soft-actioned rods coupled to double-taper lines are strictly taboo. To push out the extra weight of even small, size 00 spinners backwards and forwards, you require a fast tip-actioned carbon rod (a 9½–10 footer that throws 8–9 lines is ideal) that has some power in its lower half, matched with a bass-bug or saltwater taper line where all the weight is right up front, close to the lure. This ensures that both line and lure shoot through the air accurately and together, as opposed to fighting each other through the air 15 yd apart, which is what would happen if a double-taper line is used. Most weight-forward lines improve from being shortened at the front end by at least several feet, bringing the heavier part into play much earlier and closer to the lure.

To further reduce the distance between the forward taper line and lure, use a considerably shorter cast than you would for fly fishing. Just 5–6 ft is perfect. Also use a larger-diameter reel than is actually required and pack it well with backing. This automatically increases casting performance, because the line will have less 'memory' and leave the reel in large, loose coils.

Wherever pike and zander are expected, use a 6 in trace made from braided alasticum, incorporating a tiny size 12 swivel at the cast end, and an equally tiny American snap link at the other to facilitate quick changes from one spinner to another.

Instead of holding the rod upright when casting, angle it over at around 45 degrees, bordering almost on side casting. You can then keep an eye on the back cast to ensure you don't experience the pain of a small treble in the back of the neck. It goes without saying, although I will mention it anyway, that polaroid glasses and a hat are imperative for both improving vision and protection.

During the making of the international *Go Fishing* programmes in the North-West Territories of Canada, where grayling are incredibly prolific among the boulder-strewn rapids of the Kazan and Ferguson River systems, fly fishing with a standard wet pattern like a size 12 butcher catches grayling after grayling. They were exquisitely coloured fish, their sail-like dorsal fins liberally spotted in aquamarine blue, but all were between 2 and 10 in long.

Tie on a small spinner, however, and hey presto! You go straight through the size barrier and start thumping into those superb Arctic grayling averaging between 2–3 lb. Every now and then a big lake trout puts in an appearance (it is, of course, feeding on the very 2 and 3 lb grayling you are trying to catch) and promptly chomps on the tiny spinner through rage.

Now if there were such a thing in fishing as the 'ultimate fight', playing a 20 lb laker through boulder-strewn rapids from pool to pool on just 3 oz of carbon fibre, with the tiniest of spinners in its jaw tied to a 6 lb cast, must come pretty close. Coming right back down to earth, considerably smaller species, such as chub and perch can also be enjoyed on the fly rod. Both gobble up spinners and both hit hard into small jigs – those lightly leaded, feathered or grub-tailed hooks so beloved by Americans. All can be presented with the fly rod, but, as I said previously, it is imperative to minimize the distance between the heavy part of the line and the lure, or you will find casting impossible and dangerous.

DRIFTING FOR TROUT – LOCH STYLE

To make full use of the wind to cover vast areas of stillwaters like lochs and reservoirs, there is nothing to beat sharing a boat with a friend and drifting slowly down with the wind while presenting a team of three flies loch-style. Whether this method originated in Ireland or Scotland, I am not sure, but it has really caught on with Britain's growing army of reservoir trout fishermen in recent years, and on some of our largest stillwaters like Grafham and Rutland Water, this has now become very much the accepted method that everyone wants to enjoy.

Loch-style fishing is perfectly suited to catching the smaller stock fish, particularly rainbows, which generally tend to occupy the upper water layers through-

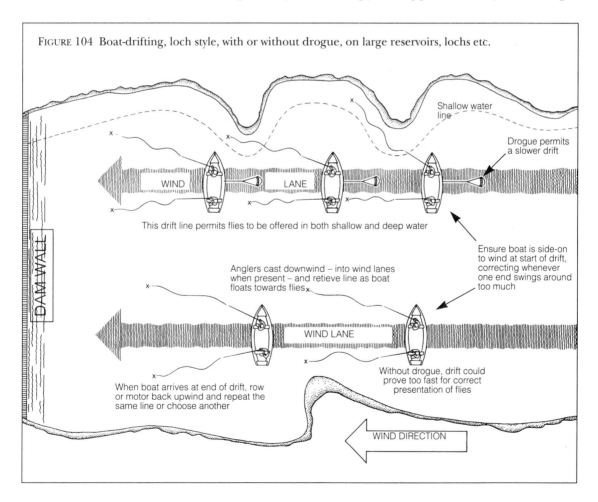

FIGURE 104 Boat-drifting, loch style, with or without drogue, on large reservoirs, lochs etc.

Shallow water line

Drogue permits a slower drift

WIND LANE

This drift line permits flies to be offered in both shallow and deep water

DAM WALL

Anglers cast downwind – into wind lanes when present – and retieve line as boat floats towards flies

Ensure boat is side-on to wind at start of drift, correcting whenever one end swings around too much

WIND LANE

Without drogue, drift could prove too fast for correct presentation of flies

When boat arrives at end of drift, row or motor back upwind and repeat the same line or choose another

WIND DIRECTION

Amid the wild, fertile crystal-clear waters of Canada's far north, small, traditional wet flies will catch tiny grayling one after another. But present a small spinner on your fly rod, and 2- and 3-pounders grab hold.

out the warmest months. They can, of course, be taken more easily with a heavy weight-forward sinking line or shooting-head set up and a powerful rod to match, on large, gaudy reservoir lures stripped in speedily. And indeed, there will be days when only this method will produce. But the beauty of loch-style fishing is that it is less hurried, less dependant upon ultimate success and on the fisherman not even wanting to take his bag limit or a specimen on every outing. It has a special magic that two anglers sharing a boat for the day can enjoy, using the most sporting of tackle in a most relaxed

fashion. You do, however, need one very important ingredient, and that is a fair blow of wind, because without it you cannot drift.

The method is to start from an upwind position (fig. 104) and put the boat side on to the wind so it slowly drifts along a particular line. And once the drift has been fished through when you run out of either wind or water, you motor or row upwind again and repeat the procedure from the same spot, or try another.

The drift could run parallel with the shoreline, for instance, so at least one of the two fishermen has the opportunity to cover fish in both shallow and deep water. Or you can drift down the fishery's entire length, always taking full advantage of wind lanes, those invaluable and defined lines of flattened bubble-strewn water aerated by wind and wave action, along which trout follow their food in an upwind direction towards the boat, rather like fish facing a current, sucking in items from just below and on the surface.

The considerably 'flattened' water of these narrow wind lanes not only makes food very much easier for the trout to see, it provides the fisherman with a very definite feature along which to present his flies in huge expanses of water, which otherwise appear very daunting when absolutely nothing can be seen rising. Another kind of feature towards which the loch-style fisherman should endeavour to work his drift is the aerators that spew enormous boils up to the surface

Caught with his waterproofs half on, Bob Church, who was John's boat partner on Rutland Water in the 1993 series of Go Fishing, *took this rainbow by loch-style fishing.*

from columns of water piped at great pressure from deep down below. These super features exist in many large reservoirs for the purpose of breaking up heavy concentrations of algae growth that form during the warmer months, and to increase the levels of dissolved oxygen. Naturally, the constant whirlpool effect is a big turn-on to trout – rainbows especially.

When I fished massive Rutland Water – Europe's largest man-made lake – for the 1993 *Go Fishing* series, in the company of Bob Church, it was always towards one of the numerous aerator boils situated between the old Normanton church and the wide dam end, where depths shelve down to over 100 ft, that we endeavoured to make our boat drift.

We were rewarded regularly in a nice chop on the surface, which continued for three days and provided us with more than enough action for the two cameras, even if all the fish were on the small side. But then, with loch-style fishing, it is the technique that continually enthrals, and not necessarily the size of trout caught. We were also subjected to sudden squalls and persistent bouts of heavy rain, which made filming extremely difficult – hazardous, in fact – because for much of the shoot the second boat carrying director, Paul Martingell, sound recordist, Steve Bowden and cameraman, Ron Tufnell was tied up parallel to our boat. The second cameraman, Paul Bennett, sat perched not 18 in away from my casting arm on the bows of our boat, and whenever the wind suddenly increased up to force 7, as it did on several occasions, panic broke out as ropes were hurriedly untied, lest we risked heavy waves breaking over the connected boats and soaking our electronic video equipment, which, even on a damp day, can prove temperamental.

I am amazed that in seven years of filming *Go Fishing*, we have never lost a camera overboard. Broken rods, and those which have mysteriously disappeared over the side – yes; but cameras – no. We have experienced several near misses, mind you. But I digress …

For the cost of a few pounds, towing a drogue behind the boat (tied mid-way along, usually around the rowlocks) can make a dramatic difference in helping to slow down the boat's drift in really strong winds. It can slow the boat down to as much as a quarter of the speed. The entire technique revolves around casting your line directly downwind and retrieving it while the boat drifts towards the flies, so if the boat is whisked along too fast you will be retrieving like a maniac, and re-casting flies that haven't had time to hit the water, let alone be seen by a trout. So always remember, there will be certain conditions when a drogue is absolutely essential, and it is wise to be so equipped.

If you value your comfort throughout a long day's loch-style fishing, you will want two other essential items: the first is a lightweight extending seat with a built- in line tray and the second is a foam cushion covered in water-proof material. You can, of course, manage with a simple boat-board, which is supplied at some fisheries and hooks over one gunnel, stretching right across the boat's width. Although not as comfortable, like the extending seat it will ensure that you are sitting up high so that casting and retrieving are much more enjoyable and efficient.

When fish are active and can be seen regularly sucking in nymphs from just below the surface or hatching flies off the top, fish a fairly short line. After just a few retrieve pulls, casually flick the line up and back behind the boat and immediately lay it down out in front again. This, of course, is floating-line loch-style fishing at its very best and most visual. Sometimes you will find that fish after fish chase the team of three flies right to the side of the boat, where they perhaps grab hold at the very last second as you run out of water and cannot hold the rod any higher. But, in truth, there will be many more occasions with precious little to see and cast to for most of the day until the evening rise, and those preferring to experience the joy of floating-line fishing throughout will need to cast their flies further downwind.

This necessitates perhaps two false casts, followed by a single haul to shoot a reasonable line out. In loch-style fishing, you are casting all day long, so powerful, horizon-style casts are simply not on, or even required. Enjoyment, rather than looking good, is very much the order of the day. The bottom or point fly (which can be a lure or a slightly weighted nymph) then has the chance to sink and attract fish from lower down during the retrieve. This is not to say that something won't come up and grab the bob fly, which is creating that enticing wake or furrow along the surface, but you are at least hedging your bets.

Of course, when absolutely nothing shows interest in flies worked through the surface film, it is time to switch over to a sinking line and explore the deeper water.

Loch-style fishing demands the use of longer, more flexible rods for ease of casting and, on average, lighter lines than are generally used for reservoir fishing. I suggest that you use an 11-footer, which handles a double taper size 7 and should enable you to handle and enjoy most situations.

Don't be tempted to construct excessively long casts, or you will find that the inevitable tangles result. One matching the rod's length should suffice, made from 5 or 6 lb test straight through. Add a couple of 12 in droppers tied using the four-turn water knot, dividing the cast into three equal portions to take the point, middle and bob fly. I prefer a dull, low-stretch mono for making up loch-style casts, because it is much less prone to tangles, and I always keep spools of 4–5 and 6 lb test handy. Once kinks or wind knots start to appear, or the droppers shorten drastically through trying too many different patterns (that's why I tie them long in the first place), it actually saves more time in the long run to put on a new one – ready-tied, of course.

I am afraid that space limits any comprehensive dialogue about fly selection here. It is a subject that demands a book in itself, and there are, indeed, many volumes on loch-style flies currently available. Suffice it to say that when trout are really up and hitting adult flies on the top, you are best off using a team of three dry flies. Otherwise, hedge your bets with a weighted nymph or lure on the point, a standard wet fly on the middle dropper, and something to provide an attractive wake across the surface for the bob fly – a G. & H. sedge, a muddler or hopper, etc. Never be afraid to experiment, no matter how ludicrous your choice may appear to be.

DOWNRIGGER TROLLING

In many of the really deep, natural, freshwater lakes of North America and in Finland, Austria, Germany, Holland and Sweden, the only workable method of fishing for species like char, lake trout and salmon (other than jigging) is to present your artificial lure or mounted deadbait by downrigger trolling. And because it can be effectively used at any depth from just 10 ft down to over 100 ft, there are numerous stillwaters within the British Isles, especially the Irish and Scottish lochs, and the English man-made reservoirs, where this devastatingly productive technique will score – not only with game fish, but with perch and pike too.

The main advantage of downrigger fishing is that once your fish is hooked, you can enjoy the ensuing fight on light tackle, with no additional weight on the line, whereas the only other way of keeping the bait or a lure down deep is to load it up with heavy trolling leads. As can be seen from fig. 105, when small-boat (dinghy) fishing, each angler uses just one rod, with the line going almost vertically down to the (5 lb) lead trolling-

How else can you possibly show a trolled lure to jumbo-sized lake trout holding station just above the bottom in over 80 ft of water, than by downrigger fishing, one of the most popular of all Canadian fishing techniques.

ball set at a pre-determined depth, where some 10–20 ft in front of the lure or bait it is held firmly by an adjustable line-release clip.

The lead ball is lowered away from the boat via an 18 in steel boom (rather like a mini rod) connected to stainless steel cable, which is housed on a large-diameter centre-pin spool incorporating a handle with a built-in braking system. Once the lure or bait has been lowered to the desired depth, the rod tip is wound right over into a tight curve so that when a fish grabs hold and pulls the line from the release clip, it springs suddenly back and helps to pick up some of the inevitable slack. At this point, a hefty follow-through strike and some fast winding will help put the hooks home.

However, there are occasions, and down-rigger trolling at depths in excess of 50 ft is one of them, when there is insufficient torque on the line to set the hook. And when hits are repeatedly missed on mono, a change over to a low-stretch dacron reel line will greatly improve the hooking ratio. As to reels, I much prefer high-speed multipliers to fixed-spool reels. The latter in fact come a very poor second for all trolling techniques, and my armoury includes Ryobi's S220, T2 and T20, which all hold at least 200 yd of 15–20 lb test.

Over on the other side of the Atlantic, downrigger rods are 7–8 ft and are made purposefully soft in the tip, which can then be wound right over. But my preference is for longer models in the 11 ft range, with a 2¼–2 lb test curve and a fairly fast taper action. I certainly found that my British-style carp/pike rods converted a greater percentage of hits into hooked big lake trout than those whippy little sticks supplied with the trolling boat when making *Go Fishing's* Canadian programmes on massive Lake Nueltin in the province of Manitoba. But then, pulling big spoons along, sometimes at depths of between 70 and 90 ft is rather specialized fishing, to say the least.

The single 6/0 and size 8/0 thick-wire, barbless hooks fitted to the giant 6–8 in long lake-trout spoons were, in my experience, all too easily shaken out by those massive fish. In truth, and at such extreme depths, the point probably never found purchase with any sort of consistency anyway. I am certain that smaller, treble hooks would have really sorted out those trout, but for the 'catch and release' laws of Canada, I am afraid it is barbless, single hooks only.

To help the process of hooking, accelerate the motor by several knots when the rod tip springs back when downrigger trolling in really deep water, but be careful not to overdo it. As for actual

Indian chief and guide, Nap, displays a superb laker taken downrigger trolling by Martin Founds on Nueltin Lake.

trolling speed, I would suggest you start off very slowly – especially if visibility is not good – at no more than 1 knot, and increase the speed gradually if hits are not forthcoming, or if only the occasional interest is shown in your bait or lure.

When lures, especially, are trolled too slowly, trout and pike may well follow behind for a while out of curiosity, perhaps even giving the lure a sideways bang or two, but afterwards swim away in disgust. Be prepared to alter or vary the speed accordingly.

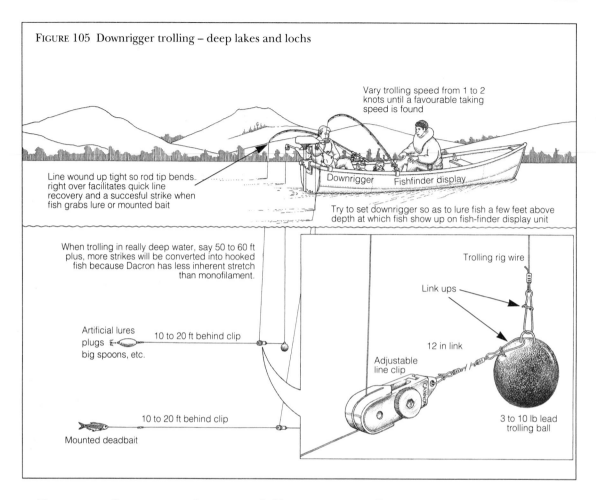

FIGURE 105 Downrigger trolling – deep lakes and lochs

Vary trolling speed from 1 to 2 knots until a favourable taking speed is found

Line wound up tight so rod tip bends right over facilitates quick line recovery and a succesful strike when fish grabs lure or mounted bait

Downrigger   Fishfinder display

Try to set downrigger so as to lure fish a few feet above depth at which fish show up on fish-finder display unit

When trolling in really deep water, say 50 to 60 ft plus, more strikes will be converted into hooked fish because Dacron has less inherent stretch than monofilament.

Trolling rig wire

Link ups

Artificial lures plugs big spoons, etc.

10 to 20 ft behind clip

12 in link

Adjustable line clip

10 to 20 ft behind clip

Mounted deadbait

3 to 10 lb lead trolling ball

You can, of course, only successfully fish a downrigger in conjunction with a sonar/fish-finder unit like a Humminbird, eagle, or lowrance, because you must first ascertain at what depth the fish are lying. Even then, you must keep a careful watch on the screen and be ready to raise the downrigger ball and take up the resulting slack line when the lake bed starts to shelve up dramatically or peak, or you could hit bottom and even become snagged. Conversely, lower the ball so the lures fish deeper when the bottom shelves down deep; if, for instance, the trout or pike are stationed just above or among the bottom terrain. Always plan to troll your lure or bait a few feet above the depth at which fish are lying, encouraging them to dash upwards to make an interception. Hits are, consequently, more violent, which increases the hooking rate. Besides, it is pointless to troll the bait along at, say, 60 ft in 80 ft of water, if the only group of lake trout to show up on the screen are holding station well above at 40 ft, due to the existence of a thermocline.

Incidentally, the salmonoide species

are attracted to thermoclines, especially during the summer and autumn months, when temperatures in the upper water layers are very high. And during this period, the thermocline separates the warmer epilimnion from the much colder hypolimnion, rather like a sandwich with a 'cool water' filling. Electronic wizardry, coupled to modern tackle and techniques does not, contrary to popular belief, automatically make fish jump into the boat. It is beneficial only if you use it sensibly. So keep a constant eye on the sonar screen for fish that suddenly show up, and the depth at which they are holding, and be especially vigilant with bottom contours. Search for those fish-holding features like dramatic peaks in the bottom strata, drop-offs, gullies and rock formations, and in man-made reservoirs, look for bushes, trees and the existence of tree-stump remains (former forests cut down prior to the valley being flooded), old fences, farms, cottages and other buildings. All attract large concentrations of small shoal fish just as reefs do in salt water, and are particularly inviting to predators.

If you intend doing any amount of downrigger fishing, it is well worth purchasing a unit with a depth counter, so that you know exactly how much cable is below the boat, and consequently, at what depth you are presenting the bait or lure.

I have used the American Cannon downriggers (sold in the UK through Normark Sports Ltd) for several years now, and can thoroughly recommend them. For sheer portability and for fishing in relatively shallow water, where gauging the depth is not so much of a problem, the Cannon 'minitroll', which quickly clamps onto the boat's gunnel, is perfect. You can hold the rod throughout, or only when runs are expected, or relax until the action warms up and you hit a particularly productive area, by sliding the entire butt below the reel into a tube-type rod holder (which, incidentally, are built into most of the larger Cannon downrigger units). All come with some 150 ft of 150 lb test stainless-steel cable, retrievable on a single-handed control, clutch and brake system for a steady, controlled descent of the lead ball.

In fact, it is possible for two anglers to clip their lures to the one downrigger by clipping a special 'stacker' release clip onto the lead ball. This is actually a double-release line clip, which allows, for instance, a spoon to be trolled along parallel to the lead ball, and a diving plug to work several feet above it. For most Cannon downrigger units, double rod holders are available that fit onto the rear mount specifically designed for stacker fishing, enabling each rod to be adjusted individually for both angle and height.

SALTWATER FISHING TECHNIQUES

UPTIDE BOAT-FISHING

This relatively new and revolutionary method of boat fishing, which permits much lighter and more sporting gear to be used for just about every species in-

Opposite *Perched on the jetty wall at Alderney in the Channel Islands, Roddy Hays wonders whether a mullet or a garfish will be next to take the bait presented on freshwater float tackle.*

Below *Uptide boat fishing at its best exists in the Thames estuary, as a* Go Fishing *research trip proved for Paul Martingell when he and John fished from Bradwell.*

habiting our coastal waters, was pioneered by enthusiasts like my good friend, John Rawle, with whom I fished in the 1993 series of *Go Fishing*. John operates a charter boat called Donna Mary out of Bradwell Marina in the mouth of the River Blackwater in Essex, which provides access to an infinite variety of marks over the undulating sea-bed of the Thames Estuary.

Uptiding is exactly what the term implies, as can be seen from fig. 106: casting a much lighter lead than you

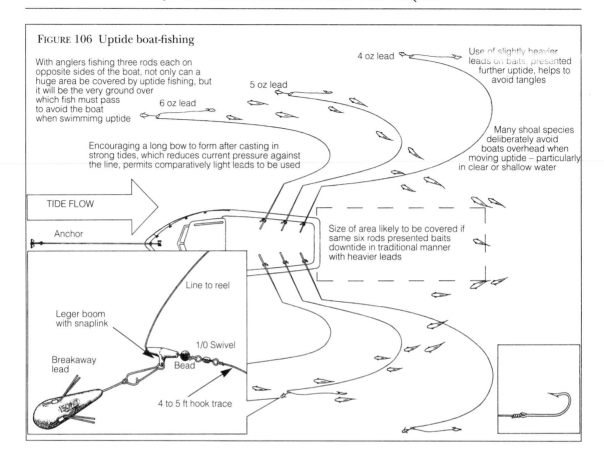

FIGURE 106 Uptide boat-fishing

With anglers fishing three rods each on opposite sides of the boat, not only can a huge area be covered by uptide fishing, but it will be the very ground over which fish must pass to avoid the boat when swimmimg uptide

4 oz lead

Use of slightly heavier leads on baits, presented further uptide, helps to avoid tangles

5 oz lead

6 oz lead

Encouraging a long bow to form after casting in strong tides, which reduces current pressure against the line, permits comparatively light leads to be used

Many shoal species deliberately avoid boats overhead when moving uptide – particularly in clear or shallow water

TIDE FLOW

Anchor

Size of area likely to be covered if same six rods presented baits downtide in traditional manner with heavier leads

Line to reel

Leger boom with snaplink

1/0 Swivel

Breakaway lead

Bead

4 to 5 ft hook trace

would if simply dunking the bait over the stern, well uptide into areas of the sea floor over which fish often travel (particularly in clear water), in order to avoid the anchored boat. That a shoal of fish splits and goes around the boat (not all do, obviously) is, perhaps, a premise that even many hardened sea fishermen find difficult to swallow. But catches taken by uptide fishing prove this fact beyond doubt. Besides, the longer, more forgiving and sensitively tipped specialist uptide rods in lengths of 9½ to 11 ft, so necessary for casting from the platform of an anchored boat, allow you to fully enjoy the fight of even small species,

compared to the rigid, broomstick, boat rods of yesteryear. And they cover much more ground. Consider fig. 106: a huge area of the sea floor is covered by just six uptide outfits compared to what those same six would cover if the baits were simply lowered downtide from the stern, as was once the normal practice.

Several points must be observed, however, when uptide fishing, to avoid tangles and accidents. Firstly, use slightly heavier leads on the baits being presented furthest uptide, stepping down progressively so the downtide outfit has the lightest lead. Refer to fig. 106. Secondly, never cast when the lead is inside the boat, or cast across the boat from one side to another. Always ensure that your lead is outside the boat and close to or beyond the stern, so it is not liable to pick up another line when you punch it out and uptide. Casts of 70 and 80 yd are easily made with a gentle swing, but search out the areas closest to the boat first.

And thirdly, get used to watching for those gentle 'nods' on the rod tip, and sudden dropback bites when the break-away lead wires 'fold', making the lead bump along the bottom downtide as a fish makes off with the bait. In so doing, the fish invariably hooks itself. For this very reason, don't use those old-fashioned, thick wire hooks that require a good clout from the rod end before they penetrate. There are several fine-wire but strong patterns now available. Indeed, those marketed under the 'Cox and Rawle' label and manufactured by Partridge are superb, having been designed by John Rawle and his partner, Bob Cox, with the specialized requirements of uptiding in mind.

Those distinct knocks and bangs from fish hanging on, but which have failed to 'pull' the lead, should be quickly wound down to in order to straighten the exaggerated bow in the line created by the current. You need to encourage such an enormous bow on the line between lead and the rod tip is, of course, because it allows you to fish with very light leads and, consequently, sporting reel lines of just 15 to 20 lb test. This, in turn, allows you to use small, high-speed multipliers for effortless casting. Mine are Ryobi T2s and T20s, which are extremely rugged, and I sometimes use the ABU 6500 range.

Boat fishermen of yesteryear demanded reel lines of at least 50 per cent heavier to match the heavy downtide leads being used, and so were committed to larger, heavier reels that restricted enjoyment and were simply not necessary.

The secret of uptiding lies in the fact that when an exaggerated bow is allowed to form in the tide by paying out excess line once the lead has caught bottom, current pressure against that bow is only severe in the middle. And this is what permits comparatively light leads to be employed (fig. 106).

If the line were straight between rod tip and lead, it would, of course, attract the full current pressure along its entire length, so the lead would be washed immediately downtide, regardless of its weight. If your lead will not hold, simply pay out more line (creating a larger bow – within reason) until it does; or, in extremely strong tides, go up a couple of ounces.

Now for the rig itself, which is very simple: just a running lead slider (to take the lead) stopped by a large bead against a size 1/0 swivel (fig. 106 inset), to the other end of which is tied a 4–6 ft hook trace of your choice.

For species like bass, where bait movement is advantageous, go for as long a trace as you can comfortably cast, whereas with flat fish like thornbacks, which need to centre the bait beneath them in order to swallow it, a shorter, 3 ft trace is ideal.

Incidentally, when uptide fishing over exceedingly rough ground on which the front end of your reel line will invariably lie, to prevent unnecessary break-offs

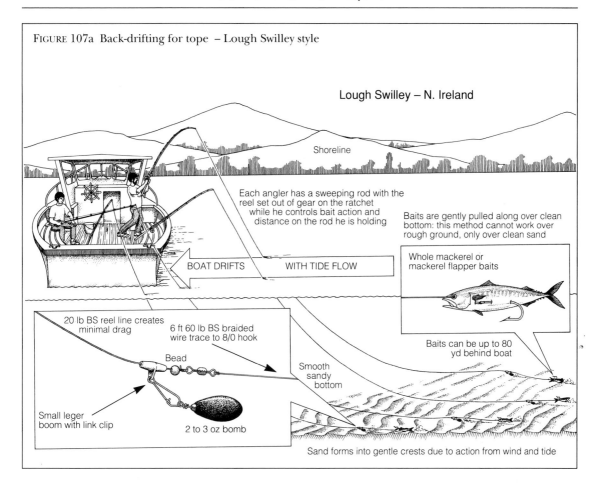

FIGURE 107a Back-drifting for tope – Lough Swilley style

Lough Swilley – N. Ireland

Shoreline

Each angler has a sweeping rod with the reel set out of gear on the ratchet while he controls bait action and distance on the rod he is holding

Baits are gently pulled along over clean bottom: this method cannot work over rough ground, only over clean sand

BOAT DRIFTS — WITH TIDE FLOW

Whole mackerel or mackerel flapper baits

20 lb BS reel line creates minimal drag

6 ft 60 lb BS braided wire trace to 8/0 hook

Bead

Baits can be up to 80 yd behind boat

Smooth sandy bottom

Small leger boom with link clip

2 to 3 oz bomb

Sand forms into gentle crests due to action from wind and tide

through chaffing, add 50 ft of 40 lb test to your 15–20 lb reel line to act as both buffer and a shock leader for really punching out an 8 oz lead well uptide.

BACK-DRIFTING FOR TOPE

I was introduced to back-drifting by Malcolm Bowden, a local skipper operating out of Rathmullen in Ireland's beautiful Lough Swilley. With this fascinating

Opposite If Paul Martingell continues smiling on cue and catching fish, like this pretty thornback, Wilson may consider a career re-think.

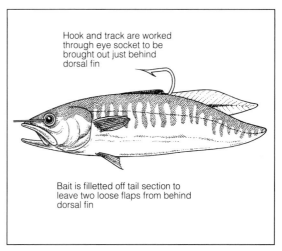

Hook and track are worked through eye socket to be brought out just behind dorsal fin

Bait is filletted off tail section to leave two loose flaps from behind dorsal fin

FIGURE 107b Lough Swilley – mackerel flapper bait

technique you do exactly what the term implies: drift your bait way back behind the boat until it reaches bottom, then simply allow the tide to pull both the boat and your bait along (fig. 107).

Obviously this method cannot be employed over rough ground, only over a perfectly clean, sandy bottom where the baits won't snag up. It is, in fact, the favourite method of fishing for tope in Lough Swilley and other Irish sea loughs where baits presented static on the bottom are liable to receive the attentions of dogfish and small thornbacks long before a tope happens along. So for tope, back-drifting is particularly selective, and is a wonderful way of searching large areas of the bottom. With the boat positioned side-on to the wind, two anglers (assuming there are just two) can happily fish two rods apiece. It pays to be active with one outfit by holding the rod throughout, and continually varying the bait's distance from the boat by gently retrieving and then paying out line again so it drifts back downtide anywhere from 50 to 80 yd.

To do this you require minimal lead on the line; just a 2–3 oz bomb stopped with a bead above a 6 ft, 60 lb braided wire trace. The hook should be a 6/0 to 8/0, and the bait a whole, medium-sized mackerel or mackerel 'flapper' that has had the tail and backbone removed so the two sides 'flap' in the tide and provide visual attraction – often a most important factor in the clear sea loughs of Ireland (fig. 107b)

The bait on the second, 'sleeper' rod can be drifted distances of 30 to 50 yd back and the reel left in gear with the ratchet on, but with the clutch slackened off sufficiently so that the line will scream out only with the run of a tope (and not from the bait momentarily catching against a ridge of sand on the bottom). The tope is, in fact, a requiem shark, so back-drifting is really small-scale shark fishing. To obtain the most enjoyment, use a rod with plenty of action in the tip. An 8–9 ft uptide-style model, matched with a small multiplier holding at least 200 yd of 18–20 lb test mono is absolutely perfect, and will allow the tope to give you a really scrappy fight.

SURF-FISHING

Fish way out from the beach into the surf and beyond is not just a matter of 'chucking it and chancing it', as many may think. If you stroll along the beach with binoculars, studying wind and tide direction, the wave patterns and surface displacement for 10 minutes without actually taking the tackle from the car, you will have a lot of information about what might lie beneath the turbulence.

After a while, what at first appears to be line upon line of waves crashing in, will seem less hostile. You will be able to spot a definite pattern, and subsequently select the most likely spot. You will be able to define shallow sand bars situated way out, where the water becomes noticeably more coloured and where a long cast could even put your bait into mere inches of water. Conversely, you will be able to isolate those valuable, much deeper gullies and troughs simply by studying the waves and breakers as they roll in.

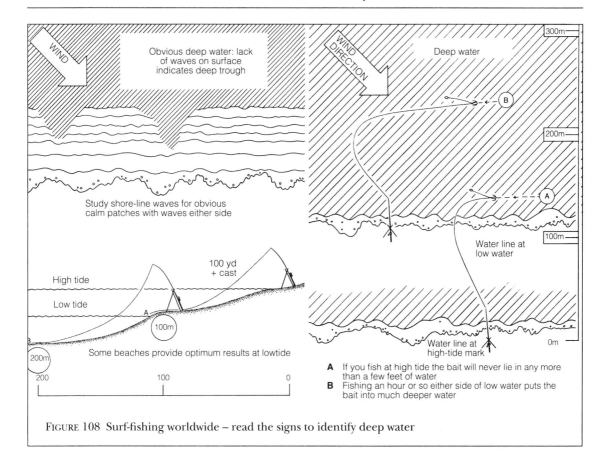

Obvious deep water: lack of waves on surface indicates deep trough

WIND

Study shore-line waves for obvious calm patches with waves either side

100 yd + cast

High tide

Low tide

A

100m

200m

Some beaches provide optimum results at lowtide

200   100   0

WIND DIRECTION

Deep water

300m

B

200m

A

100m

Water line at low water

Water line at high-tide mark

Water line at high-tide mark   0m

A   If you fish at high tide the bait will never lie in any more than a few feet of water
B   Fishing an hour or so either side of low water puts the bait into much deeper water

FIGURE 108 Surf-fishing worldwide – read the signs to identify deep water

Look for areas of noticeably calmer, flatter sea, signifying that the water beneath is too deep for surf breakers to build up over it (fig. 108). Long, flat beaches, for instance, which suddenly drop away significantly, are usually best fished at low tide, when a long cast will lay the bait on the bottom of deep water. A cast of the same length made from way up the beach at the very top of the tide will lay it in extremely shallow water – in fact, where you were standing at low water points A and B, (fig. 108).

A study of the sea bed when the sea is at its very lowest during exceptionally low spring tides will help unravel many my-steries – such as the presence of snags, shell-fish beds, rock outcrops. So plan well ahead and gain knowledge of the sea floor wherever you intend on fishing from the beach.

Note also from A and B (fig. 108), how the cast should always be made well uptide whenever a good sea is running, by walking up the beach for about 30–40 yd, and then back again once the lead digs in, paying out line so the tide bellies it out into an exaggerated bow. There will be occasions when only if you follow this procedure will the lead finally stay put and keep your bait well out there. If you cast straight out, the tide will quickly

John's initial glimpse from high up on the cliff tops of the remote Atlantic surf beaches at Dakhla, Morocco, which skirt the Western Sahara

Not exactly the monster corbine John had travelled thousands of miles to catch, but a corbine nonetheless, and not unlike a bass.

sweep the terminal rig back in along the beach.

One of the most difficult, yet immensely challenging beaches, due to there being few deep gullies close inshore, that I have explored while researching locations for *Go Fishing*, has been at Dakhla, which is virtually the most southerly point of Morocco in North-West Africa. Here, the full force of the Atlantic Ocean comes roaring in, accompanied for much of the time by the prevailing westerly winds, which are so strong you can hardly stand

up at times, let alone fish. On my first visit during the month of April (far too early) I made the mistake of wearing shorts, and nearly got my legs sandblasted off (extremely painful) through the sheer force of the wind. Throughout even the warmest months between May and September you just have to accept that you will be able to fish on maybe only two days in seven, which is a great pity. The reason a few headbangers like me even consider making the arduous pilgrimage to the remote beaches of Dakhla, on the edge of

Local anglers and Sochatour guides, Omar and Said, extract a large shovel-nosed ray (guitar fish) caught on squid strip, from the surf at Dakhla. Octopus and cuttle fish are also widely used for both rays and corbine.

the Western Sahara, is for the chance to connect with a giant corbine, the world's most exciting sea bass.

In fact, these pewter-sided monsters are found all around the West African coast and all the way round the Cape. South Africans call them kob. In the Gambia the same, or a very similar fish is called casarva. But I chose Dakhla for one very good reason; the variety to be found there is special: along the Moroccan coast corbines are commonly caught between 60 and over 90 lb. Imagine catching a bass from the wildest, most deserted of surf beaches (the beaches at Dakhla are not entirely dissimilar to those on the west coast of Ireland) and the ensuing fight it would give. Unfortunately, there is no fairy tale ending to this story whereby Wilson hooked-up and after a dramatic battle through the lashing surf, eventually dragged a double armful of gleaming pewter towards the cameras. I managed plenty of small corbinas up to the 5 lb mark, plus other bass-like species, guitar fish (shovel-nosed rays) and stingrays, but those giant corbina of the Western Sahara still await me.

DRIFT-FISHING OVER HUMPS AND WRECKS

Some of the most exciting, and without question, the most productive sea fishing for both quality and quantity around the British Isles, is to be enjoyed by those who plunder the deep-sea wrecks well off shore. Whether wartime hulks or peacetime disasters, these features lying on the bottom attract an entire ecosystem, and provide an exceedingly rich food chain for the masses of small to medium sized shoal fish that use the wreck as sanctuary and feed upon all tiny life forms, and for the larger fish like conger eels, ling, big cod, pollack and coal fish that prey upon the smaller ones. The trouble is that wrecks within easy reach of the British coastline are all too quickly fished out, and anglers nowadays must travel further and further out to maintain their standard of sport. Many boats working along the south coast, for instance, regularly work very much closer to the French coast and the Channel Islands than the shores of England in order to put their customers over choice locations.

Over some wrecks and in certain conditions, skippers anchor their craft, but generally speaking, wreck fishing involves drifting over the entire length of the wreck, starting from a position well uptide. And because spring tides are simply too strong and whisk the boat along too fast, around the British Isles at least, skippers choose the weaker neap tides when organizing their wrecking parties.

Regular viewers of *Go Fishing* may recall the superb and hectic sport with big cod, ling and pollack back in the second series on a wrecking trip filmed some 11 miles off the beautiful island of Alderney in the Channel Islands. During that shoot my boat partner was my good friend Roddy Hays (who now operates a big-game charter boat out from Funchal in Madeira), and we got through almost a tackle-shop full of pirks hauling up those lunkers lying in 180 ft of water. Lost pirks are, of course, an inescapable fact of wreck fishing, because very often the biggest cod frequent the snaggiest parts of the rusting hulk, and will only grab hold if you literally bounce the pirk off the steelwork before starting to jig it upwards.

A good-sized fish fillet is best fished in conjunction with a plastic squid skirt on a short snood, with a much weaker lead link beneath (fig. 109). It doesn't matter how often you snag up and pull for a break, because the 'rotten bottom' quickly snaps and leaves your lead (sections of old lead piping make great disposable wrecking weights) in the wreck. Shop-bought, chromium-plated pirks can really hurt your pocket, but you can construct your own from lead-filled chromium-plated tube.

The same principles apply to areas of the sea bed known as peaks or humps, which suddenly thrust upwards like an underwater mountain, because these features also attract just about everything, from colourful reef-dwellers to the largest sharks. One such sub-surface mountain, affectionately called 'the hump' by skippers who regularly tap the unbelievably

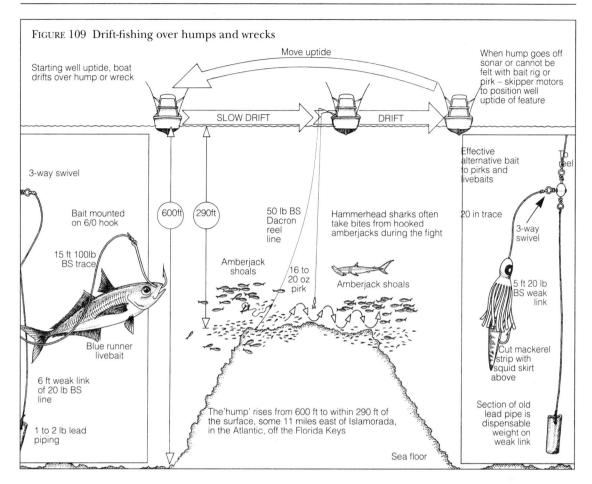

FIGURE 109 Drift-fishing over humps and wrecks

Move uptide

Starting well uptide, boat drifts over hump or wreck

When hump goes off sonar or cannot be felt with bait rig or pirk – skipper motors to position well uptide of feature

SLOW DRIFT

DRIFT

To reel

3-way swivel

Effective alternative bait to pirks and livebaits

600ft   290ft

Bait mounted on 6/0 hook

50 lb BS Dacron reel line

Hammerhead sharks often take bites from hooked amberjacks during the fight

20 in trace

3-way swivel

15 ft 100lb BS trace

Amberjack shoals

16 to 20 oz pirk

Amberjack shoals

5 ft 20 lb BS weak link

Blue runner livebait

Cut mackerel strip with squid skirt above

6 ft weak link of 20 lb BS line

1 to 2 lb lead piping

The 'hump' rises from 600 ft to within 290 ft of the surface, some 11 miles east of Islamorada, in the Atlantic, off the Florida Keys

Section of old lead pipe is dispensable weight on weak link

Sea floor

rich food chain gathered around the summit, lies several miles due east of Islamorada in the Florida Keys. (fig. 109). One of the most productive locations that I have ever researched for *Go Fishing*, it rises from 600 ft below sea level on the sea floor to slightly less than 300 ft at its peak, and rates as one of the best guaranteed hotspots in the world for a variety of big fish, despite the fact that it is regularly plundered by commercial longliners, and the charter-boat fleets working the Atlantic deeps out of Islamorada.

Many of the tuna family (plus dorado and other pelagic species in season) can be taken by trolling squids or feathers around the surface directly over the hump, which is most convenient when you need a few shark baits quickly, or alternative sport. But as far as driftfishing is concerned, the real wealth of this mountain, which has a dense coral summit of just 2 acres in size, is that it attracts hard-fighting amberjacks, (one of the strongest and most durable of fish you are ever likely to meet) by the thousand.

Immensely thick-set, these powerful fighters are plentiful in the 60–80 lb bracket, and even on a stand-up 50 lb

Pete Hazlewood congratulates a weary Wilson upon boating this thick-set hammerhead shork of close on 300 lb after a lively 40-minute battle.

Opposite:
Top *This 'double hit' included a hammerhead shark for Pete Hazlewood and a 70 lb amberjack for John. Both were taken drifting over the 'hump', 11 miles off the Florida Keys.*

Far left *This superbly streamlined and hard-fighting amberjack hits pirks or livebaits readily.*

Left *Only three amberjacks in every four came up in one piece during John's visit to the Keys. Hammerhead sharks took out huge bites, or simply removed the rear end.*

doesn't immediately snag you in the coral, or a shark doesn't relieve you of it by biting its rear end off or taking a huge chunk out of its middle on the way up. Talk about pumping adrenalin, because if you like a real tug of war and a gut-busting battle, then drifting for these big jacks is only surpassed by catching a similar-sized big-eyed tuna that zooms down to 300 ft the moment it feels cold steel, or a mahseer of the same stamp from the swirling rock-strewn, rapids of an Indian River.

A day's drifting starts with an hour's cut-bait fishing with light tackle and fresh-water-size hooks at anchor over a shallow reef, in order to stock up the live well (most of the Keys' boats have built-in live-bait tanks) with a batch of blue runners. These are a species of small jack, which, unlike grunts and most of the snappers, are not born with that really nasty habit of swimming your hook straight into the coral maze on top of the hump. They always work attractively upwards, and obviously have a certain 'something' that amberjacks cannot resist.

Once out in the blue void of the Atlantic, ready to start the drift over the hump, a blue runner is rigged up in conjunction with a three-way swivel on a 15 ft, 100 lb test mono trace. The hook is a 6/0, thick wire, gently eased into the bait's top lip (fig. 109). To the top of the swivel is tied the 50 lb reel line, and to the bottom, a 6 ft weak link of 20 lb test mono holding 1½ lb of disposable lead piping, just in case it snags. Trying to break a 50 lb test mono-filament reel line takes more doing than you would ever believe, so the weak lead link is invaluable.

class outfit, they will quickly take you into the pain barrier during the 20–30 minutes it inevitably takes to fight one up from the bottom – and that's if it

Actually, after taking several big amber-jacks on mono, I switched over to dacron, which provided a far more enjoyable and controllable tussle at such great depths due to its inherent low stretch.

The skipper locates the hump on his sonar and cuts the engine well uptide, so the boat drifts slowly over the 'peak', whereupon the bait is lowered steadily (to eliminate tangles) until the lead hits coral. You now reel up quickly a few turns so the bait works enticingly above the bottom, and brace yourself for the arm-wrenching take of an amberjack. And when this happens, there is no mistaking it. As soon as the amberjack takes, you must quickly and forcibly heave it upwards lest it reaches sanctuary within the coral. It is brute force at its best. Incidentally, the outfits I had taken along seemed to suit amberjack fishing exactly, and consisted of 6 ft Ryobl wrecking, hollow-glass rods, and Rybol S340 high speed multipliers loaded with both dacron and mono – extremely light outfits to hold, which is most important when enduring comparatively long stand-up battles without a harness. Heavy old reels and rods can tire you quicker than the fish.

It was during a hectic spell with these big amberjacks that I tried, for the very first time, an electric reel. Yes, an electric reel – the Ryobl K2S heavy-duty multiplier to be exact. For the disabled or anyone weak in the right arm or hand, especially arthritis sufferers, the reel is a boon. Initially, the concept of pushing a button to wind in did seem strange – rather like cheating. Nevertheless, I loaded it to the brim with 50 lb test

dacron and ran the reel's connecting cable to a supply line from the boat's 12-volt supply. A portable 12-volt battery can, of course, easily be taken on board, but requires a little forward planning.

Being connected by an umbilical cord from the reel sounds more inhibiting than it is in practice. You only put the connecting plug in for the retrieve, which takes up line positively and powerfully during the fight whenever you lower the rod to pump (the reel has a level wind) by pressing a simple on/off button comfortably situated beneath the thumb of your right hand. There is a cut-out mechanism in case of overload during the fight, or if a whopper grabs hold during bait retrieval, or should a shark happen along – which is exactly what happened.

More or less the same drifting technique is followed if you are using big, brightly coloured pirks to catch amber-jacks, except that they need to be continually worked in a double-handed, up-and-down, accentuated jigging motion, at a level slightly higher than the coral jungle covering the summit, for obvious reasons.

Most sane men start to slow down after busting their guts on three, or possibly four big amberjacks in one day. Some headbangers I know may even go for five, but that's sheer masochism. Far better to relax for a while and enjoy a few beers while pulling lures around to catch some bonito or small yellow-fin tuna for shark baits.

Once again, the skipper follows a similar procedure when drifting with the tide for sharks, except that he starts the drift ½ mile uptide of the hump and

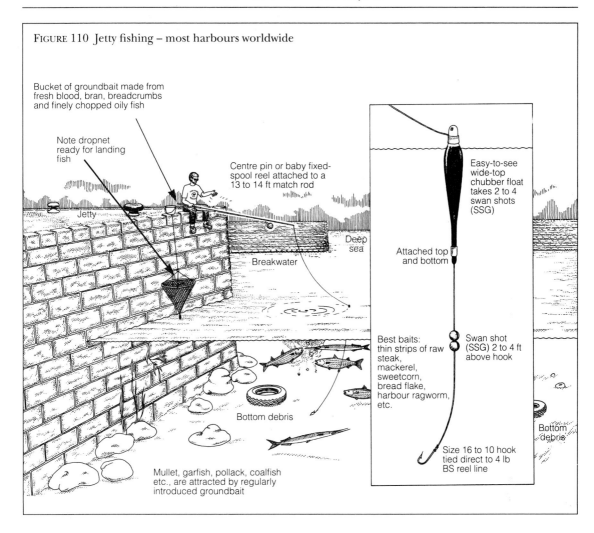

FIGURE 110 Jetty fishing – most harbours worldwide

Bucket of groundbait made from fresh blood, bran, breadcrumbs and finely chopped oily fish

Note dropnet ready for landing fish

Centre pin or baby fixed-spool reel attached to a 13 to 14 ft match rod

Jetty

Deep sea

Breakwater

Bottom debris

Mullet, garfish, pollack, coalfish etc., are attracted by regularly introduced groundbait

Easy-to-see wide-top chubber float takes 2 to 4 swan shots (SSG)

Attached top and bottom

Best baits: thin strips of raw steak, mackerel, sweetcorn, bread flake, harbour ragworm, etc.

Swan shot (SSG) 2 to 4 ft above hook

Size 16 to 10 hook tied direct to 4 lb BS reel line

Bottom debris

finishes ½ mile or more down tide, because the shark population of the area is not so concentrated around the hump's peak as the smaller shoal fish. The glut of 150–300 lb hammerheads we experienced on my last trip while drifting the hump provided some truly great sport. It was noticeable, however, that those sharks really wanted tuna flesh, even in preference to a flank of fresh amberjack, because as soon as we trolled up a few bonitos and drifted them out as flappers,

along came a hammerhead time after time again.

JETTY FISHING

Of all the saltwater locations in the world, the one that is guaranteed to provide interesting sport for at least part of the day, regardless of weather conditions, is jetty fishing. Some harbours completely dry out at low tide and will only produce for a couple of hours before and after high water when the fish move into feed, but others, deep-water harbours especially, offer virtually all-day prospects, even right at the bottom of the tide. The attraction of harbours for many species is immense, owing to a regular food supply from commercial fishing boats, which deposit the remains of their filleted catch overboard; drainage and effluent outfall pipes that feed into the harbour; and to the thick algae and crustacean growth that adheres to both wooden and brickwork jetties and walls. Species like mullet, garfish, young pollack, coalfish and wrasse are all harbour regulars during the summer months, and great fun to catch on freshwater tackle.

My preference is for a 13 or 14 ft carbon float or match rod coupled to a centre-pin or baby fixed-spool reel that has a sensitive clutch, loaded with around 4 lb test. If you do, by accident, happen to whack into something big and lose it – that's life! The secret of jetty fishing is to fish light and obtain maximum enjoyment from what, most of the time amount to smallish fish from mere ounces up to 4–5 lb – hence the freshwater tackle. Mind you, the fight of even a 4 lb mullet will certainly make you wonder why carp are held in such high esteem; their stamina and turn of speed is incredible. Mullet can prove exasperatingly difficult to tempt, so step down the hook size accordingly, using a strong pattern of eyed hooks in sizes 16 to 10 tied direct to the reel line. Drennan's 'super specialist' range, for instance, are ideal. As for floats, there is, of course, nothing to stop you using a long waggler as though bream fishing, and in flat calm conditions bites may,

indeed, prove delicate. But overall, I find that a wide-topped trotting float like a two to four swan shot 'chubber' or 'loafer' fixed both top and bottom registers bites perfectly while being easy to see even in a fair chop.

Put all the shots way down, somewhere between 2 to 4 ft above the hook so the bait behaves naturally during the last part of its fall. Garfish, especially, love to hit 'on the drop', and those found in harbours where the water is crystal clear can be clearly observed inspecting the bait and turning away when it doesn't look right. Just because they are sea fish they are not necessarily silly. Aggressive species like small wrasse, pollack and coalfish are less suspicious, however, and together with gars and mullet they are attracted to the continual introduction of groundbait. A smelly mix that breaks up well and really attracts can be made from a combination of fresh blood (your butcher will oblige), fish oils, such as herring or pilchard, bran, breadcrumbs and finely chopped oily fish or raw steak. If you don't fancy getting your hands smelly use a large, tablespoon whipped onto a 12 in section of garden cane with stout cord to flick out regular helpings.

The most wonderful aspect of jetty or harbour fishing (call it what you will) is that no two days' sport will ever be the same. One day, a seemingly endless supply of mullet will be attracted to your groundbait. Yet on the next, you won't see one – just an army of ever-hungry little pollack that won't allow anything else to approach the bait. When you can see fish can mopping up all the loose fragments of groundbait, but not your hookbait,

Top *Cutting up fish to go into the 'rubby-dubby' is an unpleasant business, that must be done on the way out to the sharking grounds.*

Above *As this big lemon shark proves, Mark Longster's 'Gambian' method of groundbaiting, using nothing other than a plastic carrier bag, really works.*

juggle about with the depth of the bait. This is why polaroid glasses are essential for jetty fishing, as they enable you to watch the bait being sucked in and to strike whether the float has registered the bite or not.

Mullet, especially, are extremely timid feeders. They will accept tiny slivers of raw steak or small segments of the tiny 'harbour ragworm', and also freshwater baits such as sweetcorn and, in particular, bread paste or flake. Whenever they can be seen grazing like sheep tight up against the harbour or jetty wall, feeding on the thick growth of filamentous algae, which is soft and fluffy, bread flake can prove most deadly. Small loose fed balls of mashed bread will help keep them interested and receptive to your flake on the hook. Floating breadcrusts also attract mullet during bouts of really warm weather.

Incidentally, when fishing high above the surface from the jetty or harbour wall, you will need the help of a dropnet. You can improvize here by using a 24 in diameter, freshwater landing-net top, to which you tie a long cord, supporting the net horizontally with a three-point fixing. There is nothing more frustrating after a hectic scrap on light tackle than the sight of a sizeable mullet lying beaten on the surface, with no way of lifting it up onto land.

DOWN-TIDE SHARK FISHING

Until I visited the massive Gambia river system in West Africa, most of the shark fishing sorties I had enjoyed in various

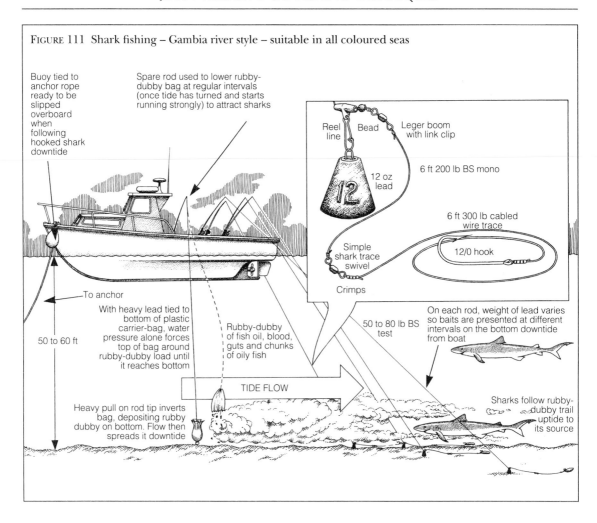

FIGURE 111 Shark fishing – Gambia river style – suitable in all coloured seas

Buoy tied to anchor rope ready to be slipped overboard when following hooked shark downtide

Spare rod used to lower rubby-dubby bag at regular intervals (once tide has turned and starts running strongly) to attract sharks

Reel line

Bead

Leger boom with link clip

12 oz lead

6 ft 200 lb BS mono

6 ft 300 lb cabled wire trace

12/0 hook

Simple shark trace swivel

Crimps

To anchor

With heavy lead tied to bottom of plastic carrier-bag, water pressure alone forces top of bag around rubby-dubby load until it reaches bottom

50 to 60 ft

Rubby-dubby of fish oil, blood, guts and chunks of oily fish

50 to 80 lb BS test

On each rod, weight of lead varies so baits are presented at different intervals on the bottom downtide from boat

TIDE FLOW

Heavy pull on rod tip inverts bag, depositing rubby dubby on bottom. Flow then spreads it downtide

Sharks follow rubby-dubby trail uptide to its source

parts of the world, from the West Indies to Australia, revolved around drifting the boat along with the tide in crystal-clear, deep blue seas. The accepted way of attracting sharks from many miles away up to the boat is to use a rubby dubby bag containing a mixture of blood, minced fish and fish oils. It is lowered over the side and tied off at waterline level so it slaps against the boat with each wave and releases a 'slick'. Wherever you have clear seas there is no more effective method. However, in heavily coloured water like the 10 mile wide mouth of the mighty Gambia River, which pours its life out into the Atlantic Ocean at depths of just 50–80 ft, where currents are exceptionally strong, and with visibility of less than 2 ft (you cannot see what you have hooked until it breaks surface), fishing at anchor is far more effective than drifting.

One way of putting out an attractive slick to these bottom-fishing sharks, is, of course, to tie a large rubby-dubby bag, such as an old onion sack, onto the rope close to the anchor itself. Another, much better technique, however, was illustrated to me by Mark Longster, skipper of *White Warrior*, with whom I fished on two international *Go Fishing* programmes. It is the 'carrier bag' method and you'll find it is simplicity itself.

Using a spare rod, you thread line through the bottom of a heavy-duty plastic carrier bag, and tie on a heavy boat lead. You then wrap a couple of strong elastic bands around the bottom of the bag and lead so it cannot pull through. Then half fill the bag with a smelly, pre-chopped and minced mixture of fish pieces, blood, guts and fish oils, and lower it over the side on a free spool until it hits bottom. Whereupon you give a couple of heavy jerks to invert the carrier bag, which instantly releases the rubby-dubby, and reel it back up, repeating the procedure half a dozen times.

This, of course, is done once the anchor has caught and the boat has swung round into position downtide. You may need to repeat the process every so often to keep sharks following the bait trail uptide towards the bottom-presented hookbaits, or as the situation dictates. It's rather like using a freshwater bait dropper on a giant scale, and just as effective. In case you are wondering why the rubby-dubby mix does not spew out of the bag on the way down to the bottom, this is due to water pressure forcing the sides of the bag tightly together until you give that hefty jerk to invert it.

Naturally, in addition to sharks, this form of groundbaiting works for all bottom species, such as stingrays, guitar fish, snappers and catfish, and creates a baited slick for several hundred yards

directly downtide of the anchored boat, exactly where your hookbaits are ledgered. And although we unfortunately did not have space in the Gambia programmes to show viewers other species that we caught in addition to the 300 lb lemon shark, I finally managed to beat some big cats, stingrays and various snappers that also came our way, plus several other sharks.

We used two 50 and two 80 lb class stand-up outfits, and varied the size of the leads between 12 oz and 1½lb, so the four rods presented baits at different distances downtide to alleviate the possibility of tangles. Traces consisted of a 12/0 hook to 6 ft of 300 lb cable-laid wire and a 3/0 swivel, to which 6 ft of 200 lb mono and a second 3/0 swivel is added, the lead slider being stopped above the trace swivel by a large bead – a simple, yet most effective set-up.

The best baits for shark are any smallish members of the tuna family, mackerel, bonito, small blue fins or yellowfins, or, as we used in the Gambia, 'bonga fish', a species not unlike our own horse mackerel or scad. And a whole bonga sandwiched between two freshly cut fillets provided a good enough mouthful, even for small fish to peck away at, until a shark arrived on the scene.

Incidentally, if the tide is minimal, the reel can be left out of gear with the ratchet on to give an audible warning and provide insurance against over-runs. As the tide picks up, it's best to put the reel into gear with a light drag setting, so the flow cannot pull line against the ratchet but a good-sized fish can.

Bites from sharks when downtide fish-

Roddy Hays' boat Anguilla, *leaves Funchal harbour in Madeira to head offshore in search of big-eyed tuna with the lures set to troll in a particular formation (fig. 113).*

ing on the bottom nearly always consist of sudden, screeching runs (occasionally the rod top might knock heavily a couple of times first) as the shark engulfs the bait and belts off. As soon as this happens then, assuming the fish is of an enjoyable fighting size, there is no reason for delaying the strike. Wind the clutch down, take the ratchet off, and allow the line to tighten under the shark's own weight. Make sure that you wait until the line has tightened fully before heaving the rod back into its bulk and waiting for the hook to penetrate. In short, it makes

good sense to use the shark's own weight combined with current strength to help the large hook find a purchase.

BLUE-WATER TROLLING

A feeling of mystery and genuine boyish enthusiasm always comes over me whenever I climb aboard a blue-water trolling boat and head towards deep water in search of the pelagic species, hopefully to do battle with the fastest, strongest and arguably the most colourful fish on our planet. Anyone who has hooked a dor-

Roddy Hayes (centre) *finally relaxes, having promised John some big-eye action, and kept his word. These two 60-pounders came from a catch of five, all between 50 and 80 lb, hooked in a mad 40-minute spell.*

ado, for instance, cannot help marvelling at the incredible mixture of metallic yellow, green, turquoise, blue and violet that radiates like a kaleidoscope along its body throughout the fight – which invariably includes one spectacular leap after another; and then felt that sad disappointment when, triumphantly standing back, one finds oneself watching the way in which those colours suddenly drain from its body literally within seconds of being caught. Sailfish, the fastest fish in the sea (said to reach speeds in excess of 60 mph), share the dorado's

ability to change and intensify their colour during the fight through an entire spectrum of blues, mauves and purples. And to catch these magnificent creatures, and also marlin, wahoo, barracuda and several members of the tuna family, you must head for deep blue water.

Sometimes the trolling grounds are just a few minutes away, and this is the case in the outer Seychelles – such as Desroche, Bird and Denis Islands – where the sea shelf falls away to over 2,000 ft into a deep blue void within a few hundred yards of the coral beaches. But such

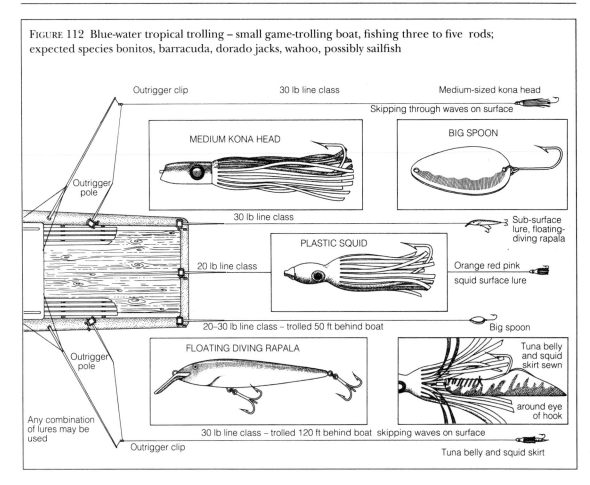

FIGURE 112 Blue-water tropical trolling – small game-trolling boat, fishing three to five rods; expected species bonitos, barracuda, dorado jacks, wahoo, possibly sailfish

Outrigger clip   30 lb line class   Medium-sized kona head

Skipping through waves on surface

MEDIUM KONA HEAD

BIG SPOON

Outrigger pole

30 lb line class

Sub-surface lure, floating-diving rapala

PLASTIC SQUID

20 lb line class

Orange red pink

squid surface lure

20–30 lb line class – trolled 50 ft behind boat

Big spoon

Outrigger pole

FLOATING DIVING RAPALA

Tuna belly and squid skirt sewn

around eye of hook

Any combination of lures may be used

30 lb line class – trolled 120 ft behind boat skipping waves on surface

Outrigger clip

Tuna belly and squid skirt

locations are comparatively rare. More often than not, and provided the seas allow it, a lengthy cruise at high speed is necessary in order for the skipper to put his punters quickly over choice locations. The places to look for are a deep channel between islands; sudden banks or humps that rise from the ocean floor and attract huge bait-fish concentrations – which in turn attract the pelagic species; or really deep waters where monsters are continually on the move in search of bait-fish shoals. And there is no more accurate method of locating the bait-fish shoals than watching through binoculars for signs of seagulls working the surface in an agitated fashion. The sight of birds by the hundred, or even by the thousand, repeatedly diving into the sea is what blue-water trolling skippers always look for and then quickly head their craft towards. The gulls are mopping up small bait fish forced up to the surface by bonito or other small tuna, and this commotion in turn attracts very much larger game fish to the scene, plus the odd shark or two.

The way in which skippers rig their rods, the choice of lures and the speed at which they are trolled depend on the

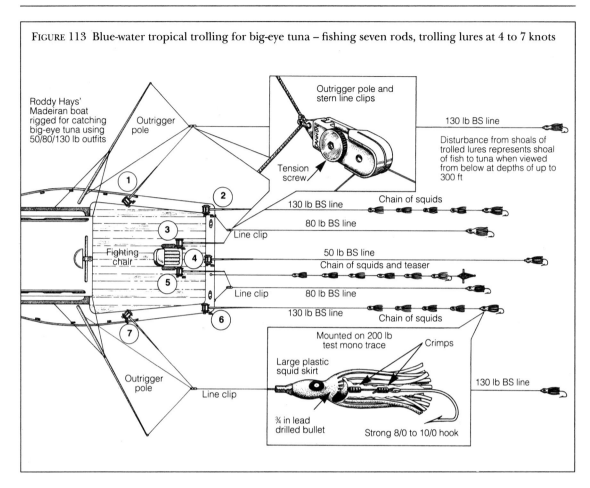

FIGURE 113 Blue-water tropical trolling for big-eye tuna – fishing seven rods, trolling lures at 4 to 7 knots

Roddy Hays' Madeiran boat rigged for catching big-eye tuna using 50/80/130 lb outfits

Outrigger pole

Outrigger pole and stern line clips

Tension screw

130 lb BS line

Disturbance from shoals of trolled lures represents shoal of fish to tuna when viewed from below at depths of up to 300 ft

130 lb BS line

Chain of squids

80 lb BS line

Line clip

50 lb BS line

Chain of squids and teaser

Fighting chair

Line clip

80 lb BS line

130 lb BS line

Chain of squids

Outrigger pole

Line clip

Mounted on 200 lb test mono trace

Crimps

Large plastic squid skirt

130 lb BS line

¾ in lead drilled bullet

Strong 8/0 to 10/0 hook

season and therefore the species that are likely to be about. When *Go Fishing* visited the island of Madeira, for instance, and I teamed up again with old friend, Roddy Hays (with whom I shared a wrecking trip off Alderney in the second series), it was April and we were out to catch not just tuna, but one species in particular for which the seas around Madeira and its neighbouring island of Porto Santos are renowned – the incredibly strong and hard-battling big-eyed tuna.

As the bait fish around Madeira tend to be on the small side, none of the trolling lures exceeded 6 in. As can be seen from fig. 113, small-headed bubblers of about 4 oz were presented on outfits 1, 4 and 7. On 2 and 6 were five lure daisy-chains made up of rubber squids with the hook in the back lure. And on 3 and 5, were heavy, straight runners of 6–8 oz. Because big-eyes tend to push lightweight lures out of the way with their own bow wave due to their relatively large heads, Roddy uses a ¾ in lead bullet threaded on the line immediately above the hook and hidden inside the head of the squid. In addition, all the lures were positioned to run on the crest of, or just behind, a wave (which is in contrast to most other tuna

The dorado hits any kind of trolled artificial lure, from feathers to squid skirts, and even spoons, plugs and mounted fish strip.

To skippers who troll off the Kenyan coast, this silvery half-beak mounted on a size 8/0 hook, with a feather or squid skirt up front, is the supreme sailfish bait.

fishing) and trolled at a speed some-where between 4 and 6½ knots, which is slower than for other tuna. Any type of lure can be used, but straight-running lures such as 'mean machines', small bubble heads and traditional Japanese feathers, seem most effective because most tuna do not have stereoscopic vision when close to the lure, and therefore need something running in a straight line, or they might easily miss it. Roddy much prefers dark colours like red and black, purple and black, blue and silver, green and silver, plus blue, pink and brown, which also work well. In fact, regardless of colour, the pattern of lures set by Roddy quite close in, some 30–50 ft behind the boat, really did look, to all intents and purposes, like a shoal of bait fish flitting from the crest of one wave to another.

During our week's visit, big-eyed tuna were, to say the least, conspicuous by their absence, and it was not until the afternoon of the fifth day that any kind of

action materialized. In fact, few birds could be seen, and nothing hit the lures prior to the big moment when all hell broke loose. With everyone either nod-ding off or deeply engrossed in books, only Roddy and I were still awake enough (yes, trolling for day upon day can border on the boring when there is nothing happening) to hear a ratchet squeal as the first big-eye grabbed hold.

Roddy continued at full trolling speed after this first strike to entice the entire shoal into a feeding frenzy, which is exactly what happened. Fish upon fish could be seen slashing at the attractor daisy-chain teaser and bird, so that within no time at all, no less than six of the seven rods were buckling heavily and short of line to the tune of at least a 100 yd apiece, as the big-eye on each zoomed straight back down to the depth at which the shoal had been holding before rising

Opposite *The menacing barracuda is a regular customer on mounted fish baits trolled in blue water. John hooked this specimen off Bird Island in the Seychelles.*

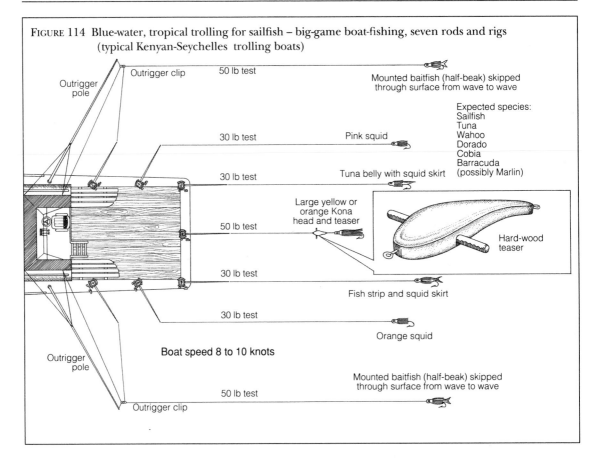

FIGURE 114 Blue-water, tropical trolling for sailfish – big-game boat-fishing, seven rods and rigs (typical Kenyan-Seychelles trolling boats)

Outrigger pole

Outrigger clip

50 lb test

Mounted baitfish (half-beak) skipped through surface from wave to wave

Expected species:
Sailfish
Tuna
Wahoo
Dorado
Cobia
Barracuda
(possibly Marlin)

30 lb test — Pink squid

30 lb test — Tuna belly with squid skirt

50 lb test — Large yellow or orange Kona head and teaser

Hard-wood teaser

30 lb test — Fish strip and squid skirt

30 lb test — Orange squid

Boat speed 8 to 10 knots

Outrigger pole

Mounted baitfish (half-beak) skipped through surface from wave to wave

50 lb test

Outrigger clip

behind the boat, attracted to our simulated bait-fish shoal of lures.

Roddy then slowed the boat down to idling speed as we went about playing the big-eyes, all between 60 and 90 lb, back up through the blue void to the boat, which is not, I might add, the kind of battle on stand-up tackle anyone frail or subject to a heart condition should ever consider attempting, even on the 50, 80 and 130 lb outfits we used. I played two of them plus the best part of another, which gave the two cameras more than enough footage for the programme (all within the space of 40 minutes) and I was truly exhausted.

In complete contrast to those lovely Madeiran big-eyes, in the same series of *Go Fishing* also trolled off the wonderful East African coast out from Malindi on board *Tina*, a comfortable 40-footer skippered by Angus Paul. And Malindi's boast of being among the top areas world-wide for hooking into the acrobatic and swift-moving sailfish proved totally justified.

It was, indeed, fascinating to observe how Angus worked his variation of lures and mounted fish-baits on a seven-rod set up, while trolling at a fast speed of somewhere between 8 and 10 knots. As can be seen from fig. 114, the two outside 50 lb class outfits had the lines held out away from the boat via clips on the long out-rigger poles, and trolled mounted baits (half beaks) that skipped most attract-ively from wave to wave. The middle rod, also a 50 lb outfit, trolled a mounted fish strip/squid skirt combo, with a wooden bird-teaser positioned a few feet in front up the trace. On both sides of this middle rod were two 30 lb outfits pulling a variety of different lures, including simple fluorescent pink or orange plastic squids, a large orange or yellow Kona head teaser, and a tuna-belly bait sewn around an 8/0 hook with a squid skirt over it.

I found it most enjoyable swapping over and experimenting with various lures as we ploughed up and down the coastline, keeping within 2 to 4 miles of the shore in deep blue water, where the largest concentrations of sailfish were known to be working.

As expected, most hits came to the outrigger baits, and sometimes two sailfish were being played simultaneously. I even hooked and played one to the boat for tagging (all the sailfish are tagged and released). It took a liking for a deep-diving plug, and was the first sailfish that Angus had ever brought to the boat on a plug. It took the very same 8 in blue mackerel rapala magnum on which I had landed the largest lake trout during our Canadian lakeland programmes in the province of Manitoba six months pre-viously. It was, ironically, also the very same plug that I found myself painfully connected to – along with a snapping, flapping 10 lb barracuda – via one of its rusty 3/0 trebles (penetrating my right

forefinger) when fishing on the Gambia River with Mark Lonster.

While I love the banter that accom-panies the usual group of four to six anglers that can comfortably attend the large-scale set up of a big trolling boat, I also enjoy trolling from much smaller, 20–25 ft craft when just two anglers share between three and five rods. As can be seen from fig. 112, if a small game-boat is fitted with outriggers, five rods are man-ageable. Medium-sized Kona heads or tuna belly/squid skirt combo rigs are trolled furthest behind the boat on, say, 30 lb outfits clipped up to the outriggers, hopefully to attract species like sailfish, dorado and wahoo. The three inside rods, 20–30 lb outfits, can then offer a variety of lures, including big spoons, shallow running plugs, small to medium Kona heads, squid skirts, feathers, and so on.

When fish such as dorado and sailfish, in particular, can be seen following a particular lure, but are loathe to grab hold, take the rod from its holder and drop the lure back several yards on a free spool before slamming the reel suddenly back into gear and speeding it up. When just one lure appears to be going at a different speed to the others, or behaves in a strange manner, it is invariably hit immediately. You need to keep a watchful eye on those lures and fish-mounted baits all day through in order to instigate a hit, and, of course, periodically to untangle lines that cross over in strong winds or as the boat turns.

Whenever small game fish like bonito and skipjack tuna are bountiful, don't moan that your 30 lb outfit is too heavy. Rig up a 10–15 lb single-handed lure rod,

The spectacularly coloured and acrobatic sailfish, in the 50–80 lb bracket, abound in Kenyan waters. And there was no shortage when Go Fishing *chartered Malindi skipper, Angus Paul (sitting), and his boat* Tina *for a blue-water extravaganza.*

or even a fly rod, and really have some fun. You won't believe the fight of, say, a 6 lb bonito, even on 10 lb line. Their stamina and endurance is incredible.

What I especially like about small game trolling is that even on a mediocre day two anglers both have more chance of catching several fish than four or six anglers who have to wait their turn on a big boat. And provided both anglers agree, you have the opportunity of switching about throughout the day, varying the set-up of trolled lures and baits to suit different species, and even to come reasonably close inshore to work over reefs in depths of 20–50 ft.

When I lived on the west coast of Barbados, for instance, many years ago, some of the most exciting sport was working big drone spoons over the inshore reefs and hooking into barracuda, hard-fighting jack crevalle and a similar species coloured jet black all over. In recent years I have even put my collection of large, deep-diving plugs to good use while trolling from small game-fishing boats. This provided some truly memorable action from the inshore reefs around the Seychelles while I was researching future material for *Go Fishing*, including carangue, green job fish, barracuda, blue-spotted trevally, and others I didn't know the name of.

The point is that trolling can be as varied and as exciting as you wish to make it, so be prepared to come closer in occasionally, and to experiment continually, rather than fishing a deep blue void that at the the time you happen to be there, doesn't contain many gladiators. At the end of the day you can be fortunate and you can be unfortunate. However, taking all things into consideration, you will, I hope, appreciate that through trial and error you actually create your own luck most of the time.

CHAPTER THREE

GO FISHING
MAGIC MOMENTS

Some of those truly magic moments that have occurred during the
making of Go Fishing

MOST DANGEROUS	Asking Mark Lonster, charter-boat skipper of White Warrior, out in the mouth of the Gambia River, to gently unhook 300 lb of thrashing lemon shark by hand with just a pair of pliers, so that viewers would not be upset by the usual blood-and-guts reality of shark fishing. Thanks Mark!
MOST UNCOMFORTABLE	Breaking a toe in southern India, which meant having to spend the entire week's shoot hobbling about across a rock-strewn flood plain, and jumping from boulder to boulder in the river's most likely mahseer runs without grimacing on camera. Served me right for not wearing trainers.
SADDEST	Hearing of the sudden death of old Bill Clarke of Barnham, Thetford, on the very day we should have filmed his favourite dace stretch on the Little Ouse, and towards which he did so much to help. The programme never materialized due to severe flooding that very week.
MOST HUMILIATING	Sitting round a huge table at the famous Sandgrund night club in Karlstad, Sweden, with the rest of the crew on a Thursday – the club's 'grab a granny night'. The women ask the fellas to dance, and I wasn't asked all evening. Brings you back to earth, though!

MOST PAINFUL No problem choosing this one. How about 10 lb of snapping, barracuda in the bottom of the boat with a large rapala in its jaws, to which one of the rusty trebles my right forefinger was connected? The point could, in fact, just be seen coming through the fingernail, with the barb well and truly in the middle of the finger. And it was entirely my own fault. However, a bit of self-surgery and a minor fracas in a Gambian hospital soon had me fishing again.

MOST SATISFYING	Eventually subduing and landing, on totally inadequate tackle – including badly frayed line and a rod broken in three places – a 60 lb vundu catfish from Zimbabwe's Lake Kariba after an arduous hour-long fight on camera.

MOST DIFFICULT	Extracting more than the occasional word from my Indian guide, Napoleon, during one of our Canadian lake-trout programmes, due to a political blunder by the Canadian government in reclaiming land from the angry Chipaweyan Indians, of whom Nap was a local chief.

**MOST
FRIGHTENING**

Being bitten on the shoulder by a scorpion hiding in my shirt during the filming of our mahseer programmes in southern India, and awaiting events with a sweating brow to find out whether or not it was the deadly poisonous kind. Luckily it was not.

MOST REWARDING

Hooking into, and finally boating live on camera, a 27½ lb pike from my local Norfolk Broads during a week's shoot when the weather had been exceptionally bad. It was particularly pleasing to score on my home waters and, in truth, I would have settled for anything approaching 20 lb for this programme. Thus, a veritable monster gave extra pleasure, and credibility to Broadland pike fishing.

MOST UNEXPECTED

Feeling the 10 ft python I was holding around my neck throughout the introduction to our sailfish programme in Malindi, Kenya, rear up, open its huge jaws and snap angrily at

camera operator, Peter Milic, having been told by the handlers it was quite tame. In fact, the handlers regularly teased this particular snake into attacking. Had I only known!

MOST DISAPPOINTING Flying all the way across the Atlantic to the North-West Territories of Canada with five clear days' fishing ahead to shoot the first of a double programme, only to spend the first 3½ days completely fog-bound in Rankin Inlet, an old mining town full of nothing but boarded-up houses and drunken Eskimoes.

MOST REVENGEFUL While camped beside the river in India, getting my own back, so to speak, on sound recordist and practical joker, Dave Lindsay, who did his utmost to wake me from a drunken stupor (too much Mahseer punch) in the early hours of the morning by lighting a fire-cracker (used for deterring elephants from approaching the camp) right beside my tent. The trouble was that just like a poorly made firework, although considerably more powerful, it fizzled out only to go off with a resounding bang in Dave's hand

when he stupidly picked it up. Worse still, Wilson carried on snoring, completely oblivious to the commotion.

MOST DAUNTING
With the pilot having to make three trips in and three out in a small Cessna float-plane each day to assemble our equipment and crew on a remote island next to the Kazan River in the North-West Territories of Canada, we did not know whether the fast-forming fog would allow the plane to return on the last trip. Three of us stood shivering in the rain, with little protection from the night ahead as the fog loomed in with dusk, accompanied by black flies and mosquitoes in profusion, listening to stories of grizzly bear attacks from our ever-jovial guide, Keith Sharp. Fortunately, pilot Harvey, a Vietnam War veteran, risked the possibility of not being able to see his way back, to pick us up. Were we relieved.

MOST UNBELIEVABLE
Hooking into and landing the very same, recognizable 8 lb sea trout from Sweden's famous River Mörrum that I had caught and carefully returned only two hours previously to a pool some 300 yd away, . Honest!

MOST REGRETFUL Not being able to land, or even catch a glimpse of, the huge mahseer that I had hooked right at the end of our double Indian programme, over 100 ft up, above the river from a dangerous rocky ledge. Viewers may have thought I was insane even attempting to hook something from such a spot, but believe me, after much careful negotiation of the rocky ledges while inching downstream during the fight, many mahseer have finally been landed.

MOST SICKENING Having to wait for the film cartridge to be loaded back on the cine camera (it was off when I hooked into the fish) while a truly massive mahseer of 80–100 lb ripped 150 yd of 40 lb line from a fast-emptying multiplier and zoomed down into the next set of rapids, where the line promptly broke on jagged rocks. If only I had listened to my guide, Suban, and immediately scrambled into the waiting coracle and disregarded the fact that those early stages of the fight would be lost on film I might have landed the leviathan and the closing stages of the fight would have been caught on camera. If only!

MOST PROFESSIONALLY REWARDING	When my partner in Kazan River Productions and Director of *Go Fishing*, Paul Martingell, and myself, received accolades from the Swedish, Austrian and Canadian Tourist Boards for the 1992 series of programmes and their accompanying fact sheets, which had attracted more interest from viewers than any previous television programmes about their respective countries.
MOST LUCKY	Having had all my carefully prepared tackle stolen from the car only an hour before driving to a shoot, I then drove past the very drunk who had taken it, still staggering along with my entire collection in his arms an hour later on the outskirts of Norwich.

MOST FRUSTRATING	Watching through the crystal-clear waters as an enormous lake trout of easily 50 lb turned away from my 6 in spoon and slunk back into the depths of the mighty Kazan and Ferguson river confluence in the North-West Territories of Canada, while two cameras were rolling. It was mere inches away from engulfing the spoon, when it caught sight of the boat.
MOST SURPRISING	Hooking into a mahseer after a timed 29 seconds from casting to strike in the fast, rocky waters of my favourite southern Indian river. I had left this particular run alone for a few days, knowing that with the tight time schedule dictated by having to film two

half-hour programmes in only six days, we could do with a few breaks. However I never envisaged a mahseer grabbing hold so quickly with the cameras rolling.

MOST PROPHETIC

I remember saying to Len Head, while we sat on the edge of a rather spongy bed of brown sedges during the perch programme shot in early December 1992, that if they were not more careful, someone was going to step right through the floating sedges we were filming from. And within minutes, two of the crew were trudging back to the car swearing between clenched teeth, their wellies full of freezing cold black sludge, which represented countless years of decomposed plant tissue. You don't think we laughed, do you?

MOST NAUSEATING

Watching a succession of carp and barbel cavorting on the surface of Spain's usually most prolific and easy-to-fish Rio Ebro, a real banker venue if ever there was one, without experiencing so much as a bite – not even a liner on ledger or float. Even Terry Smith from Sheffield, who I would choose to fish on my behalf if my life depended on the outcome (and this was, in fact, the last day of our shoot, when results were imperative), couldn't buy a bite. It was a puzzling phenomenon that obviously had something to do with millions of gallons of much colder water that was being emptied into the main channel from an irrigation canal. Fortunately, I happened to notice some carp in a small, swirling rock-pool and caught a few on freelined bread flake to save the day – and, more importantly, our programme filmed in beautiful Cataluyna. But it was close.

MOST STUPID

While I was cooling off actually in the river in India following a lengthy battle with a big mahseer, an innocuous-looking but exceptionally pretty snake of around 20 in long, banded in segments of beige and violet, came swimming by mere inches away. It stopped, looking up at me within hands' reach next to the rocks I was resting against. I said to my guide 'Suban, is this snake dangerous to pick up?' 'Lovely snake, sir' came the reply. I was about to make a quick grab behind the head, a legacy from boyhood intrigue, I am afraid, but then I thought I would ask Suban again, anyway. 'Is this snake poisonous, Suban?' 'Yes sir, most poisonous' came the reply. I later found out that it was, in fact, a banded craite, one of the deadliest snakes in India.

MOST EMBARRASSING

Having returned from Malindi, Kenya, where we filmed the sailfish programme in which our TV monitor packed up, and with just an hour to spare before flying on to Lake Victoria for its Nile perch, we watched Dave Lindsay blow up the only available (and brand new) monitor in Nairobi. 'You will be careful with it, won't you?' said our agent, a timid young colonial woman who had promised the television shop owner we would return it in good order. Unfortunately, Dave hurriedly connected it up wrongly, and the look on the poor girl's face when it exploded in a cloud of black smoke was priceless. 'Obviously needs a new fuse' said Lindsay. 'I think we'll manage without it'.

MOST IRONIC

Having warned the rest of the crew about not standing too close to the water's edge on Zimbabwe's Lake Kariba, where huge crocodiles lie patiently in wait, wonderfully camouflaged, and regularly snap up innocent victims, sound recordist, Dave Lindsay, and I spent half an hour bashing rocks into the skull of a very dead hippopotamus that lay half in and half out of the water in order to remove its huge front teeth. Having obtained our souvenirs, we suddenly realized the irony of the situation and how very stupid – and fortunate – we had been.

MOST EXASPERATING	The easiest, yet most important part of filming for the Canadian catfish programme in Winnipeg should have been my introduction piece to camera beside Chuck, the friendly channel catfish – a colourful 20 ft high statue and local landmark. Unfortunately, when we arrived to shoot the introduction on Day One, the statue could hardly be seen for scaffolding, and was in the process of being repainted. Would the workmen finish before we had to fly out four days later? Fortunately they did, but only just, and we hurriedly filmed Chuck with the paint still wet.

MOST RELIEVED   Having travelled goodness knows how many miles by helicopter up into wilderness country along the spectacular Copper River Valley in British Colombia, Canada, and after fishing hard for close on five barren days, with just one day left I hooked and eventually beached a 14 lb steelhead trout in the shallows on a barbless hook fly, following an exciting battle. It was the only take of the entire trip. Talk about cutting it fine!

FUNNIEST   Seeing Anglia cameraman, Paul Bennett, fall backwards out of the crew boat into a reed-bed, and scramble back in again without getting soaked, while filming pike fishing in the pouring rain on Hickling Broad.

HEART IN MOUTH   I watched helplessly as cameraman, Ron Tufnell, clutching £50,000 worth of video camera on the first day of a shoot, lept from the dinghy that had ferried him across the fast-flowing water of Denmark's River Guden, and promptly slid down the steep, slippery slope into the drink. Only when the camera became entangled in the dense marginal foliage was Ron saved from completely going under. The 'blackmail' footage shot by the second cameraman while poor old Ron was drying off, completely unaware, and shamelessly modelling the skimpiest of bright red underpants, lies in the tape vaults of Kazan River Productions at an undisclosed branch of Barclays Bank.

MOST IRRESPONSIBLE

Taking most of the night to pull an 18 ft aluminium boat across 2 miles of a slowly thawing ice flow on the Ferguson River system with Martin Founds and Keith Sharp in the North-West Territories of Canada, because we wanted a second boat from which to film on the following day. Our guide fell through and completely disappeared beneath the ice, and the trip could easily have ended in disaster.

MOST DUMBFOUNDED

Having spent most of the day driving high into the Austrian mountains, followed by half an hour's steep climb down into a ravine with our two heavy cameras and complement of batteries and so on, we arrived at a secluded stretch in the upper reaches of the lovely little River Gail. I was really looking forward to catching the colourful grayling and trout on dry fly from the crystal-clear water.

Fate, however, took a strong hand in the events. Heavy overnight thunderstorms had turned the water into the colour of weak, glacial tea. And if this were not bad enough, although I did manage to botch out a couple of tiny brownies on tinhead nymphs, within an hour, a succession of German canoeists came down the tiny rock-strewn river, one after another with not so much as a smile between them. I was so dumbfounded I could only laugh.

MOST HILARIOUS   During the afternoon of our first day on fabulous Rusinga Island, Kenya, in search of the legendary Nile perch, camp manager, Antony Dodds, suggested that Andy Davison and I accompany him for a spot of shore fishing. We took the landrover and drove through a breathtaking, lush valley to a remote-looking spot where palm trees line the shore of Lake Victoria, which looked as though it had never been fished before.

An incredible sight greeted us as we walked around the first bay towards a distant rocky outcrop. It was full of completely naked village women. Naturally, crafty Dodds knew exactly where he was taking us, and he and I increased our walking pace, leaving poor Andy Davison, laden down with his usual armoury of tackle, at the rear. He was soon being followed by a dozen or more voluptuous, teenage beauties, like the proverbial pied piper. I don't think I have ever seen Andy so embarrassed and so totally at a loss as to how to extract himself, because those

girls followed him for the best part of a ½ mile along the shore until we reached the rocks and starting spinning – which, incidentally, proved fruitless. Andy's entourage of lovelies sat there mesmerized throughout. Antony Dodds, the devil, had deliberately walked us through the local ladies' bathing beach.

MOST CAUTIOUS Having, over the years, bred several species of birds, and reared clutches of young barn owls for release into the wild, I was most eager to do the introduction to our Austrian programme in the province of Corinthia at Longskron Castle, where the daily 'birds of prey in flight' show is a truly spectacular event. The handler said I could hold the magnificent golden eagle. Once I had sleeved on the long, leather gauntlet, he eased it carefully onto my left arm with the words 'just watch your eyes'.

INDEX

(Illustrations in bold)